T0323625

"A good business plan can be worth billions, but how do you find one? Chander Velu explains why business model innovation is the most important and valuable innovation for your company and shows you the route to your new business model. Fascinating and enjoyable – buying this book is possibly the best investment you can make!"

Stuart Madnick
John Norris Maguire Professor of Information Technologies
at the MIT Sloan School of Management, and Professor of
Engineering Systems at the MIT School of Engineering

"Fascinating and highly relevant. Chander's book is valuable inspiration, particularly for anyone concerned with how we can boost growth and productivity, on which so much of society depends. Conventional economics assume that markets (and, by definition, those people who operate within them) are rational, moving quickly to optimise returns. In reality, businesses often aren't rational. They're full of inertia born out of the tensions between the short and long term and the way rewards are assessed and distributed. Many business leaders have good strategic instinct but transmission to results is often compromised by failure to overcome the inertia that stands in the way of changing a business model. Chander's work addresses this reality head on with a rich analysis of how business model innovation is key to successful execution of strategy."

Sir Charlie Mayfield
Chairman of Be the Business, former Chairman of the John Lewis
Partnership, and member of the Industrial Strategy Council

"Choosing a business model means choosing a particular way to compete and, for aspiring entrepreneurs as well as seasoned executives, I have found that there is nothing more important to focus on first. Professor Velu's meticulous research and focus on the role of innovation in the design of business models and the dynamics that influence business models are extremely insightful, and what sets his work apart is his ability to seamlessly bridge academic rigour with real-world examples of the link between technology advances and business model innovation. I wholeheartedly endorse this book for anyone seeking to understand the importance of business model innovation in building a competitive business today."

Lee Olesky
Founder of Tradeweb and former CEO and Chairman of the Board

"The publication of this book is very timely as the latest wave of digital technologies is challenging virtually every business model in every type of firm across the globe. The time lag in adoption and the need for greater absorptive capacity are often mentioned as barriers to firms seeing productivity gains fast. Chander Velu opens the black box on how firms can innovate their business models to obtain lasting benefits from those new technologies. His years of study of the topic come together in this comprehensive book, from which not only scholars and students of business will learn – it also shows the way for practitioners to get beyond the hype."

Bart van Ark
Professor of Productivity Studies at the Alliance Manchester Business School, and Managing Director of The Productivity Institute

"A concise account of research on the relationship between business models and organisational performance. Recommended to anyone looking to gain a thorough understanding of the drivers, obstacles, and performance impacts of business model innovation."

Panos Desyllas
Professor of Strategy at the University of Bath School of Management

"A comprehensive guide that sheds light on business model initiatives for sustained competitive advantage. This book expertly takes the business model perspective to navigate the complexities of market dynamics, digital transformation, sustainable development, and organisational adaptation, making it a must-read for academics, practitioners, and policymakers. The use of real-world examples from contemporary businesses and practical frameworks brings the principles of business model innovation to life, providing actionable strategies for today's ever-evolving digitally enabled business landscape."

René Bohnsack
Professor for Strategy and Innovation at Católica-Lisbon, and Director of the Smart City Innovation Lab

Business Model Innovation

What strategic challenges are faced by both start-ups and incumbent firms, and what opportunities do these challenges create for business model innovation? Focusing on the underpinning theory and concepts of business models, this book identifies new business models capable of creating sustainable competitive advantage and guides readers through their implementation. A detailed introduction outlines current research in business model innovation (including directions for future research), and global business cases are applied throughout to illustrate key issues. Topics covered include market creation, leadership, digital technology adoption, small- and medium-sized enterprises, start-ups, sustainability, socio-economic development and conduct risk. Also discussed are the principles of the architecting economic systems, the role of government in influencing business models design and how organisational structures must adapt in the context of business model innovation.

CHANDER VELU is Professor of Innovation and Economics in the Institute for Manufacturing (IfM) at the Department of Engineering, University of Cambridge. He heads the Business Model Innovation Research Group at the IfM. Professor Velu is Fellow at Selwyn College, Cambridge and Fellow of the Institute of Chartered Accountants in England and Wales. Prior to joining the IfM, he was a member of the faculty at Cambridge Judge Business School. He has worked as a consultant with PricewaterhouseCoopers and Booz Allen & Hamilton in London.

Business Model Innovation

A Blueprint for Strategic Change

CHANDER VELU
University of Cambridge

CAMBRIDGE
UNIVERSITY PRESS

Shaftesbury Road, Cambridge CB2 8EA, United Kingdom

One Liberty Plaza, 20th Floor, New York, NY 10006, USA

477 Williamstown Road, Port Melbourne, VIC 3207, Australia

314–321, 3rd Floor, Plot 3, Splendor Forum, Jasola District Centre, New Delhi – 110025, India

103 Penang Road, #05–06/07, Visioncrest Commercial, Singapore 238467

Cambridge University Press is part of Cambridge University Press & Assessment, a department of the University of Cambridge.

We share the University's mission to contribute to society through the pursuit of education, learning and research at the highest international levels of excellence.

www.cambridge.org
Information on this title: www.cambridge.org/9781009181716

DOI: 10.1017/9781009181709

First published 2024

A catalogue record for this publication is available from the British Library

Library of Congress Cataloging-in-Publication Data
Names: Velu, Chander, author.
Title: Business model innovation : a blueprint for strategic change / Chander Velu, University of Cambridge.
Description: Cambridge, United Kingdom ; New York, NY : Cambridge University Press, 2024. | Includes bibliographical references and index.
Identifiers: LCCN 2023041847 | ISBN 9781009181716 (hardback) | ISBN 9781009181709 (ebook)
Subjects: LCSH: Organizational change. | Strategic planning.
Classification: LCC HD58.8 .V45 2024 | DDC 658.4/06–dc23/eng/20230908
LC record available at https://lccn.loc.gov/2023041847

ISBN 978-1-009-18171-6 Hardback
ISBN 978-1-009-18169-3 Paperback

Contents

Figures

Tables

Preface

A plethora of new start-ups were launched to disrupt incumbent firms across a range of industries in the late 1990s and early 2000s, during what has come to be known as the era of the dot.com bubble. Often, people left secure employment to harness the opportunities provided by the Internet to launch new businesses that would disrupt their loyal employers or other incumbent firms that relied on the inefficiencies of the market to sustain their superior competitive advantage. During this exciting period, I joined one of the major global strategy consulting firms at the time, Booz Allen & Hamilton. My very first assignment at the firm was a strategy-evaluation project for a major global news and information service provider whose share price had declined rapidly, as the market felt it did not have a coherent e-commerce strategy. A team was assembled in London to work on this assignment in record time. After several weeks of intense work, our proposed e-commerce strategy was received with enthusiasm by the senior management; however, the firm found it challenging to implement the strategy because each department had an urgent current operational issue to address. There was a lack of common ownership of the business model, which made it difficult to coordinate the response internally to develop new business models. This resulted in a lethargic response by our client, with the consequence that they missed the opportunity to become a pioneer in leveraging the business opportunities provided by the Internet.

This experience sowed the seeds of my interest in business model innovation. I worked on several high-profile strategy-formulation assignments with major blue-chip firms, which demonstrated a similar inability on the part of management to innovate business models despite having a great deal of knowledge about Internet-based technologies. I could not fully understand the dynamics of the decision-making process and the resource-allocation issues to drive strategic business model innovation from the vantage point of a management consultant, as the demands of the next assignment did not allow for such reflection. Hence, I decided with great trepidation to pursue my doctoral studies at the Cambridge Judge Business School to develop a deeper theoretical understanding of business model innovation resulting from new digital technologies. I initially studied the global financial services market before pursuing my interest across other manufacturing and service-driven industries when I joined the Institute for Manufacturing (IfM) at the Department of Engineering, University of Cambridge. I quickly realised that many of the grand challenges of society, such as the productivity paradox and economic growth, climate change, poverty alleviation, health and biodiversity, among others, require innovative business models. Moreover, novel business models are often the catalyst to enable digital and other emerging technologies such as quantum technologies to provide benefits to society. In fact, as I learnt about business model innovation through research and discussions with senior executives, more questions arose in my mind – reminding me of Charles Darwin's insightful quote, "The pleasure of knowing things always goes on increasing the more one knows."

This book is an attempt to pause and take stock of the knowledge in the area of business model innovation and to highlight what we know and the topics we need to explore further. I hope this book will provide the scaffolding to enable scholars, managers and policy-makers to ask the right questions in a truly collaborative effort to discover and shape our understanding of business model innovation in order to build a better world for us all as we face the next generation of grand societal challenges.

Acknowledgements

Although I have been fortunate to be given the opportunity to hold the pen in writing this book, it has been a collaborative effort, with contributions from many people. Several individuals have helped to shape my thinking and the contents of this book. I would like to thank my students and researchers at the Cambridge Business Model Innovation Research Group. In particular, my current and former PhD students and Research Associates have performed a crucial role in teaching me patience and the ability to learn from their insights. It has been delightful to learn from all of you equally. Stuart Madnick at the Massachusetts Institute for Technology has been a mentor and a great role model and inspiration for my academic work ever since I visited his research group back in 2004. His enduring support provided me with the confidence to pursue an academic career. I would also like to thank Sir Mike Gregory, Tim Minshall, Duncan McFarlane and Andy Neely. Sir Mike was crucial in encouraging me to be bold in my ambition to build a research group on business model innovation when I joined the Institute for Manufacturing (IfM) at the Department of Engineering, University of Cambridge. Tim, Duncan and Andy have been great mentors ever since I joined the IfM. They have helped me to embrace and complement the strengths of the Engineering Department and have been extremely supportive in my research and personal development by encouraging me to go beyond my comfort zone to explore new areas of research at the crossroads of engineering, economics and management.

I would also like to thank Geoff Meeks for providing the intellectual partnership to develop some challenging issues on conduct risk and business models. Thanks also go to my collaborators, colleagues and friends who have provided stimulating discussions and stretched my thinking on this topic – Sergei Savin, Jonathan Gair, Philip Stiles, Marshall Van Alstyne, Jan Heidi, John Deighton, Wayne Hoyer, Michael Pollitt, Gishan Dissanaike, John Metseelar, Rita Shor, Ataman

Ozyildirim, Anne Greer, Roger McKinlay, Golnar Pooya, Philip Dalzell-Payne, Toni Vidal-Puig, Andi Smart, Svetan Ratchev, Roger Maull, Mike Jones, Sir Charlie Mayfield, Arun Jacob, Evert Geurtsen, Dominic O'Brien, Chris Noble, Keith Norman, Charles Popper, Jamie Cattell, Andy Page, Mahima Khanna, Jeff Alstott, Abdul Mumit, Rob Glew, Stefan Kurpjuweit, Stephan Wagner, Jeremy Edwards, Sheilagh Ogilvie, Maximilian Klöckner, Mark Phillips, Charles Baden-Fuller, Panos Desyllas, Steve Roper, John Nicholson, Steven Pattinson, Michael Ehret, Paul Ryan, Dan Friedman, Hyunkyu Park, Liz Salter, Janet Hao, Arnoud De Meyer, Adam Brandenburger, Richard Foster, Charles Teschner and Youngjin Yoo. I am also very grateful to various students and Research Associates, whose excellent research work contributed to various chapters of this book – Fathiro Putra, Myungun Kim, Philip Chen, Sudhir Rama Murthy, Jiashun Huang, Nikolai Kazantsev, Zurina Moktar, Fauzi Said, Feares Ben Hadj, Ghanim Al-Sulaiti, Philipp Koebnick, Chen Ye, Julius Bock, Luka Gebel, Pengbo Qi, Yuzhen Zhu and Wit Wannakrairoj. Selwyn College has provided me with a stimulating interdisciplinary intellectual environment, while also offering a sanctuary for my mind. Thank you to the Fellows of Selwyn College, and I am particularly grateful to the Master, Roger Mosey, for his friendship and encouragement. I would like to express my grateful thanks to Valerie Appleby, my Editor at Cambridge University Press (CUP), for her guidance and advice, which are much appreciated. Thank you to Carrie Parkinson and Chris Hudson from CUP and Alice Gregory for their help and editorial assistance. And thank you to Amanda George for painstakingly copy-editing the drafts of the chapters with such care and professionalism.

I would also like to thank the Engineering and Physical Sciences Research Council (EPSRC) and the Economic and Social Research Council (ESRC) for providing the funding for my research. In particular, the EPSRC Digital Economy Fellowship allowed me to pursue the broad area of productivity, digital technologies and business model innovation. The Fellowship has also given me the time to pursue new and exciting areas of research in quantum technologies and the implications for business model innovation. And it allowed me to take time out from normal teaching and administrative duties and to focus on writing the book. Thank you also to my colleagues at the IfM, in particular, Florian Urmetzer and Judith Plummer, for taking on a substantial part of my teaching and administrative responsibilities during the

Fellowship. The ESRC also provided funding through The Productivity Institute – my very grateful thanks to Bart van Ark, Tony Venables and Mary O'Mahony for their leadership and encouragement.

I would like to thank my family for their continuous support and encouragement throughout. My father, the late Mr Kathir Velu, and Mrs Thanam Velu laid the foundations for being ambitious in whatever I do and for teaching me the merits of contributing to society. My father, with the enduring support of my mother, played a crucial role in encouraging me to apply to the University of Cambridge based on reading an advertisement in the local newspaper in Malaysia for a British Council Scholarship to study for a Master's course. This was the start of my academic career – many thanks are due to my parents for their wholehearted love, prayers and the foresight to guide me. I would also like to thank my brother, Ramani, for his brotherly advice and support over the years. Thank you also to my parents-in-law, Srilata and S. R. Iyer, Soumya and Mukund, for their prayers, blessings and love.

Finally, I would like to dedicate this book to my wife, Sriya Iyer, for her undivided love and support. You have provided me with the wind beneath my wings when I needed to fly and the breeze to relax and reflect when I needed to think. You have been a most gracious and elegant intellectual and life partner, making our lives truly enjoyable and meaningful. This book was made possible through your inspiration and encouragement – My Most Grateful Thanks.

1 | The Imperative for Business Model Innovation

Nothing is so practical as a good theory.

Kurt Lewin

Introduction

The concept of the business model has become especially prominent in recent times, even though it has been in use among business practitioners and academic scholars for a long time (Massa and Tucci, 2017; Teece, 2010). Alfred Chandler, the prominent Harvard business historian, outlined eloquently that American firms transformed themselves via vertical and horizontal integration from 1840 onwards following the emergence of the railroad for transportation, telegraph for communication and coal as a major source of energy (Chandler, 1977). Moreover, Joan Robinson, the distinguished Cambridge economist – in her famous article discussing the production function and the theory of capital – posited that each production technique might display different degrees of mechanisation involving its own specific *blueprints*, and there may be no recognisable items in common between one and any other (Robinson, 1953). Although Chandler and Robinson did not explicitly use the term "business model," the spirit of their analysis describes the architecture of firms that contribute to performance differences.

The more recent prominence of business models was predominantly fuelled by the Internet and by digital technologies. Amazon.com, Uber, Airbnb, Google, Netflix and Southwest Airlines are firms that are founded on business model innovations, that is, innovations[1]

---

[1] Joseph Schumpeter had proposed that the process of technological change in a free market consists of three phases: *invention* whereby a new idea or process is conceived, *innovation* whereby arranging the economic and social processes for implementing an invention and *diffusion* whereby stakeholders adopt the new discovery or imitate it (Schumpeter, 1939, 1942).

that involve changes to a business's value proposition combined with changes to how the value is created and captured by the firm and the network of partners required to do so. Moreover, competitive pressures have pushed business model innovation high up the priority list of firms worldwide (Global Innovation Barometer, 2013; Hao et al., 2020; IBM Global CEO Study, 2006). Perhaps unsurprisingly, not a day seems to go by without some new prescription in the popular press advising managers on how to deal with the challenges and opportunities posed by such innovation. Business model innovation can create huge opportunities, while threatening traditional means of generating revenue (Zott and Amit, 2008). As a consequence, business model innovations can create the fortunes of some firms, while killing the market positions of others (Velu, 2015). Incumbent firms, who may not have implemented such innovations, are forced to wrestle with decisions that can profoundly affect their future. New firms need to grapple with decisions about how best to design new business models that disrupt existing industries or create new markets for their propositions.

One indicator of the importance of business models is the surge in prominence of the number of articles in the *Financial Times* using the term "business model": this number grew from 10 in 1995 to over 2,027 in 2021. A similar trend is evident in other major business newspapers around the world, including *The Wall Street Journal* in the United States and *The Economic Times* in India. Surveys of CEOs suggest that firms that emphasise business model innovation have grown their operating margins faster than their competitors (Hao et al., 2020). Moreover, a survey of senior executives in twenty-five countries found that business model innovation is at the top of all forms of innovation on their priority lists (Global Innovation Barometer, 2013).

Business model innovation is also a critical enabler of productivity improvements. Productivity growth has slowed down in the last decade in major economies, as well as in emerging markets, despite the prevalence of digital technologies (Bean, 2016). This phenomenon is widely known as the productivity paradox (Syverson, 2011).[2]

---

[2] Global labour productivity (output per worker) growth slowed down from 2.4 per cent to 2.1 per cent between 1996 and 2006 and between 2007 and 2014. Total factor productivity growth displayed an even larger slowdown from 1.3 per cent to 0.3 per cent during the same period (Van Ark, 2016).

Moreover, industries that are the most intensive users of information and communication technologies (ICT)[3] appear to have contributed most to the slowdown in productivity (Van Ark, 2016). There could be many reasons for the productivity paradox, including the skills' mismatch due to changes in product market structures driven by digitalisation; the slowdown in technological diffusion between firms at the front of the technological frontier and others; and the legacy of the financial crisis causing dislocated markets and mismeasurement as a result of the digital economy providing significant propositions for free. However, studies on the history of new technologies have shown that productivity improvements might be hampered by the limited redesign of business models following the adoption of new technologies by firms. For example, in the United States, productivity gains were very limited when electric motors first replaced the steam engine on an industrial scale in the late nineteenth century. It was only when firms completely changed their business processes and corresponding business models that technology had a significant impact – and that took over forty years (David, 1990).

A business model can be seen as a complex organisational system that aims to transform input into valuable propositions for customers. Business models often act as the bridge between technology and the ability to deliver a compelling customer value proposition. Hence, the ability to experiment with new technologies, and to develop associated business models, is potentially a major source of productivity gains and growth for both new and established firms (OECD, 2015). Although new technologies often act as the catalyst for business model innovation, they are not necessary for the emergence of new business models. For example, the emergence of the *Metro* as one of the leading newspapers in the world was not due to any particular new technology; its free-sheet business model is based on distributing the paper free of charge to commuters in busy cities. The *Metro* earns its revenue from advertisements, which represents a major difference when compared to conventional newspapers that earn revenue from subscriptions or sales at news-stands.

Business model innovations can be disruptive when they change the bases of competition by altering the performance metrics along which firms compete (Markides and Oyon, 2010). Such disruptive

[3] Measured by purchases of ICT assets and services relative to GDP.

business models can manifest themselves through acquiring the customers and beneficiaries of the dominant business model by improving their efficiency in the provision of the existing customer value proposition or by creating a new market for an improved value proposition. The implications of disruptive business models are evident across many industries, including low-cost airlines, for example, Southwest Airlines; the retail book industry, for example, Amazon; and Google, with its search engine and related services; and, more recently, the taxi and hotel industries, with the emergence of firms such as Uber and Airbnb, respectively. However, how these business models emerge and disrupt industries, and the leadership and organisational design challenges inherent in managing them, are among the issues that scholars and managers are trying to understand better. This book aims to address some of these issues by bringing together the research on business model innovation and identifying areas for future research while highlighting the implications for management.

1.1 Strategy, Business Models and Tactics

Scholars have provided various definitions of a business model. These definitions vary from the stories that explain how enterprises work (Magretta, 2002), the resources and processes that are put together to create and capture value (Johnson et al., 2008) or the structural template of how the focal firm connects to factor and product markets (Zott and Amit, 2008). The common theme in these definitions rests on how the revenue model and the underlying cost structure, as a result of the operations, create and deliver the customer value proposition.

Business models are a form of activity system that connects the internal aspects of the firm, such as resources and routines, with the external aspect, such as partners, markets and customers, and hence articulates how the firm goes to market to implement the strategy (Baden-Fuller and Haefliger, 2013; Zott and Amit, 2010; Zott et al., 2011). The business model as an activity system has three key design parameters, namely, *content, structure* and *governance*. Content outlines which activities are part of the business model. Structure is about how these activities are linked to one another. Finally, governance relates to who can make decisions about them. The business model acts as a mechanism for actors to collectively form a shared

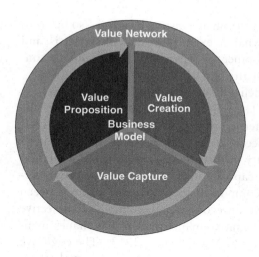

Who are your customers
and what do they value?
– Target customers
– Solutions

How is the value chain
configured?
– Production
– Inventory
– Distribution

What is the economic logic
of making a return?
– Revenue and cost
  architecture
– Financing

What is the role in the value
network?
– Partners
– Complementarities

Figure 1.1 Components of the business model
Source: Velu (2018)

understanding based on rules, norms and beliefs in order to guide their choices (Chesbrough and Rosenbloom, 2002; Doganova and Eyquem-Renault, 2009). In this sense, business models are the "architecture" that provides the bridge between the value created for customers and the value captured by the business in terms of profit.[4] A business model can be viewed as a complex system with components that connect the customer value proposition, how value is created, the means of value capture and the partners in the value network (Velu, 2017). Management's objective is to manage the *dynamic consistency* by maintaining congruence between the components of the business model in order to ensure efficiency, while enabling innovation of the business model (Velu, 2020).

We propose the 4Vs of the business model: value proposition, value creation, value capture and value network (Velu, 2018). Business models define the organisation's customer value proposition, and its approach to value creation, and the means of value capture and the partners in the value network. This is illustrated in Figure 1.1. Business model innovation involves the discovery and adoption of fundamentally different modes of value proposition, value capture and/or value

---

[4] This includes a holistic perspective covering value for all stakeholders.

creation and the value network from an existing business – so business model innovation redefines what an existing product or service is, and how it is provided to the customer, by seeking to identify unique configurations of business model attributes (Velu and Jacob, 2016).

Business models can be defined both objectively and subjectively (Doz and Kosonen, 2010). The objective definition encapsulates the economic manifestation in terms of the structure of the firm's relationships and procedures (Teece, 2010). The economic manifestation captures the financial viability of the business proposition in relation to value creation and value capture. In this sense, the objective perspective corresponds to the components and the relationship between components in order to have an economic outcome. The subjective definition encapsulates the cognitive manifestation that shapes managerial choices (Baden-Fuller and Mangematin, 2013). The cognitive manifestation captures how senior management conceptualise the business model as a model-like device as the basis for their actions in order to create and capture value.

A firm's business model is different to its business strategy, although the two constructs have some overlapping characteristics (Zott and Amit, 2008). In particular, a business model relates to the overall system that drives revenue and costs to deliver the customer value proposition, while business strategy refers to the generic choices that firms make to compete effectively in the marketplace (e.g., creating competitive advantage via differentiation, cost leadership and focus (McGahan and Porter, 1997)). The business model represents how the activities of the firm work together to execute its strategy[5] (Casadesus-Masanell and Ricart, 2010); hence, choosing a particular business model means choosing a particular way to compete.

Strategy relates to the contingency plan regarding which business model to adopt. Hence, strategy can be seen as an action plan that responds to a high-stakes challenge and requires diagnosis, guiding policies and coherent action (Rumelt, 2011). On the other hand, the business model is the underlying business logic of the go-to-market strategy. Tactics relate to how to optimise the performance of the

---

[5] Strategy formulation and implementation are an integral part of business model design and evolution (Foss et al., 2015). Strategy is determined by answering three questions: *What* is the offer, *who* constitutes the target market and *how* is the offer delivered to the customer? Business model selection constitutes the realised strategy that principally resides within the "how" question.

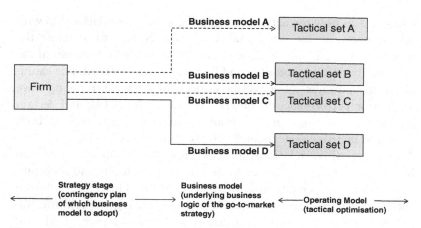

Figure 1.2 Strategy, business models and tactics
Source: Adapted from Casadesus-Masanell and Ricart (2010)

business model once a strategy is chosen – the operating model. Figure 1.2 illustrates the relationship between strategy, business models and tactics. The constructs of business models and strategy are related because the understanding of how a business model works is important when formulating an effective business strategy. For example, a firm could execute a cost leadership strategy by more effectively training its staff to use state-of-the-art technology. Such a cost leadership strategy might be implemented based on the existing business model. On the other hand, a firm that intends to develop a differentiation strategy, such as going into low-cost air travel, might require a reinvention of the business model. For example, in the early 1990s, the Ryan brothers changed their full-service regular airline business into a low-cost, no-frills airline to save the firm from bankruptcy. Such a strategic change to create differentiation requires innovation to the business model. The business model innovation that created Ryanair was not only instrumental in saving the firm from bankruptcy but also contributed to the re-emergence of the firm as a profitable airline (Casadesus-Masanell and Ricart, 2010).

1.2 Business Model Innovation and Performance

The design of new business models has been shown to affect performance (Zott and Amit, 2008). The design of the business model encompasses how the activities are configured, their relationship with one another and the actions taken by management to maintain the congruence of the link between the customer value proposition of the external market environment and how value is monetised. For example, some business model configurations in Formula 1 racing have a superior performance to others (Aversa et al., 2015), and certain service-based business models among manufacturing firms have been shown to improve performance (Visnjic et al., 2014).

Such a positive relationship between business model innovation is evident not only in larger firms but also in small- and medium-sized firms (Cucculelli and Bettinelli, 2015). However, research shows that there are contingency factors affecting the relationship between business model innovation and performance. Zott and Amit (2008) studied the relationship between strategic positioning and business model design in relation to performance by examining relatively new firms that conducted parts of their business over the Internet. They classified these businesses based on the degree of novelty (novelty-centred business model) – new ways of conducting economic exchanges – and degree of efficiency (efficiency-centred business model) – reducing transaction costs for all transaction participants. They showed that, as firms pursued a differentiation strategy, there was a positive relationship between the degree of novelty-centred and efficiency-centred business model design in relation to firm performance in terms of market value. However, high design novelty has a stronger positive relationship than efficiency-centred business model design. This is because firms that pursue a differentiation strategy need to make their customer value proposition different to that of their competitors, which might entail new ways of doing business through radically different business models rather than merely reducing the transaction costs for the customer. On the other hand, when firms try to design business models with both high design efficiency and novelty in their business model, the performance tends to decline as a result of experiencing diseconomies of scale. This is in line with the positioning school of strategy that argues that firms seeking to be cost leaders, and also to differentiate, can ultimately become stuck in the middle and hence fail to create superior competitive advantage.

Building on this early work on business model design and performance, Velu (2015) addressed the question of how the degree of business model innovation affects the survival of new firms. The research analysed new firms that launched electronic trading platforms in the US bond market between 1995 and 2004 following the advent of internet technology. The study showed that new firms with a high or low degree of business model innovation are more likely to survive for longer than new firms with a moderate degree of business model innovation. The study also showed that partnering with third-party firms with complementary assets reduces the survival of new firms as the degree of business model innovation increases. This might be because such complementary assets derived from partnering might be most effective when the business model is not altered radically, as it creates significant complexity and coordination costs. Research has also shown that the relationship between business model innovation and performance might be related to the types of skill set held by the managers (Patzelt et al., 2008). For example, in the biotechnology industry, founder-based firm-specific experience contributes more positively to performance in the case of platform firms focusing on the commercialisation of research services or enabling technologies compared to biotherapeutic firms that continuously need to come up with new drugs. This is because such platform-based firms are not radically altering the core proposition over time. However, founder-based firm-specific experience has a negative impact on performance in therapeutics firms that focus on biotherapeutic products (drugs) because new drug development requires new knowledge and skill sets.

1.3 Challenges to Business Model Innovation

Incumbent firms often find it extremely challenging to innovate their business models effectively despite ample evidence of the positive effects on performance of such innovations. Business model innovation can occur when there are changes in the components, or interdependencies between the components, in order to serve an existing, or new, market (Amit and Zott, 2012; Casadesus-Masanell and Zhu, 2013). Such business model innovation might require, among other things, *reactivating* – changing the set of activities; *relinking* – changing the linkage between activities; *repartitioning* – changing the boundaries of the focal firm; or *relocating* – changing the location in which activities are performed (Santos et al., 2015). Such decisions need to be made in order to maintain congruence between the different components of the business model to ensure that the positive reinforcing factors are harnessed, while managing the conflicts arising from the negative mitigating factors. There are two principal reasons for the difficulty that incumbent firms face in innovating their business models. First, senior management tends to get locked into a cognitive frame with a dominant business model design that it is unable to reframe appropriately in a timely manner – the *cognitive challenge*. Second, incumbent firms tend to find it difficult to reconfigure their activities and processes from an architectural perspective to change the business model – the *reconfiguration challenge*. We review these challenges next.

1.3.1 The Cognitive Challenge

The importance of the cognitive framework and the influence of the dominant design of the business model have significant implications for the ability of incumbent firms to innovate their business models. For example, Xerox was one of the major firms in terms of the number of patents held in the 1960s and 1970s. In fact, Xerox PARC (Xerox's Palo Alto Research Centre) was responsible for many science-based technological inventions, such as the mouse, word-processing software, the personal computer and the graphical user interface. However, Xerox did not commercialise these inventions (Chesbrough and Rosenbloom, 2002); the firm's success in the past was partly responsible for such a missed opportunity. In order to understand why this is the case, it is instructive to review the history of Xerox.

Xerox was originally known as the Haloid Company, which developed the first dry photocopier technology. Xerox launched the 914 dry copier in 1959 when the prevalent technology was wet copiers.[6] The 914 copier would have retailed at over $2,000, which was close to seven times the price of a regular wet photocopier, at $300. Since wet copiers were cumbersome to use, as one needed to wait for the ink to dry upon photocopying, clients only photocopied very important documents. In order to make the 914 copier attractive to clients, Xerox decided to encourage leasing of the machines at $95 per month, with the first 2,000 copies free, although at the time most clients did not

---

[6] This was called the 914 copier because the photocopier used paper that was 9 by 14 inches.

photocopy more than 2,000 copies per month so they felt that the 914 copier was good value for money. However, once they started using the 914 copier, they soon began copying more than 2,000 copies per month and paying Xerox four cents per copy above the 2,000 copies. The success of the leasing model prompted Xerox to vertically integrate into the paper business in order to make additional profits from supplying the paper to clients for photocopying. The 914 copier soon became a bestseller and accounted for two-thirds of Xerox's revenue.

The success of the photocopying business for Xerox prompted its senior management team to develop a vision for transforming how the office would work in the future, with Xerox machines central to that vision. This vision was also driven by the fear of Xerox becoming redundant following the emergence of the paperless office enabled by digital technologies such as the digital computer. Hence, Xerox set up Xerox PARC and hired some of the most brilliant scientists to work on the latest technologies, which resulted in some of the major inventions listed above. However, the new propositions from Xerox PARC did not fare well in the annual budgeting process because they did not conform to Xerox's business model. In particular, when the inventions (such as the Star workstation and the Ethernet) from Xerox PARC were presented to the senior management at Xerox, the latter asked a simple question: "How would these technologies help speed up photocopying?" This was because the volume and speed of copying were central to the success of the 914 copier, and hence to Xerox's growth. Since the scientists did not have a clear answer to the question, the inventions were not funded for further development and therefore not commercialised by Xerox. In fact, several of the key technologies and patents were sold to the founders, Steve Jobs and Bill Gates, to form Apple and Microsoft, respectively.

Another example of the cognitive framing and dominant design affecting the decisions of firms is the failure of the Polaroid Corporation to commercialise digital cameras (Tripsas, 2010). Polaroid introduced the first instant camera in 1948. The leading firm was Kodak, which had transformed the camera industry by introducing the Brownie chemical-based film camera in 1901, and the technology was still dominant in the market. However, Kodak cameras were still cumbersome to use, as the films needed to be processed separately in a lab. In 1965, Polaroid introduced the "Swinger" instant camera model. In order to encourage sales, it dropped the price of the camera to stimulate demand for the film and hence increased the price of the films. This was the "razor and blade" business model, with the razor (the camera, in the case of Polaroid) sold at a loss in order to stimulate demand for the blades (the films, in the case of Polaroid), which are sold at a premium. In 1972, Polaroid invented the SX-70, with the lab for development essentially embedded in the camera: the SX-70 provided one-step developing following the photo being taken, with no waste. The success of the Polaroid Corporation was a source of great envy for other firms. Between 1948 and 1978, Polaroid showed annual growth rates of 23 per cent in sales, 17 per cent in profit and 17 per cent in share price.

The success of Polaroid enabled it to invest heavily in research and development. The spirit of the high-risk radical invention in the firm was captured in a quote from the 1980 annual report to shareholders: "Do not undertake the program unless the goal is manifestly important and its achievement nearly impossible." Such a focused effort in R&D at Polaroid enabled the firm to file some of the early patents in digital camera technology. However, it was slow to realise the potential of commercialising digital photography because of the dominant design of the razor and blade business model of Polaroid, which influenced the cognitive framing of the senior management team in the evaluation of new technologies. This is evident in a quote from the CEO of Polaroid at that time: "...in the photographic business all the money is in the software, none of it's in the hardware ... so the fundamental objective in these things was to find ways to advance products but that would be useful for improving the software sales." Since digital photography essentially eliminates the distinction between the camera (razor) and the film (blade), the senior management team rejected commercialising digital photography despite having in-depth knowledge of the technology from its own patents. Xerox and Polaroid were leaders of not only the existing technology but also the new technologies in their respective fields. However, they struggled to leverage these new technologies in order to commercialise them. The challenge for Xerox and Polaroid was not technological know-how but overcoming the cognitive framing of their respective business models that made them world leaders. In order to enable business model innovation, there needs to be a means of systematically changing the cognitive framing of the business model by managers. How this can be done will be the subject of later chapters. Next, we look at how firms are able to overcome the reconfiguration challenge.

1.3.2 The Reconfiguration Challenge

In this section we discuss why managers, even when they are able to overcome the dominant logic of their previous business model as a result of cognitive framing, might still respond in a sub-optimal way. We call this the reconfiguration challenge. There are three broad reasons why firms might respond sub-optimally when trying to innovate their business model, namely, tactical responses, organisational design issues and leadership challenges. Let us examine these in turn.

The first reason is the result of firms using tactical responses that might destroy the economics of the business model. This is because firms change the value proposition of an existing business model via a tactical response through their operating model without altering the underlying business model. An example of this can be seen in the rental car industry (Hart et al., 2005). Zipcar is a car rental business that was launched in Boston, the United States, in June 2000. Zipcar's business model was different to the major incumbent car rental firms in the United States at that time, such as Hertz, Avis and Enterprise. Specifically, Zipcar enabled car rental by the hour, whereas the major incumbents only allowed rental by the day. Zipcar stationed its cars around cities and near residential neighbourhoods in pre-paid public parking spots where customers could pick up their cars and return them. The pick-up and drop-off processes were made very simple for the customer. Specifically, the car keys were left in the cars and members of Zipcar could unlock a car that they had booked by waving their Zipcar membership card – a unique proximity card called Zipcard – on the front windscreen during pick-up or drop-off.[7] The cars were booked via the Zipcar website when one became a member and paid the annual subscription of $75; the cars were charged by the hour directly to customers' credit or debit cards. The Zipcar model was cheaper than renting from the incumbent car rental firms, as the former included gas and insurance. Moreover, the incumbent car rental firms allowed rental by the full day but not by the hour.

The initial reaction of the incumbent car rental firms such as Hertz was to downplay the potential impact of Zipcar on their business. Indeed, Hertz did not initially respond to the launch of Zipcar but

---

[7] Zipcar extended this to a mobile phone application, whereby customers can unlock their cars using their mobile phone.

began to see a slowdown in its revenue growth from 12.5 per cent in 2004 to 7.9 per cent in 2007. Moreover, when Hertz observed the successful expansion of Zipcar across various cities in the United States, it decided to respond with a business model that leveraged its fleet of cars and brand reputation. Hertz allowed rental by the hour in the Manhattan area of New York City in 2007: customers would pick up and drop off the cars in one of the Hertz depots. It soon became apparent to Hertz that this was destroying the economics of its business model, for two reasons. First, the systems and processes of Hertz were not designed to manage the new customer value proposition of renting cars by the hour. Hence, management of the inventory of cars required a separate process, which increased the costs involved. Second, the randomness of customer's renting by the hour added complexity to managing the car fleet for regular customers who rented by the day. Therefore, the service levels decreased as a result of the firm not being able to match the customer booking preferences exactly. Hertz therefore decided to abandon its business model experiment of adding a new customer value proposition of car rental by the hour and focus on the existing business model that was designed to deliver car rental by the day. Eventually, in 2008, Hertz launched Connect as a separate business that enabled rental by the hour with a separate car fleet to the conventional Hertz business model.

The second reason for a sub-optimal response is the organisational design and its implications for how the business model is launched. This might be because the firm launches a new business model to deliver the new value proposition and tactically integrates it with the existing business model. Such an approach could create conflict among the components of the business model. An example of this is the development of a new business model that retrofits the existing business model, as seen in the response of Blockbuster to the emergence of Netflix (Shih et al., 2007). Figure 1.3 shows the stark contrast of the share price performance of Netflix and Blockbuster, respectively, between 2002 and 2010.[8] Netflix was created in 1997 and quickly evolved a business model of renting DVDs based on membership subscription. Netflix, an online business, also pioneered the delivery of DVDs by post rather than through retail stores. Blockbuster, which had more than 5,000 video rental stores across

---

[8] Netflix was listed in 2002.

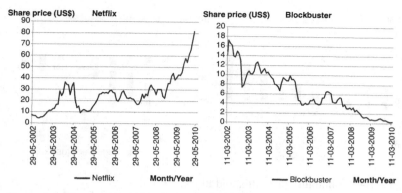

Figure 1.3 Share price of Netflix and Blockbuster
Source: Yahoo Finance

the United States, initially did not respond to the threat posed by Netflix. However, when it did respond in 2004, Blockbuster launched an online proposition, Blockbuster.com, to replicate the business model of Netflix, which was run in tandem with the Blockbuster store model. Blockbuster felt that its customer value proposition was better than that of Netflix because the customer could rent movies either online or through the store network seamlessly. This is encapsulated by a quote from the CEO of Blockbuster in 2008, Jim Keyes: "I've been frankly confused by this fascination that everybody has with Netflix ... Netflix doesn't really have or do anything that we can't or don't already do ourselves."

Two aspects of the response are worth noting, the first being the elimination of late return fees by Blockbuster. Blockbuster had a policy of charging fees for late returns; the late fees generated approximately $600 million per annum, which was roughly 10 per cent of the company's revenue. In addition to the revenue, late fees enabled Blockbuster to manage its inventory, as customers had an incentive to return the rentals in a timely manner. Since Netflix and Blockbuster.com were subscription models with no late fees, Blockbuster decided to drop its late fees for stores in 2005. Second, in order to provide an even better value proposition for its customers compared to Netflix, it allowed customers to return DVDs received by post via Blockbuster.com to Blockbuster stores. This added complexity to its inventory management system and increased costs further. Both the loss in revenue from dropping late fees and the added costs of complexity from

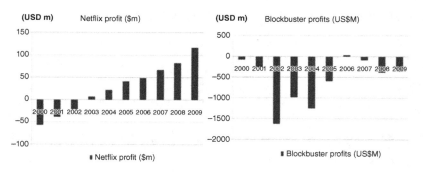

Figure 1.4 Profitability of Netflix and Blockbuster
Source: Financial statements of Netflix and Blockbuster

inventory management resulted in a poor performance at Blockbuster. The cost/income ratio of Blockbuster in 2003 prior to the year it launched Blockbuster.com was 0.72, and this had grown to 1.11 by 2009. In contrast, Netflix's cost/income ratio in 2003 was 0.80, and this came down to 0.74 by 2009. Figure 1.4 shows the profitability performance of Blockbuster and Netflix, respectively, between 2000 and 2009.[9] These factors, together with the high cost of its branch network, resulted in Blockbuster filing for Chapter 11 bankruptcy in September 2010. It is clear that the response of Blockbuster in launching a new business model, and trying to integrate new customer propositions into the existing business model, created a mismatch between the components of its business model.

The third reason for a sub-optimal response is a lack of leadership in transforming the business model. An example of this is the case of Nokia (Doz and Keeley, 2017), the leading firm in the mobile phone industry in the early 2000s. However, the firm could not transform its business model fast enough to be a leader in the smartphone industry. In 2003, Nokia had two business divisions, Nokia Mobile Phones (NMP) and Nokia Networks (NET). NMP focused on selling handsets to distributors and operators, while NET focused on selling bundled handset deals to operators. Nokia decided, in September 2003, to adopt the matrix organisational structure to enable strategic differentiation between mobile phones, multimedia and enterprise solutions.

---

[9] The last annual report available for Blockbuster was for 2009.

Such a structure would also enable the sharing of common marketing, sales, logistics and technology platforms for these businesses. However, the benefits of the matrix organisational structure did not materialise because of the lack of a clear "strategic vision" by the senior management team. This resulted in middle managers negotiating resource allocation via committees, which slowed down decision-making, with a lack of overall responsibilities for a technology roadmapping strategy. Moreover, during this period, mobile phone evolution from voice and text to smartphones meant a shift from focusing on market segmentation to mass customisation driven by software applications rather than the hardware of the phone. However, Nokia was slow to make the shift from traditional mobile phones to smartphones because of the lack of leadership, coupled with short-term quarterly sales targets, and a cap of 10 per cent on R&D over sales meant that the focus was on improving the existing mobile phones.

The above examples illustrate the importance of business model innovation in sustaining superior performance. The effectiveness of the business model in contributing to performance is based on the alignment and congruence between the value proposition, value creation, value capture and value network. As discussed earlier, there are several components to the business model: the value proposition, value creation, value capture and value network. Therefore, "fit" here refers to the internal consistency of the various components of the business model. Drazin's and Van de Ven's (1985) systems approach to fit is relevant here, whereby fit is defined as the degree of internal consistency of multiple contingencies and structural and performance characteristics. The cases provide vivid illustrations of how the lack of congruence could arise from activity and organisational design elements and, if not managed appropriately, could have detrimental consequences. Therefore, developing a business model where there is fit among the components of the business model, and continuing to maintain such congruence as tactical elements are changed, are among the biggest challenges that firms face.[10] This calls for measuring and managing such congruence of the business model components via a Business Model Coherence Scorecard (Velu, 2020).

---

[10] Drazin and Van de Ven (1985) assume that there are various ideal types that might give a superior performance. In that sense, there is equifinality among the various combinations of options to configure the tactical choices.

1.4 Discussion and Outline of This Book

The cases show that the relationship between customer value propositions and business model design is crucial in order to create and sustain competitive advantage. In particular, understanding the relationship between strategy, business models and tactics is key. This is captured well by a quote from Ronald de Jong, former CEO of Philips CL, Germany, who said: "When the business model is innovative, operations and the product will follow automatically." However, because of the functional nature of organisational design many firms tend to respond tactically to changes in the market environment by assuming that the business model is a given. Often, the product, price, promotion and distribution channels are leveraged individually and not collectively as the basis for a tactical response to changes in the strategic environment. Hence, this piecemeal response raises the question of who should be responsible for the business model. Often, in large organisations, as a result of the functional specialisation in order to drive efficiency, ownership of the business model is either dissipated or neglected altogether. Hence, firms often struggle when there are changes in the environment that call for innovation to the business model in order to serve a new market, or to serve an existing market with a different value proposition.

Management needs to overcome the cognitive and reconfiguration challenges in order to innovate the business model effectively. The challenge arises as there are always market and technological uncertainties affecting firms. Firms need some simple rules or metaphors, as managers are rationally bounded and can therefore only process so much information. Hence, management faces the cognitive challenge of refreshing the dominant logic of the business from time to time as the market environment or technology changes (Martins et al., 2015). Moreover, as management attempts to innovate the business model through reactivating, relinking, repartitioning or relocating, it is important to maintain dynamic consistency or fit between the components of the business model. This often calls for a deep understanding of the architecture of business models; therefore, management often faces the reconfiguration challenge, which is to execute the required change in the business model. This entails reconfiguring processes and competencies within the organisation, as well as its relationship with the external network of stakeholders.

We propose a holistic, systems-based perspective to better understand and manage these challenges in order to enable business model innovation (Velu, 2017). Such a holistic perspective highlights the hierarchical nature of business models, whereby the combination of activities comprises subsystems, which, in turn, can be connected to other subsystems. However, the interconnections imply that a change in one component, for example, due to the adoption of a new technology, could result in knock-on changes throughout the system before it settles into a new stable pattern or business model (Goldstein, 1999). Such patterned interconnections often harbour core processes that are crucial to how the business model evolves (Siggelkow, 2011; Velu, 2017). Identifying these core processes as part of the strategic objectives, and designing suitable business models, are often challenging tasks for management (Chaterjee, 2005). Such a holistic-systems-based approach to business model innovation will be required to leverage the benefits of new digital technologies and address some of the grand challenges of society. The innovation economy requires upstream activities in research and invention through to downstream experiments to leverage the new economic spaces opened up by innovation – and this requires new business models (Janeway, 2018; Schumpeter, 1939, 1942; Massa and Tucci, 2017). The remainder of the book will examine the opportunities that business model innovation creates and how management needs to go about overcoming the challenges in order to benefit from them. The chapters of the book are as follows.

Chapter 2: Business Models and Creating Markets
How do we think creatively about creating markets with new business models? This chapter will examine the role that business models play in the development of new markets. The chapter will also address how senior management could refresh the cognitive framing of the dominant design in order to identify and enable business model innovation.

Chapter 3: Organisational Structure and Leadership
What are the key principles of designing organisational structures and leadership challenges for business model innovation? This chapter will examine the leadership challenges, as well as the organisational design issues, for business model innovation. In particular, it will discuss how senior management could lead the business model innovation process and the organisational design issues to consider driving change within the firm. The chapter will also consider the design

principles for management information systems to enable business model innovation. The chapter will introduce the Business Model Coherence Scorecard (BMCS) as a means to manage the congruence of the components of the business model in order to achieve efficiency and effectiveness.

Chapter 4: Digital Technologies and Transformation

What are the key digital technologies affecting business model innovation? This chapter will examine the new digital technologies, such as additive manufacturing, blockchains, the Internet of Things (IoT) and artificial intelligence, and their potential to reshape industries. The chapter will also highlight an early-stage emerging technology, quantum technology, as it promises major business model innovation opportunities, as well as challenges, to provide benefits to society that would not be possible with existing digital technologies. It will examine the conceptual underpinnings to better understand the kinds of new business models that might emerge.

Chapter 5: Digital Platforms and Ecosystems

Why are digital platforms becoming ubiquitous and what are the business model implications? This chapter will examine the benefits and challenges inherent in managing platform-based business models. It will introduce the concept of layered modular architecture (LMA) and how platform business models evolve over time. In addition, the chapter will discuss the strategic issues of managing platforms within a business-to-consumer (B2C), compared to a business-to-business (B2B), setting.

Chapter 6: Small- and Medium-Sized Enterprises and Start-Up Business Models

What are the business model challenges for small- and medium-sized enterprises (SMEs) and start-up firms trying to commercialise new technologies? This chapter will explore the challenges of SMEs, which are part of major supply chains, to innovate their business model and improve performance. In addition, it will explore the process that entrepreneurs go through when developing new business models as part of commercialising new technologies such as spin-outs from university labs. In particular, the chapter will examine the challenge that start-up firms face when designing new business models to help create markets and subsequently evolve the business model into a profitable proposition.

Chapter 7: Sustainability and Business Models

What are the benefits and challenges inherent in designing business models to address the major global sustainability challenges? This chapter will examine the challenges related to climate change and the sustainability agenda, as well as the benefits of maintaining biodiversity. In particular, it will look at the different challenges involved in value creation and value capture from a multiple-stakeholder perspective. It will examine how to internalise externalities and design business models that encompass economic, social and environmental goals.

Chapter 8: Business Models for Socio-economic Development

What are the principles of designing business models to address socio-economic challenges? This chapter will examine business model design to address issues related to healthcare, poverty, education and general well-being. In particular, it will address novel business model design, where market solutions and government intervention alone might not be sufficient to address the issues.

Chapter 9: Conduct Risk and Business Models

What are the principles of designing business models to ensure fair customer and market outcomes? This chapter will explore how the global financial crisis highlighted the need to design business models in financial institutions that are profitable, while ensuring fair customer outcomes and the integrity of markets. It will introduce the concept of conduct risk and its relevance for sectors more generally beyond financial services. The principles of designing business models to manage conduct risk, and the implications, will be discussed.

Chapter 10: Conclusion

This chapter will review the role of new technologies in fostering business model innovation to enable industrial revolutions by glancing into business history. It will also revisit some of the general principles of the design of economic systems and the role of government in influencing the design of business models. This chapter will provide some concluding thoughts, from a theoretical and practical perspective, for fruitful and impactful research opportunities on business model innovation in the future.

Chapter 1 has provided an overview of the importance of understanding business model innovation and its relationship with strategy formulation and tactical choice, including its impact on performance. It also provided an overview of the cognitive and reconfiguration challenges. These aspects provided the basis for an overview of the following chapters.

References

Amit, R. and Zott, C. (2012). Creating Value through Business Model Innovation. *MIT Sloan Management Review* 53(53310): 41–49.

Aversa, P., Furnari, S., and Haefliger, S. (2015). Business Model Configurations and Performance: A Qualitative Comparative Analysis in Formula One Racing. *Industrial and Corporate Change* 24(3): 655–676.

Baden-Fuller, C. and Haefliger, S. (2013). Business Models and Technological Innovation. *Long Range Planning* 46(6): 419–426.

Baden-Fuller, C. and Mangematin, V. (2013). Strategic Organization: A Challenging Agenda. *Strategic Organization* 11(4): 418–427.

Bean, S. C. (2016). Independent Review of UK Economic Statistics. Final Report (March). https://assets.publishing.service.gov.uk/media/5a7f6034 40f0b62305b86c45/2904936_Bean_Review_Web_Accessible.pdf

Casadesus-Masanell, R. and Ricart, J. E. (2010). From Strategy to Business Models and onto Tactics. *Long Range Planning* 43(2–3): 195–215.

Casadesus-Masanell, R. and Zhu, F. (2013). Business Model Innovation and Competitive Imitation: The Case of Sponsor-Based Business Models. *Strategic Management Journal* 34: 464–482.

Chandler, A. D. (1977). *The Visible Hand: The Managerial Revolution in American Business*. Cambridge, MA: Belknap Press of Harvard University Press.

Chaterjee, S. (2005). Core Objectives: Clarity in Designing Strategy. *California Management Review* 47(2): 33–50.

Chesbrough, H. and Rosenbloom, R. S. (2002). The Role of the Business model in Capturing Value from Innovation: Evidence from Xerox Corporation's Technology Spin-Off Companies. *Industrial and Corporate Change* 11(3): 529–555.

Cucculelli, M. and Bettinelli, C. (2015). Business Models, Intangibles and Firm Performance: Evidence on Corporate Entrepreneurship from Italian Manufacturing SMEs. *Small Business Economics* 45(2): 329–350.

David, B. P. A. (1990). The Dynamo and the Computer: An Historical Perspective on the Modern Productivity Paradox. *The American Economic Review* 80(2): 355–361.

Demil, B. and Lecocq, X. (2010). Business Model Evolution: In Search of Dynamic Consistency. *Long Range Planning* 43 (2/3): 227–246.

Doganova, L. and Eyquem-Renault, M. (2009). What Do Business Models Do? Innovation Devices in Technology Entrepreneurship. *Research Policy* 38(10): 1559–1570.

Doz, Y. L. and Kosonen, M. (2010). Embedding Strategic Agility: A Leadership Agenda for Accelerating Business Model Renewal. *Long Range Planning* 43(2–3): 370–382.

Doz, Y. L. and Keeley, W. (2017). *Ringtone: Exploring the Rise and Fall of Nokia in Mobile Phones.* Oxford: Oxford University Press.

Drazin, R. and Van de Ven, A. (1985). Alternative Forms of Fit in Contingency Theory. *Administrative Science Quarterly* 30(4): 514–539.

Global Innovation Barometer. (2013). Global Research Findings & Insights, General Electric, January 1.

Goldstein, J. (1999). Emergence as a Construct: History and Issues. *Emergence* 1(1): 49–72. http://doi.org/10.5815/ijigsp.2012.01.06

Hao, J., Hicks, S., Popper, C., and Velu, C. (2020). Realizing the Full Potential of Digital Transformation. *The Conference Board*: 1–26.

Hart, M., Roberts, M., and Stevens, J. (2005). *Zipcar: Refining the Business Model.* Harvard Business School Case, 9-803-096.

IBM Global CEO Study. (2006). *Expanding the Innovation Horizon.* IBM Corporation.

Janeway, B. (2018). *Doing Capitalism in the Innovation Economy: Markets, Speculation and the State.* Cambridge: Cambridge University Press.

Johnson, M. W., Christensen, C. M., and Kagermann, H. (2008). Reinventing Your Business Model. *Harvard Business Review* 87(12) (December): 1–10.

Magretta. (2002). Why Business Models Matter? *Harvard Business Review* 80(3): 86–92.

Markides, C. C. and Oyon, D. (2010). What to Do against Disruptive Business Models (When and How to Play Two Games at Once). *MIT Sloan Management Review* 51(4): 27–32.

Martins, L. L., Rindova, V. P, and Greenbaum, B. E. (2015). Unlocking the Hidden Value of Concepts: A Cognitive Approach to Business Model Innovation. *Strategic Entrepreneurship Journal* 9: 99–117.

Massa, L. and Tucci, C. L. (2017). A Critical Assessment of Business Model. *Research* 11(1): 73–104.

McGahan, A. and Porter, M. (1997). How Much Does Industry Matter, Really? *Strategic Management Journal.* 18(Summer Special Issue): 15–30.

OECD (2015). *The Future of Productivity.* Paris: OECD Publishing.

Patzelt, H., Knyphausen-aufse, D., and Nikol, P. (2008). Top Management Teams, Business Models, and Performance of Biotechnology Ventures: An Upper Echelon Perspective. *British Journal of Management* 19: 205–221.

Robinson, J. (1953). The Production Function and the Theory of Capital. *Review of Economic Studies* 21(2): 81–106.

Rumelt, R. (2011). The Perils of Bad Strategy. *McKinsey Quarterly* 1(3) (June): 1–10.

Santos, J., Spector, B. and Van den Heyden, L. (2015). Toward a Theory of Business Model Change. In: N. J. Foss and T. Saebi (eds), *The Business Model Innovation: The Organizational Dimension*. Oxford: Oxford University Press.

Schumpeter, J. (1939). *Business Cycles: A Theoretical, Historical, and Statistical Analysis of the Capitalist Process*, vol 1. New York: McGraw-Hill.

Schumpeter, J. (1942). *Capitalism, Socialism, and Democracy*. USA: Harper and Brothers.

Shih, W., Kaufmann, S., and Spinola, D. (2007). *Netflix*, Harvard Business School Case, 9-607-138.

Siggelkow, N. (2011). Firms as Systems of Interdependent Choices. *Journal of Management Studies* 48(5): 1126–1140.

Syverson, C. (2011). What Determines Productivity? *Journal of Economic Literature* 49(2): 326–365.

Teece, D. J. (2010). Business Models, Business Strategy and Innovation. *Long Range Planning* 43(2–3): 172–194.

Tripsas, M. and Gavetti, G.(2010). Capabilities, Cognition, and Inertia: Evidence from Digital Imaging. *Strategic Management Journal*. 21(10-11): 1147–1161.

Van Ark, B. (2016). The Productivity Paradox of the New Digital Economy. *International Productivity Monitor* 31: 3–18.

Velu, C. (2015). Business Model Innovation and Third-Party Alliance on the Survival of New Firms. *Technovation* 35: 1–11.

Velu, C. (2017). A Systems Perspective on Business Model Evolution: The Case of an Agricultural Information Service Provider in India. *Long Range Planning* 50(5): 603–620.

Velu, C. (2018). Coopetition and Business Models (Chapter 31). In: P. Chiambaretto, W. Czakon, A.-S. Fernandez, and F. Le Roy (eds), *The Routledge Companion to Co-Opetition Strategies*. Oxon, UK: Routledge, pp. 336–345.

Velu, C. (2020). Business Model Cohesiveness Scorecard: Implications of Digitization for Business Model Innovation. In: S. Nambisan, K. Lyytinen, and Y. Yoo (eds), *Handbook of Digital Innovation*. Edward Elgar, Cheltenham, UK. 179–197.

Velu, C. and Jacob, A. (2016). Business Model Innovation and Owner – Managers: The Moderating Role of Competition. *R&D Management* 46(3): 451–463.

Visnjic, I., Wiengarten, F., and Neely, A. (2014). Only the Brave: Product Innovation, Service Business Model Innovation, and Their Impact on Performance. *Journal of Product Innovation Management* 33: 36–52.

Zott, C. and Amit, R. (2008). The Fit between Product Market Strategy and Business Model: Implications for Firm Performance. *Strategic Management Journal* 29(2008): 1–26.

Zott and Amit, R. (2010). Business Model Design: An Activity System Perspective. *Long Range Planning* 43(2–3): 216–226.

Zott, C., Amit, R., and Massa, L. (2011). The Business Model: Recent Developments and Future Research. *Journal of Management* 37(4): 1019–1042.

2 | *Business Models and Creating Markets*

We cannot solve the problems we have created with the thinking that created them.

Albert Einstein

Introduction

Reconstructing market boundaries is a major source of business model innovation (Geroski, 1998). Such reconstruction of the market boundary might involve identifying new customer needs that an existing proposition does not meet or the development of a new proposition that meets existing needs in a fundamentally different way. Therefore, defining a firm's market is important, as it defines the identity of the firm, the skills and expertise needed and the appropriate organisational structure.

The market for potato crisps provides an illustration of the importance of market boundaries for business model innovation (Geroski, 1998). In the 1960s, potato crisps made by Smith's – a firm with the largest market share for such snacks – used to be sold as individual packs to complement drinks in pubs in the United Kingdom. The target market was predominantly working men, who went to the pub for a relaxing drink after work. Golden Wonder, a relative newcomer, redefined the market for crisps as a children's snack as part of their school lunchbox. Hence, they were positioned as family-size packs sold in supermarkets and targeted at mums, who often made the decision about their children's school lunchbox items. Golden Wonder promoted the new family-size offering in a major national advertising campaign targeted at mothers and children. The advertising proved to be very successful in creating a new market for crisps for Golden Wonder. The expansion of this market contributed to Smith's continued growth in annual sales. Smith's then made an incorrect inference that its market was growing despite the activities of Golden Wonder.

However, because of the much larger size of the market for family-size crisps as snacks for children and for consumption by families at home, Golden Wonder overtook Smith's and became the market leader in a very short period of time. Only after new management had been installed did Smith's respond with successive innovations, which then grew the market substantially. This case shows that one way to enter a market that is well protected is by redefining the market. Hence, identifying market boundaries almost always tops the hierarchy of strategic decisions and other decisions follow.

This chapter provides an overview of the theory of market creation, and the logics of competition, and discusses some of the appropriate frameworks in the context of business model innovation. We examine the implications for both firms and the value network.

2.1 The Theory of Market Creation

Studies have focused on the business model as a description of the firm's logic of value creation (Ghaziani and Ventresca, 2005). This conceptualisation essentially focuses on the economic and financial aspects of how value is created and captured. Such a definition is an essentialist view of a description or representation of reality that exists beyond the firm (Doganova and Eyquem-Renault, 2009). The essentialist view is problematic when considering new propositions that require new markets to be created, and, as such, the reality beyond the model has not materialised. Doganova and Eyquem-Renault (2009) introduce the notion of business models as "market devices," which have both material and discursive elements that intervene to construct markets. In such a role, the business model can be seen as a "boundary object," which connects and mediates the relationship between various stakeholders and coordinates their actions (Garud and Karnoe, 2003; Star and Griesemer, 1989). Business models have been argued to have agency to shape actions and, in turn, influence the actions of constituent stakeholders, both with and across the networks of firms, which shapes the business model (Mason and Spring, 2011). In essence, the business model as a market device acts to provide a mix of storytelling and financial logic (Magretta, 2002). Baden-Fuller and Magematin (2013) argue that business models can be seen as a set of cognitive configurations that are "manipulable instruments," which can be used by either managers of established firms or entrepreneurs to categorise the business world and better explore cause and effect. Therefore, it is important to understand the interplay between the cognitive and economic aspects of business models in order to help create the market.

Markets refer to situations in which some good or service is exchanged for a price. Factors for the development of the market include latent demand, the state of the economy, competitive pressure from related markets and relevant skills, among others. However, markets might not develop, even when such factors are favourable. There are two views about how markets might come about, namely, the discovery process and the creative process (see Alvarez and Barney, 2007; Buchanan and Vanberg, 1991). In the discovery process, the market is always in a transitory state (disequilibrium) and there is asymmetric information among stakeholders. In such a context, access to information is critical and therefore the market comes about from a search and selection process of all the possible opportunities that exist. In the creative process of market creation, opportunities do not pre-exist to be recognised or discovered. On the other hand, values and meaning emerge endogenously and the market is created as a residual process of interactions, resulting from a series of transformations of the extant reality (Sarasvathy and Dew, 2005). In this sense, creation opportunities are social constructions that do not exist independently of the perceptions of the entrepreneur or manager (Aldrich and Kenworthy, 1999). The creation of opportunities is in line with effectuation theory, which takes a set of means as a given and focuses on selecting between possible effects that can be created with that set of means (Sarasvathy, 2001, 2008). This is in contrast to causation processes, where a particular effect is given and the focus is on selecting between the means to create that effect. The market develops "causally" (has the nature of cause and effect) in the discovery process, while it develops "effectually" (capable of producing the effect) in the creative process.

There are several key implications of discovery and creation processes (Alvarez et al., 2013). First, in the case of the discovery process, objective opportunities exist because of exogenous shocks to existing markets, such as technological, regulatory or consumer preference changes. In the case of the creation process, opportunities are enacted and formed endogenously by entrepreneurs seeking to exploit them. Second, there are differences in the information and decision-making settings. In the case of the discovery process, information exists objectively in physical and social artefacts in such things as technologies, routine operating procedures and processes. This enables data collection for risk-based decision-making. By contrast, in the case of the creation process, information does not yet exist and hence the creation of opportunities forms new context-specific information. Therefore, decision-making is incremental and inductive.

Alvarez and Barney (2007) argue that it will always be possible after an opportunity is formed to describe the actions of a particular entrepreneur or manager in both "discovery" and "creation" terms. Recent studies show that the early stages of a venture appear to place greater emphasis on the creative process than the discovery process (Berends et al., 2014). The balance between these two processes reverses over time, with greater emphasis on the discovery process and less on the creative process, as the opportunity is articulated more precisely.

The emergence of casinos as a legitimate business proposition in the United States provides an example of the creation of markets as a social process (Humphreys, 2010). Although casinos had been in existence in the United States for a long time, they were often perceived as crime-laden. In order to make casinos a viable business, the stakeholders – regulators, public policy activists and financial investors involved in the industry – had to change the perception of casinos to become a legitimate leisure activity. The concerted efforts of these stakeholders through social, cultural and legal frameworks enabled the transformation of casinos from being perceived as related to crime to a financially viable entertainment business. Humphreys (2010) was able to demonstrate the evolution of casinos by analysing the content of the major newspapers in the United States – *The New York Times*, *The Wall Street Journal* and *USA Today* – to show how this positive framing took place, with an increasing number of articles discussing casinos as business enterprises for entertainment, and less emphasis on crime, over the period between 1980 and 2006. Hence, the number of casinos grew from fewer than 10 in the early 1980s to close to 150 by 2006.

Religious views and spirituality could have a significant effect on institutions and markets (Iyer et al., 2014; Iyer, 2016; Yin and Mahrous, 2022). This is exemplified by the time it took for the life insurance industry in the United States to take off. America was largely an agricultural economy during the eighteenth century (Zelizer, 1978). The mortality rates among breadwinners in the farming community were relatively high as a result of the poor health conditions in rural areas. The insurance industry saw this high mortality rate as an opportunity to provide life insurance cover for the families of farmers. However, the product did not take off, as widows and orphans were provided with assistance to overcome economic hardship by neighbours and relatives and mutual aid groups. Moreover, the farmland provided security in terms of a subsistence level of food and other income.

From the early nineteenth century, America started to industrialise, which provided opportunities for people to work in factories located in cities. The increasing urbanisation encouraged the population to migrate to the cities for jobs, which resulted in the fragmentation of the close-knit family ties that had existed before in the farmlands. As a result, the risk of economic hardship was high for families that had migrated to the cities in the event that the breadwinner passed away. The insurance industry again saw this as an opportunity to provide life insurance cover for these families, who no longer had neighbours and relatives or the farmland to protect them from hardship. However, the life insurance industry still struggled to take off despite the evident need for it. In fact, the reason for the lack of demand for life insurance was the prevailing religious view that planning for one's death through the purchase of life insurance could hasten one's death, as it profanes the sanctity of death. The insurance industry had to overcome this religious and moral view by working with the pastoral community through the Sunday church service to change the view of the public by saying that a good death equates to wise and generous provision for dependents. This is exemplified by the quote below:

The necessity that exists for every head of family to make proper provision for the sustenance of those dear to him after his death is freely acknowledged and there is no contingency whereby a man stands excused from making such a provision. (Life Insurance, Journal of the Manhattan Life Insurance Company, 1852) (Zelizer, 1978, p. 603)

The examples from the casino and life insurance industries show that markets need to be created in order for firms to develop a viable business. It is widely accepted that both discovery and creation processes are critical for market creation. Scholars have emphasised the importance of examining the role of the business model in the creation of new markets (see Doganova and Eyquem-Renault, 2009; Santos and

Eisenhardt, 2009). Next, we discuss the concept of business model inno-vation requiring creative thinking about markets through changing the meaning of the proposition (products/services), analogical reasoning and conceptual combinations (Martins et al., 2015; Verganti, 2009).

2.2 Changing the Meaning of the Proposition

The meaning of a particular artefact could change depending on the problem it is trying to solve. Let us consider the development of the bicycle (Pinch and Bijker, 1987). Early forms of the bicycle had a large front wheel, such as the Penny Farthing. The attractiveness of the larger front wheel lay in the fact that for a fixed angular velocity one way of getting a higher translational velocity over the ground was to enlarge the radius of the wheels. However, this created a hazard for the rider, as the disparity in the size of the wheels and the location of the rider's position over the centre of the wheel meant that a hitting a stone on the road could easily throw the rider over the handle bar. Hence, bicycles with a smaller wheel base were developed with safety considerations in mind. These low-wheeled bicycles resulted in bumpy rides. In order to address this issue, firms such as Dunlop introduced pneumatic tyres, which had air pumped into the types to help mitigate the vibrations from the road. Initially, this was ridiculed, as they were prone to slipping on muddy roads and did not have a particularly aesthetic look. Moreover, when air tyres were first introduced in a bicycle race, they were met with derision. However, the laughter was silenced when, to everyone's astonishment, the air-tyre-based bicycle achieved high speeds and left its rivals in its wake. The proponents had reformulated the meaning of air tyres – from an artefact meant to solve the vibration problem – to achieve speed. Such a redefinition of the problem gave air tyres prominence and acceptability, resulting in the development of business models to make and sell them.

Changing the meaning of the key customer value proposition could result in the emergence of new markets and hence business models. Let us consider the evolution of the watch market (Verganti, 2009). Watches were predominantly seen as a luxury item, and Swiss watchmakers had a global market share of over 40 per cent up until the mid-1970s. The Swiss watch manufacturers invented the Quartz movement but did not adopt it as a core technology for their watches, as they felt that it did not fit their core competencies of precision mechanics and assembly. The

Japanese company, Seiko, was the first to adopt the Quartz technology and develop a watch with LED (light-emitting diode) and LCD (liquid crystal display) technologies in the early 1970s. These cheaper watches were positioned not as luxury items but as time-keeping pieces that customers were socialised to wear on their wrists every day. In response, Swiss watchmakers made their watches even more luxurious in order to avoid competition from the Japanese watchmakers. However, as a result of the emergence of the Japanese watchmakers with their low-end time-keeping pieces, the Swiss watch industry market share dropped to less than 3 per cent by the end of the 1970s, with the closure of more than 1,000 watchmakers among the 1,600 in business at that time.

In the early 1980s, a consultant for Swiss bankers, Nicholas Hayek, came across the crisis unfolding in the Swiss watch industry and suggested that two of the major Swiss watchmakers, SSIH and ASUAG, combine to form Swatch. Swatch aimed to change the meaning of the watch industry again to make watches a fashion item. In order to do this, Swatch had to change the nature of watch manufacturing. They used the latest Quartz technology but with analogue displays, which allowed the firm to change the process whereby traditional Swiss watches were made in their entirety and assembled inside the casing. However, Swatch made all of the components separately and bonded them to the lower part of the casing, which allowed them to use more automated technology, to make the watches thinner and also, importantly, to change the casing depending on the fashion without altering the core watch. Swatch was then able to position the watches as fashion items, which was a major success, enabling the firm to grow exponentially in the 1980s. Hence, the evolution of the watch industry was enabled by changes in its meaning from its initial beginnings as a luxury item, to a time-keeping piece, and then to a fashion item supported, in turn, by the development of new business models. Figure 2.1 provides a summary of the watch industry and changing the meaning of markets.

The meanings of a proposition to support the development of markets are often based on schemas. Schemas are the knowledge structures that contain categories of information and their relationships (DiMaggio, 1997). One needs to understand how schemas emerge in order to understand how meanings change and hence new markets develop. Bingham and Kahl (2013) discuss the three stages of the emergence of a new schema: assimilation, deconstruction and unitisation. Their study shows that the insurance industry was one of the

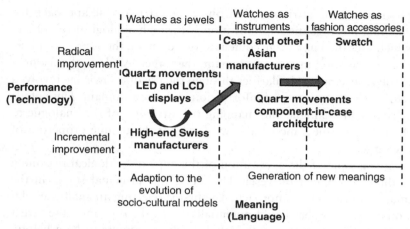

Figure 2.1 Changing the meaning of markets
Source: Adapted from Verganti (2009)

first to adopt computers after they were developed for business use following the Second World War. The insurance industry identified two opposing schemas, namely, "machine" and "brain" analogies, respectively, to describe the computer. The "machine" schema was adopted first, as it related more closely to the automation of routine processes in the insurance industry. This is the assimilation process. The machine schema did not significantly emphasise the novel features of the computer. However, as the technology improved and the insurance industry became more accustomed to the use of computers, the industry started to adopt the "brain" analogy, which was aided by the computer's ability to be programmed and provide support to management in decision-making. This is the deconstruction process. Hence, computers were adopted for their novel features rather than merely for the automation of existing processes. This process eventually resulted in the emergence of a new schema for business computers, which is termed the unitisation process.

2.3 Analogical Reasoning

An important aspect of business model innovation happens through changing its schema. The schema is defined as cognitive structures that represent knowledge about the business model attributes and the relations among attributes (Martins et al., 2015). One approach for enabling business model innovation is through analogical reasoning, which uses the knowledge content in one domain, the source, to interpret information in another domain, the target. Analogical reasoning involves leveraging similarities through the use of knowledge involved in one schema to interpret information in the new domain. This entails selecting an analogue and mapping the attributes of the analogue to the target business model and working out the unique properties of the target.

An example of the application of this type of analogical reasoning is the development of Tesla. There are four principal stages in the analogical reasoning approach. The first is selecting an analogue relational structure that could potentially be used to organise the target concept. For example, Tesla found Apple computers to be a helpful analogue in seeking to differentiate its electric car technology from internal combustion engine cars. It is important that managers look outside the immediate domain in which they are operating to find such analogues. The key is to find industry contexts that have been trying to solve a similar problem to the ones currently being addressed. For example, the Tesla model's founder, Elon Musk, refers to Model S as his Apple Macintosh, which acts as the target analogue for the design of Tesla cars. The second stage involves mapping the relational structures and similarities. Often, managers focus on the attributes that are similar between the source and the target. Although this is helpful, the more important concept is to identify the relationship between attributes and the underlying structures in order to inform the activity system of the target business model scheme. For example, there is a need to compete on high-end design, with Tesla having some very Apple-like design characteristics, including attention to detail, in order to make the Tesla Model S as distinctive as possible.

Third, one needs to determine which elements of the analogue to incorporate. For example, Tesla was emulating the Apple model by placing all stores in high-end malls and shopping centres instead of relying on dealer franchises, which is the common mode of sales for conventional cars. This approach enables sales staff to help configure their cars using giant touchscreens for potential customers. Moreover, these salespeople do not receive commission, as would be the case with regular car dealerships. Such a distribution system, owned by Tesla, allows the firm to launch new models in luxurious surroundings with invitation-only events. The design of such a system requires managers to have a deep understanding of the overall architecture of the activity system of the source domain, and the types of problems it is trying to solve, in order to be able to have an impact on the new business model. In the fourth stage, one needs to identify how to modify elements borrowed from the analogue. In the case of Tesla, the delivery of cars to high-end malls occurred later than was conventionally the case for Apple Macintosh as a result of the high costs of holding inventory of cars in showrooms. Managers need to have a good understanding of not only the similarities but also the principal differences between the source and the target in order to be able to design appropriate business models.

2.4 Conceptual Combination

An alternative way of creating new business models by changing the schema is the use of conceptual combinations (Martins et al., 2015). Unlike analogical reasoning, conceptual combinations leverage the differences between the source schema and the target. The use of conceptual combinations involves four steps. For example, we can illustrate the development of the Starbucks business model, a major global coffee chain, by using conceptual combinations. First, managers need to select a modifier concept. In the case of Starbucks, the firm selected bars as the modifier concept; in doing this, conceptual combinations allowed multiple modifiers to be used. For example, Starbucks used not only the bar as a modifier concept but also the concept of a gallery in terms of store design. Choosing a modifier concept could be purposeful or accidental. For example, Best Buy came up with the idea of the fire sale as a result of one of its stores being damaged by a tornado; the subsequent creation of temporary tents in order to dispose of the inventory helped the firm to come up with the idea of creating a carnival-like atmosphere in its regular stores.

Second, managers need to compare the modifier concept of the target business model schema to identify differences. For example, in the case of Starbucks, there is usually a difference in the roles of the bartender, in the case of the bar, and the barista, in the case of the coffee shop. The bartender tends to know his or her regular customers well and has conversations with them, while the coffee retailer might have a more impersonal relationship with the customer. Moreover, in the bar, the drinks are customisable, whereas in traditional coffee outlets, there are standard coffee options. The idea is to identify the key differences between the modifier and the target in such a way as to be able to select prototypical concepts so that their meaning can be transferred from the modifier to the new concept (Wisniewski, 1997). This process would enable managers to understand the true differences between the target and the modifier. For example, the founder of Starbucks, Howard Schultz, started to question the initial business model of Starbucks when he visited Italy and discovered how emotionally attached the Italians were to their coffee, which prompted Starbucks to embrace the more personal-connection-based model.

The third step involves the ability to integrate selected values, fillers of the modifier concept, to the slots that need to be filled in the target concept. For example, in the case of Starbucks, baristas provide a customisable menu of drinks and develop a more personalised relationship with their regular customers. Moreover, values from the schemas of an office are used to attract business people for prolonged use, while the gallery-like atmosphere enables Starbucks to increase the aesthetic value of the coffee-drinking experience. Fourth, there is the ability to adapt new fillers in the new business model schema to make it fit the characteristics of the target business model and its context. For example, in the case of Starbucks, there are no barstools and customers do not chat with the baristas while consuming their coffee. It is possible that the combination of new fillers borrowed from the modifier concept might create the opportunity for new combinations of value and hence possible new business models. This is a major difference between conceptual combination and analogical reasoning. In the case of analogical reasoning, the concepts are borrowed at systems level, while in conceptual combinations, the concepts are identified at each element. Therefore, in the case of conceptual combinations, there is the potential to combine unrelated elements and hence create new dimensions of value for the possible emergence of new business models.

The different ways that schemas or logics are combined to enable innovation and create new markets are also called recombinant strategies. Different approaches are used by firms to implement these recombinant strategies (Dalpiaz et al., 2016). For example, Alessi, an Italian manufacturer of consumer utensils for the kitchen, combined the logics of art with industrial manufacturing to create a new market for artistic kitchenware. Alessi's early attempts to combine the two schemas were based on getting artists such as sculptors to suggest designs for the kitchenware. This approach ran into technical difficulties, as the sculptors proposed designs that were not compatible with large-volume manufacturing processes. Alessi subsequently revised its approach by following an enrichment approach to its recombinant strategy. Alessi proposed that the functional value of the product needed to be retained while being enhanced by using arts and culture. This approach would maintain the industrial manufacturing logic while being enhanced by the art and cultural logic. Alessi worked with external designers with an artistic background who appreciated industrial design challenges. This process created several new designs that were appealing to hotels and bars, which made it a major success.

Alessi leveraged lessons from this stage to make new products that were simultaneously tools with functionality while also being art. For example, it introduced tea and coffee sets designed by artisan workshops by making them in silver first, which overcame the constraints imposed by steel-based manufacturing. These became a major success and were purchased by museums around the world. Once the products received positive acclaim as a result of being purchased by museums, less radical versions were designed to conform to the large-scale manufacturing processes. Hence, Alessi was able to adopt innovation in organisational practices, resulting in fundamental changes to its design and manufacturing processes, which provided the basis for creating the new art-based kitchenware market.

2.5 The Logics of Competition and Strategy

The logics of competition are an important aspect of understanding the development of markets (Barnett, 2017). The logics of competition determine the principles of *who can compete, how they compete,* on *what criteria they compete* for success or failure and *what outcomes they compete on* in order to determine the consequences of success or failure. Such principles are determined by the notion of meta-competition. The conventional notion of competition involves firms trying to learn to be better than their competitors. Once a firm is able to pull away from its competitors, the competing firms often try to outdo the lead firm, and when this succeeds the process begins again. Such competition is seen as the "Red Queen" effect (Barnett, 2008), an analogy from Lewis Carroll's *Through the Looking Glass,* where Alice needs to run as fast as possible only to stay still. The concept of trying to continuously be better than the competition has limitations, for several reasons. First, there are limits to learning and managers also tend to forget, which implies that firms often react to the latest competitive effects. Second, firms tend not to respond to just one competitor but rather co-evolve their strategies with the requirements to replicate different rivals. This approach to competition makes it challenging to manage resources and is potentially risky. Third, firms have limited cognitive capacity and tend to display myopic learning from within a small context.

Studies have also shown that firms often do not learn from failures because there is a "success bias" in learning. In order to overcome the "Red Queen" effect, firms need to engage in wider meta-competition by setting the logics of competition themselves. This might involve indirect or direct meta-competitions. Indirect meta-competition arises when there are multiple possible logics for an industry and the competition revolves around establishing one of them as the dominant paradigm. The leaders within an organisation try to establish the framing by influencing the social acceptance by working with the relevant stakeholders, such as customers, employees and governments, among others. For example, Uber is trying to position itself as a technology firm, and not a taxi firm, in order to treat its drivers not as employees but as casual workers.[1] Direct meta-competition arises when the broad contours of the industry have been set. The competition is based on different firms competing based on different logics. The issue is whether a firm is playing the right game, as opposed to playing the game well. For example, in the IT industry firms that offer "off-premises" IT services compete on the basis of scale and utilisation, which is alien to traditional enterprise IT firms providing "on-premises" services.

Barnett (2017) provides an illustration of such meta-competition in the music distribution business. Three distinct business models co-existed in the digital music distribution industry in 2003, namely, the free music downloading service, the commercial music downloading service and the commercial subscription streaming service. Although large firms and musicians consider free downloading to be illegal, there was an alternative discourse that claimed that major music labels were seeking exorbitant returns. Moreover, firms such as Apple

---

[1] The UK Supreme Court ruled in 2021 that Uber needs to treat its drives as employees rather than self-employed workers (*The Guardian*, 2021).

were initially committed to commercial music downloading services and were opposed to streaming services. For example, Steve Jobs, the CEO of Apple, at the time claimed that people should own their music albums, as they had done with LPs and CDs, and therefore they should not subscribe to streaming services. However, the increasing popularity of streaming services due to companies such as Pandora and Spotify convinced Apple to reframe its digital music proposition based on the streaming service.

Barnett (2008) emphasised that technology, regulation and the sociopolitical environment could influence the logics of competition. New technologies offer firms the ability to propose new logics of competition. For example, with the advent of the Internet, WR Hambrecht + Co, a new firm formed in 1998 and staffed by outsiders to the industry, came up with an idea whereby initial public offerings (IPOs) would be done via Dutch auctioning technology rather than by building a book through contacts, which was the traditional form practised by investment banks at the time. The auctioning approach was positioned to firms that tended towards IPOs as providing a more accurate valuation of the firm compared to investors getting the benefit through a large increase in share price immediacy after the listing, partly driven by under-pricing the IPOs. Moreover, Hambrecht promoted accessible research through the Internet rather than roadshows, which was the traditional method at the time to promote the IPO. This new logic of competition attracted significant attention when firms such as Google used Hambrecht for its IPO.

Regulation and the sociopolitical climate could affect the logics of competition, as was the case in early twentieth-century America. During the early years of the US telephone industry, the Bell System was growing and acquiring other smaller independent telephone companies. The independent telephone companies responded by cooperating with one another to fend off the threat posed by the Bell System. Legal changes and the political system at the time mandated protection to the independent companies. Counter-intuitively, such a change in regulatory setting removed the threat of the common enemy, resulting in the independents competing with one another. In essence, the legal changes due to the sociopolitical pressures at the time changed the landscape of the industry from a collective to an individualistic logic. Sometimes, firms also use the logic of predation, whereby mergers and acquisitions are used as the basis for eliminating rivals and hence maintaining the logics of competition. For example, during the early 2000s, more than a hundred electronic trading platforms were launched in the US bond trading market (Velu, 2016; Velu and Jacob, 2016). Many of these were start-up firms trying to disintermediate the market-making role of the investment banks that were dominant in the secondary trading of bonds. Some of the investment banks acquired these start-up electronic trading firms in order to help maintain the status quo of their lucrative bond trading business.

Brandenburger (2018, 2019) proposed a major question that was at the heart of competitive strategy and key to understanding market creation: *"Where do strategies come from?"* The study proposed an analytical framework for the creative process of strategy formulation that has four elements, namely, contrast, combination, constraint and context. Contrast comes from being able to make an assumption that underlies conventional thinking in an industry and challenges it. PayPal, a global online money-transfer firm, had initially taken a widely held but untested assumption in banking – namely, that transferring money between institutions, but not individuals, was fine – and then disproved it. The combination comes from connecting products and services that have traditionally been separate. For example, Apple and Nike joined forces by enabling Nike shoes to communicate with an iPod or Apple Watch to track steps. A constraint is turning a limitation or conventional liabilities into an advantage. For example, Audi converted the disadvantage that its cars could not go faster than its competitors in the Le Mans race into an advantage. It decided to build diesel-powered racers, which required fewer fuel stops than gasoline cars, and it subsequently won Le Mans three years in succession between 2004 and 2006. Context is the ability to bring ideas that at first seem disconnected to shed light on pressing problems. Intel borrowed from the notion that branded ingredients such as Teflon and NutraSweet are important drivers of brands. Intel used this insight to develop the Intel Inside marketing strategy as a way to brand the invisible computer component, the microprocessor, to help grow the PC industry.

2.6 Discussion and Frameworks

Scholars have suggested that market boundaries, and hence the conception of strategic boundaries, are based on two dimensions. The first is based on schemas, which are people's interpretational-based theories and concepts of the world. The second is based on resources, which are materially tangible and observable (Pontikes and Rindova, 2020). Structure comes about when there is an appropriate pairing between schemas and resources. Such schema–resource pairings are dynamic but stabilised when there is a consistent pattern in the use of resources that is defined by the schema; in turn, the allocation of resources is validated by the schemas. However, it is instructive to note that structure is not objectively determined, as structures can often intersect with one another at different social levels. Schema are often transposable from one area of application to another, and resources can take on different meanings depending on the context. Market structure can be seen as a schema–resource pairing that is driven by routines, technologies and business models, among others. Hence, on the one hand, markets display stability, and on the other hand, there is scope for agentic transformations.

Successful business model innovation requires the creation of new markets by changing the cultural, social and legal frameworks (Fligstein, 1996; Humphreys, 2010). There are three reasons for this. First, the demand for the proposition might not exist. Second, we need to understand how consumer needs themselves come about. Third, institutions such as property rights, governance structures and rules of exchange are required. In particular, social institutions are necessary for the existence of markets. Institutions refer to shared rules, which can be laws or collective understanding (custom, explicit and tacit agreement), which cover property rights, governance structures, conceptions of control among stakeholders and, finally, the rules of exchange. Property rights refer to the residual claimants of assets and profits. Governance structures refer to rules that define competition, cooperation and the structure of firms. Conceptions of control refer to the structure of perceptions of how the markets work, which allows the actors to interpret the actions of others and also to control situations. The rules of exchange define who can transact with whom and the conditions for transactions between parties to take place. These sets of principles that define institutions require agency from stakeholders in order to be created, maintained and changed.

Stakeholders in the marketplace need to exercise their agency in order to influence the development of markets. Scholars have proposed three forms of agency: constructive, temporal and interactive

(Pontikes and Rindova, 2020). Constructive agency involves the ability of agents to apply new schemas to the endowed resources. Therefore, constructive agency enables stakeholders to apply new schema–resource combinations in order to improve their position and transform the market structures. Moreover, such constructive agency also influences the resource accessibility of other stakeholders. Temporal agency involves the ability of agents to individualise their position by integrating their unique past and present experiences with their view of the future in order to derive their vision. Such a vision acts as the cornerstone for agents to transform the structure, which is enacted through constructive agency. Interactive agency involves interaction with others in order to learn, as well as shape their experiences of the world, which contributes to reimagining possibilities. Hence, interactive agency contributes to either enhancing or changing the vision provided by temporal agency through harmonisation or conflict with other agents. Interactive agency involves persuasive activities to influence other market actors, which entails coordinating one's actions to persuade or coerce heterogeneous market actors in order to align incentives and form a collective common purpose.

Often, there are challenges inherent in overcoming existing institutional structures for new markets to develop. These are due to practices that have created legitimacy as accepted norms by the stakeholders. In order for new markets to emerge, this accepted legitimacy of practices needs to change. In particular, studies have shown that cognitive and sociopolitical legitimacies are key aspects to consider in developing new markets (Aldrich and Fiol, 1994). Cognitive legitimacy relates to the extent to which a new form is taken for granted, the knowledge about a new activity and, finally, what is needed to succeed in an industry. Sociopolitical legitimacy relates to the extent to which a new form conforms to recognised principles or accepted rules and standards, the value placed on an activity by cultural norms and political authorities, and the process by which key stakeholders (the public, opinion leaders and government officials) accept a venture as appropriate and right. Changes to the cognitive and sociopolitical legitimacies need to be made across organisational, inter-industry and intra-industry levels. Research shows that, at organisational level, the use of inclusive language with the relevant stakeholders is key to obtaining buy-in and trust. In addition, at intra-industry level, the building of new markets calls for convergence around a dominant design by positioning the new proposition close to the existing design and encouraging collective action among stakeholders. For example, when the electric light was developed to replace oil lamps, the industry pioneer at the time positioned the lights to be similar to the design of oil lamps in order to conform to the brightness of the existing technology; they also worked with road developers to help bury the wiring below ground level (Hargadon and Douglas, 2001). At inter-industry level, the recognition that often the success of a new industry is dependent on another industry is a key factor. Hence, the ability to develop new activities by negotiating and compromising with other industries is a crucial step to enabling cooperation and building the market. For example, the development of a new healthcare provision would require the cooperation of the insurance industry.

One of the main challenges in business model innovation is the prevalence and embeddedness of the dominant logic or mental models (Prahalad and Bettis, 1986, 1995). The dominant logic is important because management often displays bounded rationality, where there is limited ability to process all of the information. In addition, scholars have emphasised the importance of formulating a strategy using simple rules or metaphors. The benefit of using simple rules is that it provides a clear and concise set of criteria for making decisions and communicating to employees. On the one hand, strategy formulation using simple rules is a powerful proposition when markets are relatively stable. However, when there is significant market and technological uncertainty, and hence there is a need to develop new markets, the use of simple rules or metaphors can be detrimental (Dunbar et al., 1996). This is because the existing dominant logic in most firms is based on the principles of deductive logic, which has an underlying premise that the world we operate in has an objective reality, and therefore any variance from the expected outcomes can be explained through a set of deductive propositions.

Much of the financial management system within organisations is based on periodic budgets and variance reporting that have a strong bias towards deductive reasoning. Such financial management practices underpinning strategy formulation are premised on explaining the variance based on a particular expected outcome and the reasons for either not achieving or overachieving the outcome. The budget-variance approach to financial management is important for

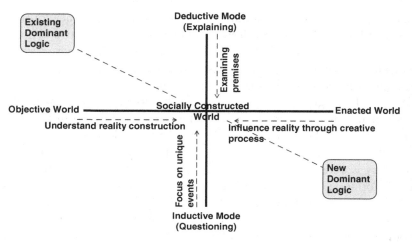

Figure 2.2 A frame for deframing the dominant logic
Source: Adapted from Dunbar et al. (1996); Prahalad and Bettis (1986, 1995)

improving the efficiency of the existing business model. However, this approach based on deductive reasoning is less appropriate for the creation of new markets – in terms of effectiveness in delivering the right value proposition. Often, new markets are socially constructed, which requires the use of inductive reasoning, whereby schemas from other sectors are used to creatively construct the new market through analogical reasoning or conceptual combinations. Therefore, it is important that there is diversity in the senior management team in order to be able to use deductive reasoning to improve the efficiency of the existing business model, while enabling the emergence of new business models through inductive reasoning.

Figure 2.2 summarises the framework for deframing these two aspects, whereby firms need to leverage the existing dominant logic while fostering the development of the new dominant logic. These two modes of thinking need to be managed and balanced in organisations in order to achieve the optimal balance between executing well on the current business model and facilitating renewal of the business model. This calls for abductive informed reasoning, whereby there is iteration between deductive and inductive reasoning in order to achieve the optimal outcome. For example, the CEO of Future Group, a major retailer in India, appointed a chief mythological officer (CMO), who often plays a major role in senior management strategy away days.[2] Based on the proposed strategic and business model innovation discussion, the CMO is often tasked with designing the first-day discussion based on a mythological story that might be connected, but not directly related, to the new business model being proposed. The objective of the first-day discussion is to try to help senior managers to deframe their dominant logic of the existing business model and to begin to consider alternative propositions. On the second day, the key strategic issues and the proposed new business models are discussed. This approach helps managers to give thoughtful consideration to any new business model proposition without dismissing it based on the metrics and success criteria of the existing business model of the firm.

Conclusion

Markets are social constructions that enable the exchange of goods and services. Reconstructing market boundaries to enable the development of new markets is a major source of business model innovation. Business models can be seen as market devices with characteristics of boundary objects that connect and mediate the relationship between various stakeholders and coordinate their actions. In doing this, business models help the functioning of markets but they also need markets in order to operate effectively. Therefore, firms need to pay adequate attention to how markets come about and strategies to influence the development of new markets as they consider business model innovation. The development of new markets is a creative process. Studies have highlighted the three approaches to thinking creatively about market creation. The first is by changing the meaning of the proposition of products or services. The second is through the use of analogical reasoning by leveraging similarities through the use of knowledge involved in one schema to interpret information in the new domain in order to help create new markets. The third approach involves the use of conceptual combination leveraging the differences between the source schema and the target to help develop new schemas.

One of the major issues that the development of new markets creates is the notion of meta-competition, whereby the logic of competition determines the principles of who can compete, how they compete, on

---

[2] Based on an interview with the founder of Future Group, Kishore Biyani.

what criteria they compete for success or failure and what outcomes they compete on in order to determine the consequences of success or failure. Firms need to ask not only how to play the game effectively but also the rules by which the new game of competition is created. Firms that are able to influence the development of such rules will become gatekeepers of the new markets and help to define the design of business models that are likely to be effective. One key element of such meta-competition and the creation of new markets and business models is to understand where strategies come from. Strategies could come from being able to make contrasting observations, combining initially unrelated elements, imposing constraints and making them advantageous and, finally, understanding the context of other innovative ventures and learning how to graft them. In developing new markets, firms need to overcome existing institutional structures that have created legitimacy as accepted norms by the stakeholders. Firms need to actively seek to change the cognitive and sociopolitical legitimacies.

Often, there are challenges inherent in overcoming existing institutional structures for new markets to develop. These are due to practices that have created legitimacy as accepted norms by the stakeholders. In order for new markets to emerge, this accepted legitimacy of practices needs to change. In particular, studies have shown that both cognitive and sociopolitical legitimacies are key aspects to consider in developing new markets. Finally, it is important for firms to understand the balance required between the deductive approaches to decision-making within firms, which is often needed to improve efficiency, and inductive logic to create new markets and improve the effectiveness of business models. Firms need to have senior management teams with the skills to do both of these things and to manage the contradictions that this might entail in order to create and capture value effectively.

There are several areas in market creation and business models that require further study covering the role of senior management, engagement of the ecosystem and the decision-making processes within firms. First, how do we develop a senior management team that has the ability to play the game of meta-competition and strategy formation to help create and shape markets? Senior management might be rooted in being in the business where the rules of the game have been predominantly defined. In such a market, marginal improvement might be fairly limited, with competition often copying innovations that provide a competitive advantage. Senior management needs to develop the skills and acumen to think about how to play the larger competition game. Defining the skills needed in the senior management team, and how they should interact with one another, is an important and relatively understudied area in top management team composition.

Second, there is the question of what kind of decision-making processes would be needed to enable schema changes and facilitate new market development. The decision-making system in firms needs to strike a balance between improving the operational efficiency of existing business models and thinking about new business models and creating new markets. Defining the principles of the governance model to enable the right balance between these two complementary, yet conflicting, processes also requires further investigation. Moreover, does such a governance model differ between the type of industries or the rate of technological change being experienced? The third area requiring further study encompasses the question of how to engage with an ecosystem of firms to enable schema changes and business model innovation. Often, there are conflicting objectives among stakeholders about what the appropriate schema change needs to be. Therefore, the notion of the interactive agency of persuading other stakeholders on the new schema – and hence the market to create – is not well understood. In particular, strategies of persuasion and coercion work better than others. Moreover, there are some powerful players in the marketplace. Hence, are there different strategies for the different players depending on their power relations in the marketplace? These are some of the research issues that require more systematic study.

This chapter has provided an overview of the principles of market creation for business model innovation and some of the outstanding research issues on this topic.

References

Aldrich, H. E. and Fiol, C. M. (1994). Fools Rush In? The Institutional Context of Industry Creation. *The Academy of Management Review* 19(4): 645–670.

Aldrich, H. E. and Kenworthy, A. (1999). The Accidental Entrepreneur: Campbellian Antinomies and Organizational Foundings. In: Joel A.C. Baum and Bill McKelvey (eds), *Variations in Organization Science: In Honor of Donald T. Campbell*. Thousand Oaks: SAGE Publications, Inc. 19–33.

Alvarez, S. A. and Barney, J. B. (2007). Discovery and Creation: Alternative Theories of Entrepreneurial Action. *Strategic Entrepreneurship Journal* 1: 11–26. Wiley InterScience.

Alvarez, S. A., Barney, J. B., and Anderson, P. (2013). Forming and Exploiting Opportunities: The Implications of Discovery and Creation Processes for Entrepreneurial and Organizational Research. *Organization Science* 24(1): 301–317.

Baden-Fuller, C. and Mangematin, V. (2013). Business Models: A Challenging Agenda. *Strategic Organization* 11(4): 418–427.

Barnett, W. P. (2008). *The Red Queen among Organisations: How Competitiveness Evolves*. Princeton, NJ: Princeton University Press.

Barnett, W. P. (2017). Metacompetition: Competing over the Game to Be Played. *Strategy Science* 2(4): 212–219.

Berends, H., Jelinek, M., Reymen, I., and Stultiens, R. (2014). Production Innovation Processes in Small Firms: Combining Entrepreneurial Effectuation and Managerial Causation. *Journal of Product Innovation Management* 31(3): 616–635.

Bingham, C. B. and Kahl, S. J. (2013). The Process of Schema Emergence: Assimilation, Deconstruction, Unitization and the Plurality of Analogies. *Academy of Management Journal* 56(1): 14–34.

Brandenburger, A. (2018). Where Do Great Strategies Really Come From? *Strategy Science* 2(4): 220–225.

Brandenburger, A. (2019). Strategy Needs Creativity: An Analytic Framework Alone Won't Reinvent Your Business. *Harvard Business Review* 97 (March–April): 50–66.

Buchanan, J. M. and Vanberg, V. J. (1991). The Market as a Creative Process. *Economics and Philosophy* 7: 167–186. Printed in the United States.

Dalpiaz, E., Rindova, V., and Ravasi, D. (2016). Combining Logics to Transform Organizational Agency: Blending Industry and Art at Alessi. *Administrative Science Quarterly* 61(3): 347–392.

DiMaggio, P. (1997). Culture and Cognition. *Annual Review Sociology* 23: 263–287.

Doganova, L. and Eyquem-Renault, M. (2009). What Do Business Models Do? Innovation Devices in Technology Entrepreneurship. *Research Policy* 38: 1559–1570. Elsevier.

Dunbar, R. L. M, Garud, R., and Raghuram, S. (1996). A Frame for Deframing in Strategic Analysis. *Journal of Management Inquiry* 5(1): 23–34.

Fligstein, N. (1996). Markets as Politics: A Political-Cultural Approach to Market Institutions. *American Sociological Review* 61(4): 656–673.

Garud, R. and Karnoe, P. (2003). Bricolage versus Breakthrough: Distributed and Embedded Agency in Technology and Entrepreneurship. *Research Policy* 32: 277–300.

Geroski, P. A. (1998). Thinking Creatively about Markets. *International Journal of Industrial Organization* 16: 677–695.

Ghaziani, A. and Ventresca, M. (2005). Keywords and Cultural Change: Frame Analysis of Business Model Public Talk, 1975–2000. *Sociological Forum* 20(4): 523–559.

Hargadon, A. B. and Douglas, Y. (2001). When Innovations Meet Institutions: Edison and the Design of Electric Light. *Administrative Science Quarterly* 46(3): 476–501.

Humphreys, A. (2010). Megamarketing: The Creation of Markets as a Social Process. *Journal of Marketing* 74: 1–19.

Iyer, S. (2016). The New Economics of Religion. *Journal of Economic Literature* 54(2): 395–441.

Iyer, S., Velu, C., and Mumit, A. (2014). Communication and Marketing of Services by Religious Organizations in India. *Journal of Business Research* 67(2): 59–67.

Magretta, J. (2002). Why Business Models Matter. *Harvard Business Review*. HBR Spotlight: Practical Strategy.

Martins, L. L., Rindova, V. P., and Greenbaum, B. E. (2015). Unlocking the Hidden Value of Concepts: A Cognitive Approach to Business Model Innovation. *Strategic Entrepreneurship Journal* 9: 99–117.

Mason, K. and Spring, M. (2011). The Sites and Practices of Business Models. *Industrial Marketing Management* 40: 1032–1041. Elsevier.

Pinch, T. J. and Bijker, W. E. (1987). *The Social Construction of Facts and Artefacts: Or How the Sociology of Science and the Sociology of Technology Might Benefit Each Other*. Cambridge, MA: MIT Press.

Pontikes, E. G. and Rindova, V. R. (2020). Shaping Markets through Temporal, Constructive, and Interactive Agency. *Strategy Science* 5(3): 149–159.

Prahalad, C. K. and Bettis, R. A. (1986). The Dominant Logic: A New Linkage between Diversity and Performance. *Strategic Management Journal* 7(6): 485–501.

Prahalad, C. K. and Bettis, R. A. (1995). The Dominant Logic: Retrospective and Extension. *Strategic Management Journal* 16(1): 5–14.

Santos, F. M. and Eisenhardt, K. M. (2009). Constructing Markets and Shaping Boundaries: Entrepreneurial Power in Nascent Fields. *Academy of Management Journal* 52(4): 643–671.

Sarasvathy, S. D. (2001). Causation and Effectuation: Toward a Theoretical Shift from Economic Inevitability to Entrepreneurial Contingency. *The Academy of Management Review* 26(2): 243–263.

Sarasvathy, S. D. (2008). *Effectuation: Elements of Entrepreneurial Expertise. New Horizons in Entrepreneurship*. Cheltenham, UK and Northampton, MA: Edward Elgar.

Sarasvathy, S. D. and Dew, D. (2005). New Market Creation Through Transformation. *Journal of Evolutionary Economics* 15: 533–565. Springer-Verlag.

Star, S. L. and Griesemer, J. R. (1989). Institutional Ecology, "Translations" and Boundary Objects: Amateurs and Professionals in Berkeley's Museum of Vertebrate Zoology, 1907–39. *Social Studies of Science* 9: 387–420. London, Newbury Park, and New Delhi: SAGE Publications.

The Guardian. (2021). Uber Drivers Entitled to Workers' Rights, UK Supreme Court Rules. 19 February.

Velu, C. (2016). Evolutionary or Revolutionary Business Model Innovation through Coopetition? The Role of Dominance in Network Markets. *Industrial Marketing Management* 53: 124–135.

Velu, C. and Jacob, A. (2016). Business Model Innovation and Owner-Managers: The Moderating Role of Competition. *R&D Management* 46(3): 451–463.

Verganti, R. (2009). *Design-Driven Innovation: Changing the Rules of Competition by Radically Innovating What Things Mean*. Boston, MA: Harvard Business Press.

Wisniewski, E. J. (1997). When Concepts Combine. *Psychonomic Bulletin & Review* 4(2): 167–183.

Yin, E. and Mahrous, A. (2022). COVID-19 Global Pandemic, Workplace Spirituality and the Rise of Spirituality-Driven Organisations in the Post-Digital Era. *Journal of Humanities and Applied Social Sciences* 4(2): 79–93.

Zelizer, V. A. (1978). Human Values and the Market: The Case of Life Insurance and Death in 19th-Century America. *The American Journal of Sociology* 84(3): 591–610.

3 | Organisational Structure and Leadership

Whether you believe you can, or whether you believe you can't, you are absolutely right.

Henry Ford

Introduction

Firms are often reluctant to cannibalise an existing business until the new business model is shown to be viable. The challenge for the top management team is to implement a new business model alongside an existing one and to manage the contradictions between the two (Velu and Stiles, 2013). For example, Kodak did not shrink the volume of chemical-based film, even when sales were declining as a result of digital cameras becoming prevalent. The continued production of colour films was driven by the incentives provided by the costing system that allocated the overhead costs of the capital equipment (Shih, 2016). Hence, Kodak could not reduce the volume of films to match the sales decline, as this would have increased the costs of producing the films and accelerated the decline in sales. The reluctance to reduce the volume of chemical films delayed the adoption of digital cameras and was ultimately fatal for Kodak.

Moreover, studies have shown that the type of leadership required to enable business model innovation might vary depending on the degree of systemic change that needs to be managed (Stock et al., 2016; Stacey, 1995; Van der Hoven et al., 2021). The more radical and architectural business model innovation would need top management to be actively involved (Stieglitz and Foss, 2015). We often see leadership changes when firms want to develop a new business model or reorient their existing one. For example, Tetra Pak, one of the largest and most successful packaging companies, appointed a new CEO to lead the new business, Tetra Recart, which produced retortable cartons as an alternative to cans for food packaging (Deschamps, 2008).

Moreover, Tetra Recart was set up as a separate organisation through a fully owned subsidiary company.

This chapter will provide an understanding of the leadership challenges that management face when implementing business model innovation and the types of organisational issue that need to be considered. In particular, it will focus on how management makes decisions to implement business model innovations. The chapter will also explore how the organisational structure and performance metrics used can influence the design and success of new business models.

3.1 Theory of Leadership and Business Model Innovation

Business model innovation is not straightforward because changes in one element of the business model often entail changes in another (Velu, 2017). Maintaining coherence of the business model as a system is important, and often such interdependencies between different elements of the business model might not be apparent (Velu, 2020). Hence, a sequence of substitutions or additions to the activities would change the business model from being one complex system to another, with possible unintended consequences (Schoemaker et al., 2018.

Business model innovation requires organisational adaptability to manage such complexity and ambiguity. Studies have shown that leadership for organisational adaptability requires organisations to be flexible, agile and adaptive in response to a volatile and often unpredictable world (Miller and Lin, 2015; Uhl-Bien and Arena, 2018). Leadership in such a setting is a multi-faceted concept that uses a systems-level approach to foster collaboration through building social capital, as well as individual performance, by emphasising human and intellectual capital. Organisational adaptability involves managing the tension between the need to innovate and the need to produce. This requires the delicate balance of organisations as semi-structures that are not over-structured and hence mechanistic, but which are not under-structured and chaotic either. New ideas for a business model often conflict with the existing business model. Leadership involves managing such tensions by enabling adaptive space by creating the conditions for conflicting and connecting to enable the emergence of new business models (Uhl-Bien and Arena, 2018). Conflicting involves engaging the tension between innovation and production.

Such tensions can be created internally by injecting tension into the system or externally by the environment. However, such conflicts need to be balanced by connecting and linking the conflicting areas in such a way as to scale up the innovative ideas into some form of beneficial order to enable the new business model to emerge. Such leadership for organisational adaptability requires both ambidexterity and dynamic capabilities (Teece, 2007).

Firms need to exhibit ambidexterity by managing exploitation and exploration activities (March, 1991; Tushman and O'Reilly, 1996). This requires a high-performance behavioural context that enables employees to use their own judgement, while the leadership provided by the top management team acts as an integrative unit in making strategically important decisions (Hambrick, 1998; Neely, 2005).

Research has shown that business model change requires dynamic capabilities, whereby leaders are able to sense, seize and transform opportunities (Schoemaker et al., 2018; Teece, 2007). Sensing is the ability to scan the environment and develop peripheral vision about what is around the corner; it requires the ability to anticipate and challenge the conventional wisdom. Seizing is the ability to innovate and implement new systems to take advantage of the external changes; it requires leaders who are able to synthesise information from different perspectives and balance speed with rigour to reach a decision. Finally, transforming is the ability to reshape the firm and the ecosystem to take full advantage of the new business models; it involves the ability to align conflicting viewpoints to reach a decision and also to view success and failure as critical sources of learning.

The above principles of leadership require three mega-capabilities to manage the strategic discontinuity brought about by changes to the business model: strategic agility, leadership unity and resource fluidity (Doz and Kosonen, 2010). Strategic agility is the ability to display anticipation and experimentation – to gain insights through experiments; distancing and abstracting – nurturing an "outside-in" perspective; and reframing – encouraging reframing of the business (Doz and Kosonen, 2010). The key is not merely to increase the lead time to enable transformation as a result of better forecasting. Forecasting tools work best when there are known uncertainties to manage the continuity of existing business models. When firms face discontinuous change, such forecasting methods need to be enhanced, for example, by technology roadmapping of radical new possibilities. For example, the investment of IBM and Google (and other firms) anticipates the development of quantum computing to complement classical computing because of its ability to do significantly more complex tasks efficiently despite the technology's commercial value being future-based.

Building leadership unity involves dialoguing: sharing assumptions among the senior team; integrating and aligning – a common agenda and interest; and caring – personal safety and compassion for trying/ failing (Doz and Kosonen, 2010). Such leadership unity requires not only that incentives be aligned but also, more importantly, the creation of a compelling mission to serve the customer. SAP reorganised itself from vertical business units by product application domains to a platform business with a more open application suite, by allocating responsibilities to board members for different phases or activities, with the mission of creating an integrated customer value proposition. This is part of providing a culture of personal safety, which is important to encourage trial-and-error learning. Resource fluidity involves: decoupling and modularising – it is easy to assemble/disassemble the activities; switching – trying different models in parallel; and grafting – importing business models from the outside (Doz and Kosonen, 2010). Business models evolve because the pressure to change in one element creates tension for other elements, which then need to adapt and change as well. Thompson (1967) suggested that this requires firms to build a technical core but also to have a more adaptable periphery that is more modular. Such modularity creates semi-structures to move resources freely (Baldwin and Clark, 2000).

3.2 Cases on Leadership and Decision-Making

The adoption of a radical business model in the US bond trading market illustrates some of the senior management decision tensions (Velu and Stiles, 2013). The US bond market is the largest securities market in the world – at the end of 2000, over US$17 trillion in bonds were outstanding, with over US$2 trillion being issued in that year alone. The US corporate bond market is highly concentrated, with twelve dealer banks having a total market share of over 90 per cent between them. Bond trading was traditionally carried out by dealer banks via a telephone-based business model. They act as intermediaries, matching buyers with sellers, and so they are able to price these securities, generating their revenue from the spread between the purchase and sale prices. The dealer banks often buy securities and hold them in inventory before selling them to other investors, during which time they assume the risk of price fluctuations, which requires economic risk capital. The advent of the Internet enabled new entrants to propose business models to allow direct trading between buyers and sellers and potentially to disintermediate the banks (Velu, 2016). In response, the smaller banks moved first to adopt an incremental business model innovation whereby trading still took place, with the banks acting as intermediaries, but over the Internet rather than the telephone. In response to the smaller banks, some of the larger dealer banks later formed a consortium to adopt the radical direct trading model via the Internet, as this contributed to lower costs by helping banks avoid holding inventories of securities.

Strategic decision-making is typically classified into three phases: intelligence – involving the identification of opportunities, perhaps highlighted as a result of problems; design – which relates to the development of solutions; and choice – choosing between possible alternatives (Mintzberg et al., 1976). Senior management needs to be aware of both procedural rationality and politics in enabling the adoption of the radical business model while running the existing business model. On the one hand, procedural rationality is about the decision-making process reflecting the intention to make the best decision possible for the organisation under the given conditions (Dean and Sharfman, 1993). On the other hand, politics is about the impact of individuals or groups who try to influence decision-making to enhance or protect their interests above those of the organisation (Pettigrew, 1973).

In the case of the large banks launching the radical direct trading business model in the bond trading market, senior management needed to bridge the tension that arose at each stage of these decision-making processes by combining procedural rationality and politics (Velu and Stiles, 2013). In the intelligence phase, management consulted widely before deciding to adopt. From a rational perspective, this made sense as, on average, one makes fewer mistakes, as different points of view are taken into account. From a political perspective, it provides buy-in via engagement by encouraging the expression of conflicting views and debate. Hence, the tension is managed via transcendence – by reframing a tension within a different perspective. In the design phase, management highlighted the business model innovation in terms of small changes. Rationally, this enables management to buy an option to execute business model innovation later, for example, to equities trading, only if the first is successful, while being politically astute in presenting the adoption of the new business model as incremental change, which makes it palatable. Hence, the tension is managed via separation – keeping apart the tension through a temporal process. In the choice phase, management leveraged different beliefs by putting forward additional strategic considerations, even if these were not the preferred choice for the radical business model. Rationally, this enables managers to see the contrasts between the business models more clearly, and hence the benefits of the radical business model. Politically, it helps to reduce conflict and encourages "give and take." Hence, the tension is managed via integration – neutralisation – whereby the opposing parties compromise to resolve the tension.

Moreover, it is important to ensure in fast-changing environments such as high-technology markets that the leadership team maintains a strategic focus within a defined framework. This strategic focus needs to be complemented with a technological focus whereby both radical and incremental technologies need to be aligned with the strategic objectives. Three firms – GE Medical Systems (GEMS), Motorola and Corning – that developed business models to become leaders in the 1990s in their respective high-technology markets, provide exemplary cases (Morone, 1993). GEMS was in the medical diagnostic imaging equipment business and one of its key products in the early 1970s was X-ray equipment, with a declining market share; it was the leading provider of X-ray equipment but its product was seen to be of lower quality than its competitors, Siemens and Philips. Initially, GEMS started to diversify into other areas of medical equipment before deciding to focus on X-ray machines in 1973. The GEMS senior management team decided to focus more specifically on computerised tomography (CT), which uses X-rays to provide detailed images of the cross section of the anatomy. Although initially slow to adopt, GEMS developed a superior CT scanner using fan beam technology rather than a pencil beam, which allowed for faster computerised reconstruction of the body part being scanned and was extremely beneficial to medical practitioners and patients. This enabled GEMS to build its leadership in CT scans with the policy of "continuum," whereby each new CT product enhancement would be compatible with the previous system so that customers could upgrade seamlessly. The firm's success in CT scanners induced its competitors to move into a new technology, magnetic resonance imaging (MRI), a non-invasive technology using a combination of magnetic fields and radio frequency technology that provides superior images of organs. GEMS reoriented its strategic positioning from an X-ray equipment business to a diagnostic imaging business. Initially, it was developing magnetic resonance technology such as magnetic resonance (MR) spectroscopy (imaging of the chemical composition of the tissue) for biochemical analysis as a complement to its CT imaging and hence to protect its CT business. MR spectroscopy needed a more powerful superconducting magnet than MRI. However, this stronger superconducting magnet was within the capability of the parent company, General Electric (GE), because its R&D department had developed the capability in its electrical power business. This superior ability to develop and produce a powerful superconducting magnet enabled higher-resolution brain images when using MRI, which enabled GEMS to develop superior MRI equipment to become the leader in the market. However, it positioned itself as a world-leading supplier of diagnostic imaging equipment in CT and MRI systems. In this way, the leadership team's ability to set targets of continuous improvement for quality and cost through learning by doing helped the firm to think about the next "big idea."

Having a strategic framework is important when creating focus but the leadership team should not be ruled by it. Motorola's move to become a leader in the mobile and portable communications market by the 1990s, despite heavy competition from Japanese giants such as Matsushita and NEC, is an example of this. George Fisher of Motorola (CEO in 1988 and CEO and Chairman from 1990) said (Morone, 1993, p. 119)[1]:

So we have a strategic framework within which we make a lot of these decisions.... We don't totally focus within the framework, but if it fits there, it gets a better chance of being funded than if it doesn't. So we have a strategic framework, but at the same time, there is a lot if Babylonian thinking, as opposed to Euclidean thinking, that goes into the process.

Often, the decision-making has to be bold and the financial analysis should act as the constraint on the pace of investment and not the determinant. Corning, a leader in an array of speciality glass and

---

[1] Babylonian thinking is akin to inductive logic, as the Babylonians often learnt to develop theorems by solving many mathematical problems. Euclidean thinking is more akin to deductive logic, whereby mathematical theorems are derived logically from axioms (Feynman, 1964).

ceramic products, which transformed itself to become a leader in the optical fibre market, had such a philosophy. Tom MacAvoy, President of Corning (Morone, 1993, p. 185), said:

The organisation has the desire to allocate resources in a rational and democratic process. Ultimately though, [to bring a big-hitting candidate to fruition], something irrational has to be done, and by irrational I mean ... requires resources that transcend the normal allocation process.

Dave Duke, Chief Technology Officer (Morone, 1993, p. 191), explains that Corning used discounted cashflow analysis to get a feel for how much it would cost and what the market shares would be but experiments and intuition were needed to make the necessary assumptions for the analysis.

3.3 Dual Business Model

Strategic renewal often involves sub-processes such as competence definition, deployment and modification and affects different levels of management (Floyd and Lane, 2000).[2] One of the major challenges of such strategic renewals faced by firms is how to adopt a new business model while running the existing business model effectively. These firms face a dilemma. On the one hand, the new business model might be able to provide great growth opportunities. On the other hand, the new business model might conflict with the existing business model and hence destroy value for both. For example, in 1998 British Airways launched a low-cost airline, Go. The idea was for British Airways to get a share of the growing low-cost airline market to cater for travellers flying to destinations in Europe. British Airways expected new passengers who had never flown before to travel with Go to European destinations. It replicated many of the processes of its regular passenger business for its Go subsidiary to ensure that capabilities were leveraged appropriately. For example, Go leased its aircrafts, which was easier but more expensive in the long run compared to Ryanair, another low-cost European carrier that bought its fleet at that time (Michaels, 2001). However, this replication of processes meant that

---

[2] Within these sub-processes the roles of the different layers of management might vary across the time horizon, information requirements and core values, which results in conflicts that need to be managed (Floyd and Lane, 2000).

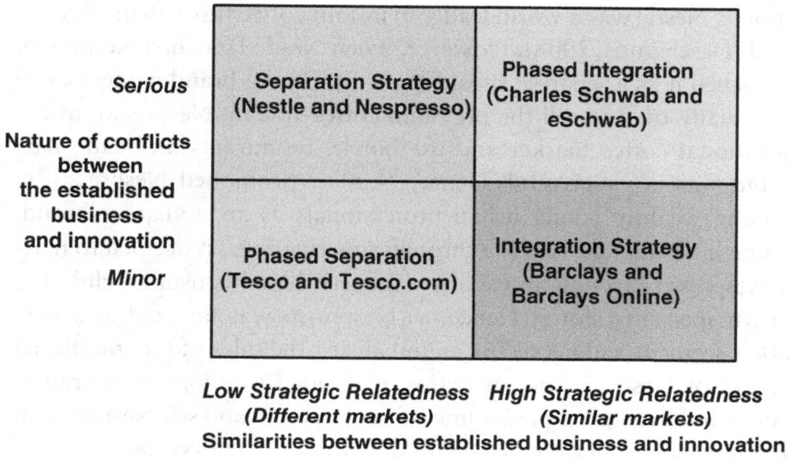

Serious	Separation Strategy (Nestle and Nespresso)	Phased Integration (Charles Schwab and eSchwab)
Nature of conflicts between the established business and innovation Minor	Phased Separation (Tesco and Tesco.com)	Integration Strategy (Barclays and Barclays Online)

Low Strategic Relatedness   High Strategic Relatedness
(Different markets)   (Similar markets)
Similarities between established business and innovation

Figure 3.1 Dual business model strategies
Source: Adapted from Markides and Charitou (2004)

British Airways never fully appreciated the differences between the business models of low-cost airlines and full service airlines (Boon, 2018). Hence, it decided to sell Go to a management buy-out backed by a private equity firm called i3, which in turn sold the airline in 2002 to EasyJet, a major competitor in low-cost airlines (Odell, 2001). This example shows that it is appropriate for firms to manage how best to leverage the existing capabilities when launching new business models.

Markides and Charitou (2004) proposed a framework to think about managing such dual business models. The principles of the framework consider two primary factors: the first is the similarities in the target market between the established business and the new business, and the second is the nature of the conflicts between the established business and the new business. The nature of the conflicts could arise as a result of location, brand, equity, value chain activities and organisational factors, among others. The proposed framework implies four broad strategies to manage dual business models, as shown in Figure 3.1.

At the two extremes are full separation or full integration strategies. Full separation, by launching the new business model within a separate organisation, is optimal when the new business model aims to serve a different market with low strategic relatedness to the existing market. For example, Nestle was a world leader in instant coffee through its Nescafe brand (Deschamps, 2008). However, when Nestle launched Nespresso, it launched it as a separate subsidiary with its own brand name. Nestle had initially tried to sell the premium coffee system, Nespresso, to the institutional coffee market and the hotels, restaurants and cafe market but was not successful. Hence, Nestle repositioned Nespresso by targeting wealthy young urban professionals as an upmarket brand. Although Nestle sold Nescafe through supermarkets, it decided to market Nespresso through an exclusive internet-based consumer club and its own speciality stores. Hence, as Nespresso was targeted at a new market segment and it was not cannibalising the sales of the traditional business of Nestle in instant coffee, it decided to adopt a separation strategy of forming a separate unit to manufacture and sell Nespresso in order to minimise the conflicts with the production of Nescafe.

The integration strategy, on the other hand, involves launching a new business model within the existing organisational structure. Barclays, for example, when it launched Internet banking in the 1990s, decided that the proposition was targeted at its existing customers and that online banking would be complementary to branch-based banking. As there was very little conflict with the activities of its branch banking, it decided to launch Barclays online as an integrated business model within the existing business. This is in contrast to some of the building societies, such as Abbey National,[3] which launched a separate unit for its online banking, namely, Cahoot; it was aiming for a new cohort of more wealthy customers compared to its current customer base and felt there would be more conflicts with the existing branch-based business model.

The other two extremes are phased separation or phased integration strategies. Tesco, a large supermarket chain in the UK, adopted a phased separation model when it launched its online business, Tesco .com (Enders and Jelassi, 2009). Initially, in order to leverage the benefits of its extensive store network, Tesco.com fulfilled its online customer orders by asking its stores that were nearest to the homes of its customers to fulfil the orders. This involved a store worker visiting the stores and filling the orders from the shelves of the supermarket, an approach that initially worked well. However, as the online business started to increase, the business of fulfilling online orders using

---

[3] The Santander Group acquired Abbey National in 2004.

the physical stores started to affect the experience of customers who came in to shop in these stores, as the number of workers moving around the store with a trolley increased dramatically. Tesco realised that it needed to develop separate fulfilment centres for its Tesco.com customers to avoid and reduce these conflicts with the in-store customer experience. It even started to launch dark stores, which might resemble a regular store but with no customers, and these stores were used exclusively for fulfilling online orders. Tesco has moved to using robotics to fulfil orders in these dark stores.

The phased integration strategy involves launching the new business model as a separate business first and then integrating it within the existing organisational structure over time. For example, Charles Schwab, a major financial services firm in the United States, launched eSchwab, its online retail broking business, as a separate entity (Markides and Charitou, 2004). eSchwab was meant to cater for new customers, and therefore the business model was launched as a separate entity with a different brand name to avoid conflict with the existing brokerage business. However, over time, the regular customers of Charles Schwab's brokerage business became more sophisticated and were using online brokerage services; Charles Schwab therefore decided to integrate eSchwab into its core business model.

The original organisational design might have to change as the product category evolves; hence, the business model required to support it needs to be redesigned. IBM's development of the PC is a case in point. IBM dominated enterprise computing and was the leader in mainframe computers (Bresnahan et al., 2012). Initially, IBM ignored developments in the PC market as being a niche for individuals and not corporate clients. However, IBM observed that PCs started to be sold to IBM customers in the 1970s. IBM's Boca Raton Group, which monitors small developments and proposes responses, prepared a presentation for IBM's Corporate Management Committee (CMC) in the late 1970s. IBM had a policy that any employee could write a note to the CMC if they disagreed with any strategic decisions made by the senior team. However, the PC was deemed to be an important strategic investment for IBM so it adopted a "no complaints" policy to the CMC.[4]

---

[4] This employee complaints policy was frozen for the PC business.

The lab director of the Boca Raton facilities was given the opportunity to build the PC business as a separate unit with independent decision-making authority to the mainframe business. Initial studies had shown that PC adoption was slow as a result of the lack of software applications. Executives at IBM felt they could develop a PC quickly and the Boca Raton team was given the authority to come up with a PC in less than a year. As a result of the limited time frame, the group's PC development team decided to use tested vendor technologies, a standardised one-model product and open systems architecture. Hence, IBM decided to build the first PC by sourcing parts from outside suppliers, which was unconventional in terms of its vertically integrated model for the mainframes. IBM chose Intel's microprocessor and operating system from a little-known company at the time, Microsoft, to enable others to participate in the open-architecture-based PC business (Bradley, 2011). Moreover, the firm decided not to use IBM's distribution network but to use third-party sales channels for getting the product to the consumer quickly. IBM's first PC, the IBM 5150, was launched in August 1981, a year after it was given the go ahead by the management committee. The company's PCs were very successful until the advent of the PC-jr, a small PC for home users, which was a failure because of keyboard and other issues, which were sourced externally when building the PC. The incident with the PC-jr damaged the reputation of IBM in other business areas, including the core mainframe business, because of conflict and diseconomies of scope. First, there was distribution channel conflict because sales did not generate commissions for PCs, which were sold via retailers, unlike mainframes, which were sold directly by the IBM sales team. Moreover, there were increasing overlaps in customers as corporate customers started buying PCs. Therefore, IBM decided to integrate the PC business into the main business.

3.4 Metrics and Incentives

Business model innovation requires the appropriate alignment of incentives and metrics in the firm. Intel's transformation from a memory business to a world-leading microprocessor illustrates this. Intel was founded in the late 1960s and became a leader in the memory business – dynamic random access memory (DRAM) – by the mid-1970s, with over 80 per cent of the global market share (Burgelman,

1994). Intel's initial investment in microprocessors came about because a Japanese calculator company, Busicom, wanted a chipset designed for its calculators. This is encapsulated in a quote from Intel's VP for sales, Ed Gelbach (Burgelman, 1994, p. 37): "Originally, I think we saw it (microprocessor) as a way to seek more memories and we were willing to make the investment on that basis." These advanced chipsets for calculators later became known as microprocessors. However, Busicom initially owned the rights to the chip design. One of Intel's technologists realised that these chipsets could be used as a general-purpose solution to other applications and persuaded the senior management of Intel to renegotiate the rights to the chip design. Busicom eventually sold the rights of the chipset back to Intel for all non-calculator applications.

During the same period PCs were becoming important and beginning to be widely used. PCs required microprocessors; however, the enormous importance of personal computers was not evident to Intel's senior management. Intel's list of top 50 priorities for the 80286 microprocessor did not include personal computers. However, its ability to provide development tools for its customers and demonstrate the upward compatibility path for its next-generation products convinced IBM to choose Intel's 8088 microprocessor as the central processing unit for its PCs. However, there was still significant emotional attachment to the memory business, as it had made Intel successful. The memory business was commoditising rapidly, with many competitors by the 1970s having thinning margins. This is encapsulated in the quote from Andy Grove, who eventually became Intel's CEO, replacing Gordon Moore, Intel's founder and CEO at the time (Burgelman, 1994, p. 43): "I recall going to see Gordon (Moore) and asking him what a new management would do if we were replaced. The answer was clear: get out of DRAMs. So, I suggested to Gordon that we go through the revolving door, come back in, and do it ourselves." Intel therefore decided to transform itself from a memory firm into a microprocessor firm.

The memory and semiconductor business shared fabrication plants. The senior management gave the local fabrication plant managers the responsibility to choose how many memory chips and microprocessors to manufacture. The monthly load to the factories was based on maximising "margin-per-wafer-start," which did not maximise immediate profits but selected niche over commodity markets. Since microprocessors had a higher margin, the managers gradually provided more resources in factories to manufacture them, resulting in an exit from DRAM. The key performance metrics, and hence the resource allocation method, provided alignment between internal and external conditions to match the competitive reality in order to help transform Intel from a leading memory firm into a global leader in microprocessors.

In designing business models and appropriate metrics, scholars have suggested that the strategy of the firms be translated into some simple rules (Morris et al., 2005). Such a process involves three steps. The first step is to define the foundational premise of the business in terms of what the business will be, and what it is not, and to ensure that such decisions are internally consistent. The foundational elements cover the core value creation and value capture mechanism, including the competitive positioning of the firm. Second is the proprietary level, which encompasses the development of unique combinations of activities and processes that result in marketplace advantage. Finally, the foundational and proprietary levels need to be translated into some simple rules that provide guidance and discipline to the business operations. Rules delineate guiding principles governing the execution of the foundational and proprietary elements. For example, in the case of the low-cost airline, Southwest, the key foundational premise related to the offering was a standardised and narrow service offering. The proprietary level was based on designing the activity and processes for a short-haul, high-frequency point-to-point service with direct sales to customers. The foundational and proprietary levels were translated into simple rules such as a maximum one-way fare per passenger of less than a certain dollar value. Eisenhardt and Sull (2001) proposed the use of simple rules as key operational measures to help translate strategy into action. The authors suggested that firms should have between two and seven simple rules. These rules could include: how-to rules – spelling out the key features of how a process is executed; boundary rules – which opportunities to pursue and which are outside the scope; priority rules – helping to rank opportunities or options; timing rules – helping to synchronise the firm's operations to speed and timing to get things done; and exit rules – helping to decide when to pull out of an opportunity.

Several leading firms have also adopted the Hoshin Kanri (HK) policy deployment matrix as a means to translate strategy objectives into operational targets and to manage continuous improvements (Da Silveira et al., 2017; Jolayemi, 2008). HK has been defined as the process of developing plans, targets and controls and identifying areas for improvement based on previous levels of policy and an assessment of previous performance. Although originally developed in Japan, the HK policy deployment matrix has been used extensively by Western corporations, including Texas Instruments, Lucent Technologies, AT&T, Xerox and Hewlett Packard (Witcher and Butterworth, 2000). The HK approach has been given various names, such as management by policy, policy deployment and planning for results. The HK planning methodology essentially identifies medium-term breakthrough objectives and translates them into annual objectives. Once the annual objectives have been agreed, a set of top-level improvement priorities are identified and operationalised into targets for improvement with the appropriate allocation of responsibilities for them (Tortorella et al., 2018). The annual planning table (APT) is used to document and deploy items and activities that constitute the annual plan. At each level of the organisation, the strategy and objectives of the APT from the level above are used to develop an APT for that level based on its expertise and technical strengths. Hence, at each succeeding level, strategies are owned, expanded and converted into implementation plans in order to contribute to achieving the overall strategic objectives of the firm (Mulligan et al., 1996). One of the key aspects of the HK planning methodology is to achieve both horizontal and vertical alignment across the firm (Mannix and Pelham, 1996). This alignment is achieved through a process called "crossball" to encourage dialogue between the different levels of the organisation during the deployment process.

3.5 Tools and Frameworks

Identifying a new business model and managing business model innovation are often challenging and risky ventures for organisations. We discuss two tools and frameworks that are helpful in managing the change process from one business model to another: the innovation readiness level (IRL); and the business model coherence scorecard (BMCS).

3.5.1 Innovation Readiness Level

Lockheed Martin, a US-based aerospace and defence firm, developed a tool to manage the risk–return trade-off related to business model innovation (Evans and Johnson, 2013). The firm set out to answer two questions related to its investment decision on new business models. First, if the new business model goes to plan, will it be financially material to the business? Second, what are the risks of implementing the new business model? The first question is answered using various measures of return on investment and net present value based on the best available estimates. In answer to the second question, the risks typically increase, as the new business model differs from the existing business model. Hence, one way of estimating risk is to develop a metric that quantifies the difference between the existing business model and the new one. An alternative approach adopted by Lockheed Martin is to measure the innovation readiness level (IRL) of its various functions with respect to the proposed new business model. Such a measure of readiness provides a proxy for the degree of "stretch" that the firm needs to go through in order to adopt the new business model.

The concept of the IRL is borrowed from NASA's technology readiness levels (TRLs). Under the TRL, readiness levels vary from 1 to 9, where 1 refers to basic principles that have been observed and reported and 9 refers to an actual system that is proven in successful mission operations. A similar concept can be developed for IRLs, as shown in Table 3.1. The IRLs are measured at a functional level, say, manufacturing readiness level, human resources readiness level, and others. IRLs are not a measure of maturity or goodness but are intended to capture the degree to which the function has demonstrated the capabilities needed to migrate from the existing business model to the new business model. The IRL scale can be seen as logarithmic, whereby taking a function from 4 to 6 might require considerably more resources than taking it from 2 to 4. Once the evaluation is done at a functional level, IRLs can be plotted on a radar diagram with scales from 1 to 9 in order to obtain a picture of the readiness levels of the different functions, which enables a dialogue about how the capabilities of the different functions can be enhanced to adopt the envisioned business model. Moreover, IRLs for the different functions can be summed, perhaps weighted according to their criticalness and plotted against the financial returns for the different proposed new business models. In this way, the management team is able to consider the return and risk profile, which helps when making informed decisions about de-risking the decision to adopt business model innovation.

Table 3.1 *Technology readiness levels and innovation readiness levels*

Level	Technology readiness level	Innovation readiness level
1	Basic principles observed and reported	General specification of capabilities required by function to execute business model generated
2	Technology concept and/or application formulated	Detailed specification of capability requirements generated for each function
3	Analytical and experimental critical function and/or characteristic proof of concept	Active development of capability begun
4	Component and/or breadboard validation in laboratory environment	First general demonstration of capability achieved
5	Component and/or breadboard validation in relevant environment	Good demonstration of capability achieved
6	System/subsystem model or prototype demonstration in relevant environment	First demonstration of capability in the market (e.g., sale of beta product)
7	System prototype demonstration in operational environment	First transaction involving full product in final form
8	Actual system completed and qualified through test and demonstration	Capability successfully used in business (generally in cash-positive operation)
9	Actual system proven in successful mission operations	Capability in routine use to support full-scale production

Source: Adapted from Evans and Johnson (2013)

3.5.2 Business Model Coherence Scorecard

Understanding and managing business model innovation requires "big picture" systems thinking (Velu, 2017). The systems thinking approach of a business model conceptualises the difference between the components with reference to the whole and its constituent parts, the relationship between components, and the perspectives of the agents who are part of the system[5] (Cabrera et al., 2015;

---

[5] The notion of perspectives or viewpoints encompasses the subjective beliefs held by agents, which can then influence the evolution of the system.

Midgley and Wilby, 2015). The objective of management is to manage the *dynamic consistency* by maintaining coherence between the components of the business model in order to ensure the efficiency of the existing model while enabling business model innovation (Demil and Lecocq, 2010). Therefore, a systems thinking approach of business models is beneficial when new technologies are implemented to enhance the efficiency, and effectiveness, of the business model.

As discussed earlier, most large firms are organised by function. In this context, often no one "owns" the business model. It is often seen as a "given," something that each function needs to optimise but which no one questions. One of the dangers of such organisational silos is that it may make sense for one part of a firm to adopt a new technology in order to make a particular process more efficient. However, if the system is not looked at in its entirety, this can be problematic and create conflicts with other processes. As a result, the cohesiveness of the business model as a system and the associated information to manage are often overlooked.

The "balanced scorecard" is an established method of augmenting financial reporting with other key measures, such as how the business is creating value for its customers, what internal processes it has for satisfying customer and shareholder needs, and how it is developing its people, systems and culture to achieve growth (Kaplan and Norton, 1996). More recently, the approach has been extended to emphasise the alignment needed to capture synergies across the business through mechanisms such as having a clear business strategy. While this more nuanced approach is a significant improvement in financial reporting, it still does not give managers the information they need to understand and manage the evolution of the business model.

Another inhibitor of business model innovation is that many firms rely on profitability from management information systems (MIS) as their principal indicator of success.[6] Furthermore, most accounting systems tend to look at the profitability of different parts of the business independently, without taking into account the value they might be generating elsewhere in the organisation or ecosystem. Profitability is based on the accounting principle of matching revenue and costs during a reporting period (Hergert and Morris, 1989). Profitability might be measured at a product, business-unit or geographical level within

[6] MIS encompasses business information systems that provide financial and non-financial information to help senior management make decisions.

the organisation. Profitability reporting is necessary to understand the economic and financial viability of a business and hence for capital allocation and decisions about business growth. However, profitability reports tend to supress the information on the interactions of the activity system that constitutes the business model and therefore the dynamic consistency of the components of the business model. Systems dynamics thinking could be valuable for understanding the interactions of the activities (Sterman, 1984; Sterman et al., 1997). Measuring the interactions of the activity system in a way that identifies both the enhancing and mitigating effects of a change of activity following the adoption of new technologies is essential in order to help identify opportunities for business model innovation. Studies have emphasised that managing linkages across the value chain, business models and ecosystems is one of the most challenging and complex tasks for management and is a major source of competitive advantage (Demil and Lecocq, 2010; Porter, 1985). Therefore, profitability reports that are complemented with a Business Model Coherence Scorecard (BMCS), which provides information on interlinkages – both within and across the value chain of firms – and hence measures the cohesiveness of the system, would enable senior management to better identify opportunities for business model innovation (Velu, 2020).

The BMCS uses systems dynamics thinking to model the behaviour of the system as a whole rather than piecemeal. It aims to measure the alignment between the different components of the business model, from four perspectives:

(1) Physical flow: Are the raw materials and finished products and services delivered at the right time and in the right place?
(2) Information flow: Is the information for decision-making delivered to the right people or systems at the right time?
(3) Decision rights: Do the right people or systems have the authority to make decisions?
(4) Incentives system: Are people appropriately incentivised to make timely and joined-up decisions?

By asking these questions of all the elements in the business model, it is possible to see if the firm is delivering on its customer value propositions while making a satisfactory return. In doing so, the BMCS complements traditional financial reporting in enabling business model innovation while evaluating its financial viability.

To help us think about the complexities of business model innovation, let us look at the following scenario with a consumer durable product such as a washing machine. The same principle could be applied to a more complex product such as the spare part for an aeroplane engine. Typically, for a washing machine, there are a number of key players such as the consumer, the retail store that sells and repairs the machine, and the manufacturer of the washing machine. If, for example, a component in a washing machine were to become faulty beyond repair, the consumer might have to contact the retailer, which then contacts the manufacturer – which has to hold a large number of spares in stock – asking for that specific component to be sent out from its storehouse located elsewhere. The entire process may take several weeks to complete, causing substantial inconvenience for the consumer during the wait. Now, in an integrated additive manufacturing network of the future, the appliance may be embedded with sensors capable of diagnosing the machine's integrity, making notifications about failure or upcoming potential failure of parts. This information can be connected with manufacturers in real time, which then share data files with a third-party 3D printing firm in the local vicinity to punctually produce, deliver and install the parts. Once the work has been completed, payment can be automatically deducted via a smart contract. The entire network can be managed using distributed ledger technology, which permits accurate recording of the contracts and various procedures, ensuring security via encryption. The interconnectivity between different parties requires advanced digital connectivity infrastructure such as 5G, which also enables the functioning of cloud computing to provide the computational resources needed by AI algorithms for the purpose of predictive maintenance and to optimise various processes. Distributed ledger technology combined with additive manufacturing could lay the groundwork for new business models such as shared factories and secure design marketplaces (Klöckner et al., 2020). The above example illustrates how a range of digital technologies are brought into play via the additive manufacturing network. In order to take advantage of the opportunities, firms in the relevant sectors need to collectively seek to adopt new business models around the new technologies.

This is an example of a whole-system innovation that could result in more agile customer service, greater efficiency for the manufacturer and less waste, thanks to a better repair service. However, if only parts

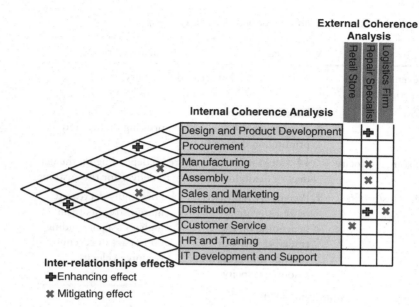

External Coherence
Analysis

Retail Store | Repair Specialist | Logistics Firm

Internal Coherence Analysis

Design and Product Development	+	
Procurement		
Manufacturing	✖	
Assembly	✖	
Sales and Marketing		
Distribution	+	✖
Customer Service	✖	
HR and Training		
IT Development and Support		

Inter-relationships effects
+ Enhancing effect
✖ Mitigating effect

Figure 3.2 BMCS coherence matrix
Source: Adapted from Velu (2020)

of the process are adopted piecemeal – for example, if the manufacturer uses 3D printing to make new parts and hold them in stock – then the benefits of business model innovation will not be realised.

We need a structured way to evaluate the pros and cons of changes to the business model. The first step is to examine its potential impact on the firm's coherence internally, across all functions (product design, procurement, manufacture, sales, distribution, customer service, HR and IT), and then externally, to include ecosystem partners such as the logistics firms, repair specialists and retail stores.

Internally, the effects could be both positive (better customer service and opportunities for product innovation, for example) and negative (challenges for IT in supporting a new, standalone machine, which may take longer to get the part to the customer). Similarly, there are pros and cons for ecosystem partners. Providing a bespoke service for customers' needs to be traded off against the complexity of managing, for example, the logistics of delivery when the logistics firm might not know when the part is going to be ready. Such analysis could be done using a BMCS coherence matrix, as illustrated in Figure 3.2.

Table 3.2 *Revenue and cost coherence analysis report*

	Value creation	Value network
Revenue/value proposition	↑ Increased flexibility ↓ Increased time to delivery	
Cost	↓ Reduced inventory ↑ Uncertainty from printing on demand	↑ Due to uncertainty from printing on demand
Resource velocity	↕ Could increase or decrease depending on the net effect of flexibility and time to deliver for the customer	
Margins/profits	↑ Potentially increased margins/profits depending on the trade-off between revenue and costs and resource velocity	↓ Potentially decreased margins/profits from higher costs depending on impact of revenue and resource velocity

Source: Adapted from Velu (2020)

Having assessed the possible impacts of the new business model on the firm and its ecosystem, the next step is to look at how it would generate revenue while delivering the value proposition to the customer.

In our example, the greater flexibility for product design could increase revenue but the increased delivery times could negate the benefits to the customer and decrease revenue. For the manufacturer, holding less inventory could lower costs but the uncertainty and complexity of printing on-demand could increase them. Combining an analysis of revenue and costs with the rate at which assets are turned over to make a profit – the resource velocity – will indicate the likely impact of margins and profit. Such analysis could be captured with a revenue and cost coherence analysis report, as shown in Table 3.2.

Applying this value lens in conjunction with an analysis of the aspects of business models discussed earlier (physical and information flows, decision rights and incentive systems) is likely to highlight some of the challenges with the proposed business model and catalyse discussions for improvements, such as moving the printing nearer to the customer, in partnership with the retailer or a repair firm.

The benefit of the BMCS is that it gives the management team a mechanism for discussing the cohesiveness of a complex system and a method for evaluating its effectiveness. It is important to stress that it is not designed to be a one-off but a tool to enable continuous dialogue among managers, both within and across the firm, to identify and enable business model innovation.

Conclusion

One of the key insights from the work of Alfred Chandler in studying the American enterprise is that organisational structure follows strategy (Chandler, 1962, 1977). For example, changes in strategy, such as product market diversification, require subsequent alterations in structure, such as divisionalisation. However, scholars have also shown that the organisational structure might influence the strategy (Miller, 1986). This is because the design of an organisation implies certain activities, process architecture and information flows that might make it difficult for it to change its strategy. For example, strategies of differentiation and innovation might be difficult to implement in organisations that have fairly mechanistic structures that place significant emphasis on cost control and standardised repetitive processes. Similarly, organisations that have fairly organic and dynamic structures might be too flexible and inefficient to serve as cost leaders. The formulation of strategy is the contingent plan about which business model to choose. Hence, strategy formulation influences the design of the business model. However, the design of the business model, in turn, might determine the architecture of the activities and the information flow to influence the cognitive aspects, as well as the capability of the management team to alter their strategy.

Studies have argued that one of the challenges for management is to maintain the congruence between the external environment, such as new technologies, customer preferences and internal processes. Often, firms need to make a trade-off between the need to alter the activities on a piecemeal basis, to match the changing environment, and the need to keep the business model as a system coherent (Miller and Friesen, 1978, 1982). There might be hidden costs in making frequent piecemeal changes to the organisational structure to cope with a changing environment because of the disharmony that it creates in the business model functioning as a system (Burns and Stalker, 1961; Miller, 1982, 1987). Hence, there might be performance benefits of delaying change and making a more quantum or multifaceted revolutionary change.

Such a decision and the management of the trade-off would depend on uncertainty and the rate of change in the environment and the design of the business model in terms of modularity (Baldwin and Clark, 2000).

Thompson (1967) provides the context for different forms of leadership styles to deal with uncertainty and preferences. The study articulates the uncertainty relating to the inability to establish cause and effect (Spender and Kessler, 1995). Preferences relate to different outcomes preferred by managers. When both preferences and cause and effect are clear, the decision-making style of the leader becomes computational and often deals with fairly unambiguous short-term situations. When the outcome preferences are clear but the cause and effect are uncertain, the decision-making of the leader will be based on judgement. When the cause and effect are fairly well established but the preferences among managers are uncertain, the decision-making style will be based on a compromise between different groups. Hence, there would be political coalitions and the leadership style would need to focus on negotiating and bargaining among the groups. Finally, when both preferences and cause and effect are uncertain, the leadership style needs to be inspirational and charismatic to bring people along. Often, when there are significant technological shifts and changes in consumer preferences, there will be uncertainty in both preferences and cause and effect. This is when radically new business models are needed, which calls for a charismatic leadership style.

The challenge for leaders is to keep the rewards system aligned with the objectives of the firm in enabling business model innovation. Given that business models are complex organisational systems requiring coordinated change across many functions, the senior management team needs to work as a coherent team in order to implement business model innovation. In most management by objective systems, goals in areas where quantification is difficult go unspecified (Kerr, 1975). Hence, often the softer aspects of intangible capital, such as working collectively as a team, ensuring that information is shared and empowered decision-making are less well measured and rewarded (Kaplan and Norton, 2006). The more individualistic measures at the activity, process or functional level are easier to measure and are rewarded. Such a tendency to measure and reward individualism over collectivism (Morris et al., 1994) could result in firms focusing on efficiency improvement rather than rethinking the business model to focus on effectiveness.

There are several areas in organisational structure and leadership that require further study, covering aspects of business model design, strategic decision-making and leadership styles. First, when and how should senior management adopt evolutionary business model innovation compared to revolutionary business model innovation? On the one hand, when the environment in which the firm operates changes, one can make incremental changes to the activities and processes in order to better fit the environment. However, this causes the internal coherence of the business model to be altered and could make the firm less efficient and effective. On the one hand, waiting to make a radical business model innovation later, while not making any incremental changes, could be more beneficial, albeit riskier. How the leadership of a firm should think about this trade-off, in terms of both theoretical framework and practical implications, requires further research.

Second, how senior management should manage the potential conflicts between a new and an existing business model requires further exploration. The issues to consider here are the optimal organisational design, the governance structure that needs to be put in place and the process of conflict resolution. Related to this is a better understanding of the composition and governance models of the top management team that would enable business model innovation. Third, the interplay between business model design and strategic choices, and vice versa, requires further elaboration. In particular, do particular business models provide management with certain types of information and hence make it more difficult to change business models in the future? In this context, the frameworks that would enable managers to make better decisions about future business model innovation opportunities that are less certain and riskier than the existing business model require further study.

This chapter has provided an overview of the principles of organisational design and leadership for business model innovation and proposed some outstanding research issues on this topic.

References

Baldwin, C. Y. and Clark, K. B. (2000). *Design Rules, Vol. 1: The Power of Modularity*. Cambridge, MA: MIT Press.

Boon, T. (2018). Was Selling Low Cost Carrier "GO" BA's Greatest Mistake? *Simply Flying*.

Bradley, D. (2011). A Personal History of the IBM PC. *Computer* 44(8): 19–25.

Bresnahan, T. F., Greenstein, S., and Henderson, R. M. (2012). *Schumpeterian Competition and Diseconomies of Scope. Illustrations from the Histories of Microsoft and IBM in Lerner, J. and S. Stern. The Rate and Direction of Inventive Activity Revisited.* Chicago, IL: University of Chicago Press, pp. 203–271.

Burgelman, R. A. (1994). Fading Memories: A Process Theory of Strategic Business Exit in Dynamic Environments. *Administrative Science Quarterly* 39: 24–56.

Burns, T. and Stalker, G. M. (1961). *The Management of Innovation.* London: Tavistock Publications.

Cabrera, D., Cabrera, L., and Powers, E. (2015). A Unifying Theory of Systems Thinking with Psychosocial Applications. *Systems Research and Behavioral Science* 32: 534–545.

Chandler, A. (1962). *Strategy and Structure.* Cambridge, MA: MIT Press.

Chandler, A. (1977). *The Visible Hand.* Cambridge, MA: MIT Press.

Da Silveira, W. G., De Lima, E. P., Gouvea da Costa, S. E., Deschamps, F. (2017). Guidelines for Hoshin Kanri Implementation: Development and Discussion. *Production Planning & Control* 28(10): 843–859.

Dean, J. W. and Sharfman, M. P. (1993). Procedural Rationality in the Strategic Decision-Making Process. *Journal of Management Studies* 30(4): 0022–2380.

Demil, B. and Lecocq, X. (2010). Business Model Evolution: In Search of Dynamic Consistency. *Long Range Planning* 43: 227–246.

Deschamps, J.-P. (2008). *Innovation Leaders: How Senior Executives Stimulate, Steer and Sustain Innovation.* San Francisco, CA: Jossey-Bass.

Doz, Y. L. and Kosonen, M. (2010). Embedding Strategic Agility: A Leadership Agenda for Accelerating Business Model Renewal. *Long Range Planning* 43: 370–382.

Eisenhardt, K. M. and Sull, D. N. (2001). Strategy as Simple Rules. *Harvard Business Review*: 105–116.

Enders, A. and Jelassi, T. (2009). Leveraging Multichannel Retailing: The Experience of Tesco.com. *MIS Quarterly Executive* 8(2): 89–100.

Evans, J. D. and Johnson, R. O. (2013). Tools for Managing Early-Stage Business Model Innovation. *Research-Technology Management* 56(5): 52–56.

Feynman, R. (1964). Lecture 2 on "The Relation of Mathematics and Physics," *Messenger Lecture Series*, Cornell University. www.microsoft.com/en-us/research/project/tuva-richard-feynman/

Floyd, S. W. and Lane, P. J. (2000). Strategizing throughout the Organization: Managing Role Conflict in Strategic Renewal. *The Academy of Management Review* 25(1): 154–177.

Hambrick D. C. (1998). Corporate Coherence and the Top Management Team. In: D. C. Hambrick, D. A. Nadler, and M. L. Tushman (eds), *Navigating Change: How CEOs, Top Teams, and Boards Steer Transformation*. Boston, MA: Harvard Business School Press, pp. 123–140.

Hergert, M. and Morris, D. (1989). Accounting Data for Value Chain Analysis. *Strategic Management Journal* 10(2): 175–188.

Jolayemi, J. K. (2008). Hoshin Kanri and Hoshin Process: A Review and Literature Study. *Total Quality Management* 19(3): 295–320.

Kaplan, R. and Norton, D. (1996). *The Balanced Scorecard: Translating Strategy into Action*. Boston, MA: Harvard Business School Publishing.

Kaplan, R. and Norton, D. (2006). *Alignment: Using the Balanced Scorecard to Create Corporate Synergies: How to Apply the Balanced Scorecard to Corporate Strategy*. Boston, MA: Harvard Business School Publishing.

Kerr, S. (1975). On the Folly of Rewarding A, While Hoping for B. *Academy of Management Journal* 18(4): 769–783.

Klöckner, M., Kurpjuweit, S., Velu, C., and Wagner, S. (2020). Does Blockchain for 3D Printing Offer Opportunities for Business Model Innovation? *Research Technology Management* 63(4): 18–27.

Mannix, P. M and Pelham, J. C. (1996). Hoshin Planning/Strategic Policy Deployment. *American Hospital Publishing*, Chapter 10.

March, J. G. (1991). How Decisions Happen in Organizations. *Human-Computer Interaction* 6: 95–117.

Markides, C. and Charitou, C. D. (2004). Competing with Dual Business Models: A Contingency Approach. *The Academy of Management Executive* 18(3): 22–36.

Michaels, D. (2001). British Airways's Budget Unit Lures Offers from KLM and 3i – Low Cost Go Airline Could Require Buyer to Make Significant Investment – Sale of Carrier Could Occur within the Next Few Weeks. *The Wall Street Journal Europe*.

Midgley, G. and Wilby, J. (2015). Learning across Boundaries: Exploring the Variety of Systems Theory and Practice. *Systems Research and Behavioral Science* 32: 509–513.

Miller, D. (1982). Evolution and Revolution: A Quantum View of Structural Change in Organizations. *Journal of Management Studies* 19(2): 131–151.

Miller, D. (1986). Configurations of Strategy and Structure: Towards a Synthesis. *Strategic Management Journal* 7(3): 233–249.

Miller, D. (1987). The Genesis of Configuration. *The Academy of Management Review* 12(4): 686–701.

Miller, D. and Friesen, P. H. (1978). Archetypes of Strategy Formulation. *Management Science* 24(9): 921–933.

Miller, D. and Friesen, P. H. (1982). Structural Change and Performance: Quantum versus Piecemeal-Incremental Approaches. *The Academy of Management Journal* 25(4): 867–892.

Miller, K. D. and Lin, S. J. (2015). Analogical Reasoning for Diagnosing Strategic Issues in Dynamic and Complex Environments. *Strategic Management Journal* 36: 2000–2020.

Mintzberg, H., Raisinghani, D., and Theoret, A. (1976). The Structure of "Unstructured" Decision Processes. *Administrative Science Quarterly* 21(2): 246–275.

Morone, J. (1993). *Winnings in High-Tech Markets: The Role of General Management: How Motorola, Corning, and General Electric Have Built Global Leadership through Technology*. Boston, MA: Harvard Business School Publishing.

Morris, M. H., Davis, D. L., and Allen, J. W. (1994). Fostering Corporate Entrepreneurship: Cross-Cultural Comparisons of the Importance of Individualism versus Collectivism. *Journal of International Business Studies* 25(1): 65–89.

Morris, M., Schindehutte, M., and Allen, J. (2005). The Entrepreneur's Business Model: Toward a Unified Perspective. *Journal of Business Research* 58: 726–735.

Mulligan, P., Hatten, K., and Miller, J. (1996). From Issue-Based Planning to Hoshin: Different Styles for Different Situations. *Long Range Planning* 29(4): 473–484.

Neely, A. (2005). The Evolution of Performance Measurement Research; Developments in the Last Decade and a Research Agenda for the Next. *International Journal of Operations & Production Management* 25(12): 1264–1277.

Odell, M. (2001). BA Completes Sale of Go to Management. *Financial Times*.

Pettigrew, A. M. (1973). *The Politics of Organizational Decision-Making*. London: Tavistock.

Porter, M. (1985). *Competitive Advantage*. New York: New Press.

Schoemaker, P. J. H., Heaton, S., and Teece, D. (2018). Innovation, Dynamic Capabilities, and Leadership. *California Management Review* 61(1): 15–42.

Shih, W. (2016). The Real Lessons from Kodak's Decline. *MIT Sloan Management Review* 57(4): 10–13.

Spender, J. C. and Kessler, E. H. (1995). Managing the Uncertainties of Innovation: Extending Thompson (1967). *Human Relations* 48(1): 35–56.

Stacey, R. D. (1995). The Science of Complexity: An Alternative Perspective for Strategic Change Processes. *Strategic Management Journal* 16(6): 477–495.

Sterman, J. D. (1984). Appropriate Summary Statistics for Evaluating the Historical Fit of System Dynamics Models. *Dynamica* 10(2): 51–66.

Sterman, J. D., Repenning, N. P., and Kofman, F. (1997). Unanticipated Side Effects of Successful Quality Programs: Exploring a Paradox of Organizational Improvement. *Management Science* 43(4): 503–521.

Stieglitz, N. and Foss, N. (2015). Business Model Innovation: The Role of Leadership. In: N. J. Foss and T. Saebi (eds), *Business Model Innovation: The Organizational Dimension*. Oxford, UK: Oxford University Press, pp. 104–122.

Stock, R. M., Zacharias, N. A., and Schnellbaecher, A. (2016). How Do Strategy and Leadership Styles Jointly Affect Co-development and Its Innovation Outcomes? *Journal of Product Innovation Management* 34(2): 201–222.

Teece, D. J. (2007). Explicating Dynamic Capabilities: The Nature and Microfoundations of (Sustainable) Enterprise Performance. *Strategic Management Journal* 28: 1319–1350.

Teece, D. J. (2016). Dynamic Capabilities and Entrepreneurial Management in Large Organizations: Toward a Theory of the (Entrepreneurial) Firm. *European Economic Review* 86: 202–216.

Thompson, J. D. (1967). *Organizations in Action: Social Science Bases of Administrative Theory*. New Brunswick, NJ: McGraw-Hill.

Tortorella, G., Cauchick-Miguel, P. A., and Gaiardelli, P. (2018). Hoshin Kanri and A3: A Proposal for Integrating Variability into the Policy Deployment Process. *The TQM Journal* 31(2): 118–135.

Tushman. M. L. and O'Reilly III, C. A. (1996). Ambidextrous Organizations: Managing Evolutionary and Revolutionary Change. *California Management Review* 38(4): 8–30.

Uhl-Bien, M. and Arena, M. (2018). Leadership for Organizational Adaptability: A Theoretical Synthesis and Integrative Framework. *The Leadership Quarterly* 29: 89–104.

Van der Hoven, C., Probert, D., Phaal, R., and Goffin, K. (2021). Dynamic Technology Leadership. *Research-Technology Management*: 24–33.

Velu, C. (2016). Evolutionary or Revolutionary Business Model Innovation through Cooperation? The Role of Dominance in Network Markets. *Industrial Marketing Management* 53: 124–135.

Velu, C. (2017). A Systems Perspective on Business Model Evolution: The Case of an Agricultural Information Service Provider in India. *Long Range Planning* 50: 603–620.

Velu, C. (2020). Business Model Cohesiveness Scorecard: Implications of Digitization for Business Model Innovation. In: *Handbook of Digital Innovation*. Edward Elgar, pp. 179–197.

Velu, C. and Stiles, P. (2013). Managing Decision-Making and Cannibalization for Parallel Business Models. *Long Range Planning* 46: 443–458.

Witcher, B. and Butterworth, R. (2000). Hoshin Kanri at Hewlett-Packard. *Journal of General Management* 25(4): 70–85.

4 | *Digital Technologies and Transformation*

Computers are useless. They can only give you answers.

Pablo Picasso

Introduction

It is common knowledge that a number of major firms such as Amazon, Google and Uber have transformed industries using digital technologies. All of these firms are founded on business model innovations: offerings that involve systemic changes to how value is created and captured (Appio et al., 2021; Bharadwaj et al., 2013). There are many newspaper articles and blog posts providing advice to managers on how to deal with the opportunities and challenges created by digital technologies. Digital technologies can offer new forms of value creation while posing a threat to conventional means of customer value propositions (Aversa et al., 2020; Bresciani et al., 2021; Velu, 2016). Digital technologies can help to transform organisations, opening up possibilities for new firms to emerge while destroying the viability of others (Berman, 2012; Velu et al., 2019; Berman and Dalzell-Payne, 2018; Broekhuizen et al., 2020). Established firms who are considering implementing digital technologies need to decide how to do so, as it can profoundly alter their prospects for the future.

Today, several digital technologies and critical infrastructures, such as AI, cloud computing, additive manufacturing and 5G, are developing rapidly and may transform the economic landscape in which firms compete. The transformation may be compared to several general-purpose technologies from the past, including steam and electricity (David, 1990; Rosenberg and Trajtenberg, 2004; Velu, 2020; Dosi, 1982).[1] Electric motors were introduced around 1879 to

---

[1] General-purpose technologies tend to display the characteristic of general applicability, whereby it performs some generic function that is vital to the

replace steam engines, yet productivity initially declined slightly up to 1920, before beginning to rise rapidly (David, 1990). The rapid productivity growth in US manufacturing may be attributed to new organisational structures and business models that only emerged in the 1920s. The new business models involved putting multiple electric motors where they are needed and leasing them from external firms with specialist support services. This enabled productivity growth through lower energy consumption, improved production flows and greater resilience.

Studies suggest that there are multiple stages or phases to digital change, ranging from relatively simple to comprehensive changes (Verhoef et al., 2021). These phases can be classified into three broad categories: digitisation, digitalisation and digital transformation. Digitisation is the encoding of analogue information into a digital format (i.e., into zeros and ones) such that they can be stored, processed and transmitted by electronic means (Yoo et al., 2010). Digitalisation refers to how digital technologies can be used to alter existing business processes (Pagani and Pardo, 2017). Digital transformation refers to a more comprehensive change across the firm that contributes to new business models (Iansiti and Lakhani, 2014).

Digital technologies enable products and services to be delivered electronically and hence provide new value propositions to customers (Andal-Ancion et al., 2003). Moreover, digitally enhanced products and services encode much more information and are significantly more customisable. Hence, firms could better engage with customers and also obtain information about their processes on a real-time – or near real-time – basis. Digital technologies enable a more integrated set-up, both within and across firms. This enables the disintermediation of some existing firms but reintermediation with different roles, depending on the flow of material and information required to develop and deliver propositions to customers. Such an integrated approach implies that firms need to change their business models from primarily "make and sell" products and services to "sense and act" based on the information flow between the customer and firms across the network (Koebnick et al., 2020). Hence, digital transformation can be challenging for firms. In this chapter, we provide an overview of

functioning of a large number of products or production systems (Rosenberg and Trajtenberg, 2004).

the theory behind digital technologies and the implications for digital transformation. We then discuss some of the recent developments in digital technologies based on developments in artificial intelligence. Following that, we preview a new and emerging general-purpose technology based on quantum mechanics that is likely to change the landscape of computing and the Internet in years to come, as well as provide a basis for major digital transformation opportunities. Finally, the conclusion section provides some of the societal challenges related to business model innovation in the digital economy.

4.1 The Evolution of Digital Technologies and Transformation Challenges

Information-technology-driven competition that has shaped strategy can be classified into three waves (Porter and Hepplemann, 2014). The first wave, in the 1960s–1980s, involved the automation and digitisation of individual activities across the value chain, such as order processing, procurement and manufacturing resource planning. This involved standardising processes, and the challenge for firms was how to differentiate effectively. The second wave came with the rise of the Internet in the 1990s and 2000s, which enabled the integration of activities across suppliers, customers, channels and geography, enabling more globally distributed supply chains. In the third wave, which is happening today, IT is being embedded into products and hence changing the nature of products and services. Products with embedded sensors, increased connectivity and cloud-based data storage and analysis enable new product features and service functionalities. This could potentially reshape the value chain dramatically. There is a good example of this from the agricultural context (Porter and Hepplemann, 2014). Imagine a tractor that is used on a farm to move earth and cultivate crops. Such a tractor could be embedded with sensors, which inform the farmer about its performance and how to optimise its use. In the next stage, the tractor could be connected to other farm equipment such as tillers, planters and combine harvesters. This would make it a product system; hence, the basis of competition shifts away from being a product to a product system. The manufacturer of the tractor could alter its business model from being a farm equipment manufacturer to farm equipment optimisation as a service proposition. The next stage could be expanding beyond a product system to a system of systems proposition, whereby the connection is not only to farm machinery but to irrigation systems, weather, crop prices and seed-management systems. Moreover, the connected processes enable increased granularity in segmenting customer needs and require enhanced flexibility of value-adding activities to meet these needs. Such features will require firms to transform their business models from the traditional "make-and-sell" into a "sense-and-act" business model (Koebnick et al., 2020). Such a connected system of systems proposition blurs industry borders and throws up major challenges for firms in designing the appropriate business models to create competitive advantage.

Smart products could change how consumers consume the product from buying outright to pay-per-use. Alternatively, the firm could go into a hybrid model, whereby product ownership is transferred to the user but there is a performance-based service contract to ensure that the product performs to a certain specification, such as uptime (Martinez et al., 2017). This fundamentally changes the incentive structure of firms. For example, Rolls-Royce traditionally might have had a business that gains from selling spare parts and service contracts on its aircraft engines (Grubic and Jennions, 2018). However, such a business model might lessen the incentives to design engines that are reliable and durable. Hence, following pressure from its customers, the firm decided to include sensors in its aircraft engines and to sell a service contract by the hour, known as power-by-the-hour, which pays based on the hours that the engine is in the air (Smith, 2013). This is often known as servitisation (Baines and Lightfoot, 2013; Martinez et al., 2017; Smith et al. 2011; Neely, 2008; Neely et al., 2005). Such a trend is happening in many industries, from personal home and office space to personal and public transportation systems. For example, automotive firms such as Scania, a Swedish commercial vehicles manufacturer, have connected 500,000 vehicles on the road to manage the optimisation of routes, predictive maintenance and more efficient staffing of trucks as a service (Bjorkdahl, 2020). However, the generation of technological shifts from product systems to systems of systems might prove challenging for truck companies. The truck industry is facing a technological shift from diesel engine powertrains to electric road system (ERS) powertrains, whereby there is continuous electric power transfer to trucks via the road surface (Tongur and Engwall, 2014). Although, from the customers' perspective, there might be little change, this represents a radical change from the truck manufacturers' perspective. Such ERS powertrain systems will be more integrated into other subsystems, such as roads, fuel supply and billing systems, than the diesel-engine-based powertrain system. Truck manufacturers' core capabilities need to be transformed from engine technology to knowledge of customer behaviour, logistics and fleet-management services as customers adapt to wanting transportation services. Hence, the challenge for firms is to decide the scope of the firm, what core competency it would need and who it needs to partner with to enable complementary assets to come together to provide the product and service offering to the customer (Leonard-Barton, 1992).

4.2 Theory of Digital Technologies

Digital technologies are increasingly prevalent in enabling new sources of value. The Von Neumann architecture of digital technologies enables the instructions to manipulate the data and the data itself to be stored in the same format and location, which enables reprogrammability (Langlois, 2007). Digital technologies enable the decoupling of information from its related physical form or device, which has been termed resource liquefaction (Normann, 2001). This enables digital technologies to have two features. First, there is the separation of content from the medium (Yoo et al., 2010; Faulkner and Runde, 2013). For example, in the physical world, the content of a book in terms of, say, its story is tied to the physical copy of the book. However, with the digital medium, the content of the book can be read or listened to in various ways, such as the phone, computer or tablet, among others. The second feature is the separation of form and function. For example, a private car has often been used as a personal vehicle, and hence the form and function are relatively fixed. However, with the advent of Uber, the personal car is being used as a taxi and reverting back to being used for private purposes. Hence, digital technologies enable the procrastinated binding of form and function, whereby new capabilities can be added to a proposition once they have been designed and created (Zittrain, 2006). These, in turn, provide new ways to recombine resources and enable generativity, the capacity to produce unprompted change and innovation from uncoordinated and heterogeneous audiences (Yoo et al., 2010).

Moreover, digital technologies can create and shape physical reality, a phenomenon called ontological reversal (Baskerville et al., 2020). Typically, the physical reality takes precedence over the digital reality. For example, as one drives, the blue dot representing the location of the car on Google Maps follows the physical location of the car. Ontological reversal happens when the digital version of an object is created first, before the physical version. For example, in the case of autonomous cars, the blue dot that represents the car is created first and is computed to move from point A to point B on Google Maps. The real car then moves based on the movement in the non-material digital blue dot. Hence, the non-material digital object,[2] the blue dot, comes before the material real object, the autonomous car. In this way, digital reality takes precedence over physical reality and the ontology is reversed. This ontological reversal could have profound implications for human experiences and how value is created and captured. The vertical and horizontal scope of the firm, in terms of the activities within its hierarchy, as well as across the network of the value chain, will determine the boundary of the firm. These features of digital technologies enable new combinations of digital and physical assets to redefine the boundaries of the firm.

The transaction costs theory of the firm helps to provide an initial framework to understand the boundary of the firm. Transaction costs theory suggests that each actor will require payment of its resources' marginal productivity in order to provide incentives to recombine resources (Townsend and Busenitz, 2008). The transaction costs theory of the firm focuses on the balance between the costs of transacting in the market compared to the firm. Coase (1937) argued that firms exist when the transaction costs of using the markets are higher than those within the hierarchical structure of a firm. Transaction costs in markets can arise because of uncertainty; asset specificity – how specific the assets are to the required transactions; and the degree of opportunism (Williamson, 1985). Economists start with the premise that markets are an efficient way of coordinating economic activity in cases in which a pure exchange economy exists (e.g., spot contracts) (Williamson, 1985). Markets, however, prove to be inefficient if business dealings require coordinated investment where the composition

---

[2] Digital objects have the properties of a binary system, are editable, and display replicability (Faulkner and Runde, 2013).

of the assets is very specific to the transactions, and if the business dealings are of a non-contractable nature as a result of uncertainty (Grossman and Hart, 1986). Non-contractability can arise from asymmetric information between trading partners, bounded rationality and difficulty in specifying and measuring output (Gibbons, 2005). Non-contractability is also an issue in team-based production, which faces challenges measuring the input of each party precisely, making it difficult to apportion the value created (Hart and Moore, 1990). This gives rise to the metering problem, which is caused by shirking by the parties in the team, which is a form of moral hazard (Alchian and Demsetz, 1972). Organising team-based production is often therefore more efficient within the hierarchical structures of firms than markets.

Modularity is important in understanding how transaction costs determine the boundary of the firm (Baldwin, 2007). Transactions are defined as mutually agreed transfers between actors with compensation. The costs of the output being transacted need to be defined and measured, which are called mundane transaction costs. The mundane transaction costs are minimised at the thin crossing points of the task network, which creates module boundaries. Tasks within such a boundary are called transaction-free zones, and transactions occur between modules. Therefore, tasks that correspond to problem-solving, as well as routine activities where transfers are dense, need to be located within these modules. These modules are called transaction-free zones, where the cost of the transactions is less than the value of the transfer. Transactions need to be located at module boundaries where mundane transaction costs are minimised; this corresponds to the thin crossing points of the task network and where the boundary of the firm lies. Hence, transaction costs theory explains how tasks are bundled into modules in such a way that transactions occur across modules, known as thin crossing points, in order to minimise costs – the breakpoints where firms and industries may split apart (Baldwin, 2007). An alternative methodology to the transactions costs approach to determining the boundary of the firm is to examine the capabilities and resources (including knowledge generation) that maximise the resource portfolio of the firm, as well as the market demand for new customer value propositions (Jacobides and Billinger, 2006; Nikerson and Zenger, 2004; Priem et al., 2018).

A valuable way to understand how such organisation of activities and tasks might be affected by digital technologies is to consider the firm as a multi-agent system with an identifiable boundary and goal, in which an individual agent's efforts are expected to make a contribution (Puranam et al., 2014; Kretschmer and Khasabhi, 2020). In this context any functioning organisation involves solving two fundamental and inter-linked problems, namely, the division of labour and integration of efforts. The division of labour involves how to divide the task – task division – and how to allocate the tasks to individuals or teams – task allocation. The integration of efforts involves the provision of appropriate incentives and motivation to complete the tasks – the provision of rewards – and what information needs to be provided in order to execute the tasks and coordinate the actions – the provision of information.

Digital technologies fundamentally alter the division and integration activities. First, digital technologies can provide significantly more information as a result of the liquefication process that we outlined earlier. Moreover, digital technologies could create a new wave of critical elements for creating customer value, and hence certain new activities might need to be added while others are eliminated. For example, Cemex, a Mexican-based global cement firm, was able to eliminate a substantial proportion of its human-based inspection tasks for cement supply because it could monitor inventory levels in real-time at client sites using sensors (Kretschmer and Khasabhi, 2020). Second, such a process requires the regrouping of tasks, not only in how they are to be divided but also in the integration process. The regrouping of tasks needs to be done by putting tasks that are complementary together in order to augment their combined value, as well as optimising coordination (Milgrom and Roberts, 1990). Such complementarities might arise by working with other firms. For example, Vodafone, a UK-based telecommunications firm, worked with Microsoft to provide the underlying technology infrastructure for its digital transformation efforts (Correani et al., 2020). Vodafone adopted Microsoft's conversational autonomous interface using neural networks processing natural language when redesigning its customer care services. Vodafone is able to interact with its customers through multiple channels such as voice, social networks and home assistance, in order to listen, understand and assist customers.

Digital technologies also affect information flow for communication, monitoring and coordination. Research shows that information technologies and communication technologies have different impacts on autonomy and control (Bloom et al., 2014). On the one hand, information technologies, such as enterprise resource planning (ERP) systems, increase the autonomy of employees and hence enable decentralisation. On the other hand, technologies that improve communications, such as data intranets and electronic communications systems, could potentially decrease the autonomy of employees and encourage centralisation. Hence, these two forces could impact how organisations divide and integrate activities, both within and across firms. Such division and integration as a result of digital technologies will affect the design of business models.

4.3 Realising the Full Potential of Digital Transformation

A report by the Conference Board titled "Realizing the Full Potential of Digital Transformation" noted that firms that have successfully executed digital transformation share two common characteristics (Hao et al., 2020). First, these firms have the discipline to undertake digital initiatives only if they are aligned with the overarching corporate or business unit strategy. Second, they can enable business model innovation through new value propositions for their customers through the adoption of digital technologies. The research study was based on interviews with executives such as chief digital officers, chief IT officers and R&D directors from fourteen companies across ten industries in the United States and Europe. The study provides three insights on digital transformation: first, digital transformation must be integrated within the business strategy; second, business model innovation is often a key part of digital transformation and leads to creating competitive advantage for firms; and, third, firms measure and manage digital transformation using a multifaceted approach. We discuss these insights from the Conference Board research report below.

The first insight of the Conference Board report highlights that of the biggest challenges that firms face is ensuring that their digital adoption fits the overall corporate strategy. Often firms might be tempted to adopt a new digital strategy, such as blockchain, sensors or additive manufacturing technology, because it is a novel technology, without necessarily thinking through how it will improve customer solutions. Digital technology adoption often requires continuous adjustment of activities and processes that needs to be closely aligned with the strategic planning process. Moreover, the adoption of digital technologies might inspire a pivot in an existing strategy or a shift to an entirely new one. However, the continuous alignment between digital technology adoption and corporate strategy needs to be maintained by the firm. This is especially challenging when firms are organised across functions and geographies where there could be a disconnect between digital technology adoption and the corporate strategy as a result of the misalignment of interests and rewards.

A US-based car-rental firm was able to learn from the acquisition of a new car-rental firm that rents cars by the hour and which had superior on-board electronics monitoring systems in order to manage the car-rental system. The firm learnt that having on-board electronics car technology on its regular longer-term rentals would be helpful in monitoring the performance of its cars and replacing vehicles if the system predicted a possible breakdown. The rented vehicle is normally replaced by exchanging another car with the faulty vehicle wherever the rental vehicle has been taken, for example, to a holiday destination. The firm learnt that this increases service quality and contributes to customer loyalty. With the increasing possibility of autonomous vehicles, the car-rental firm is looking to develop a business for fleet-management services as the result of on-board digital technology management systems – digital transformation that inspires a new business model.

There are several ways that firms can align their corporate strategy with digital technology adoption. The first approach involves the definition of a major customer solution outcome based on the technology trend. A large European personal care company has a strategy of helping customers to visualise and personalise their beauty products. Once this has been done, using cross-functional teams, IT develops feasible, cost-effective digital solutions. De Beers defined the need to have end-to-end traceability of its diamonds, because of the risk posed by lab-manufactured diamonds, and, with partners, it developed a blockchain system to do this, from the digital exploration of diamonds to omni-channel sales and distribution. The second approach involves organising cross-functional teams to develop the capabilities to achieve major strategic goals. At a major US-based semiconductor manufacturer, the firm identified thirteen competencies such as demand creation, product information management and order fulfilment to grow the market share and profitability of the firm. These major competency areas are then organised and led by a cross-functional team consisting of senior management from the various divisions of the firm, which reports to the executive leadership team. A third approach is followed by BBVA, the Spanish multinational financial services firm, which established a corporate venture fund to observe and invest in promising fintech start-ups that could be integrated into the bank's business strategy. The fourth approach is to develop trends from the bottom up. For example, at 3M, a multinational conglomerate based in the United States, business units are encouraged to draw up strategic plans that address megatrends in technology and how they are likely to impact the business. Through a recursive process these are aligned with the corporate strategy and the strategy is refreshed when required.

The second insight of the Conference Board Report emphasises that digital technology adoption is most beneficial when firms re-examine how they create and capture value (Christensen et al., 2016; Cennamo et al., 2020). For example, a leading US publishing company has transformed the delivery of books from a physical to a digital format, which enables it to collect information on usage patterns, which can be used to provide additional services such as tutorials to improve students' exam performance. Moreover, the digital model has also allowed the firm to explore new approaches to developing value, such as selling products directly to consumers and disintermediating distributors and developing subscription models for students, professors and institutions.

Two major challenges that firms face when leveraging digital technologies to change their business models are the piecemeal syndrome and incentive misalignment (Velu, 2020). The piecemeal syndrome arises from the fact that managers are typically risk-averse, according to prospect theory, whereby disutility from failure is higher than the utility from gain. Hence, in most firms, the incentives are typically aligned to conduct incremental changes at the process or functional level, with less regard for the systemic changes needed for business model innovation, as the latter is often riskier than the former. This piecemeal adoption effect was seen with the introduction of PCs to replace mainframe computers (Steinmueller, 2000). Many firms treated PCs similarly to mainframes, with users continuing to procure services from the IT department as a centralised function while not fully benefiting from the more customisable opportunities provided by the PC. Hence, PCs took a long time to benefit firms, and they only did so when they facilitated the growth of more generic software, for word processing and manufacturing operations control, which was more customisable and could be upgraded, thus quickly displacing dedicated computers.

The second challenge relates to incentive structures that are misaligned with the new business model. For example, 3M sold furnace filters that keep air filtered and clean in buildings. The emergence of sensor-based technologies enabled 3M to develop a servitised business model based on selling "clean air" to its customers on a subscription basis; the company operates on the basis of promising a certain quality of clean air and is responsible for monitoring and cleaning – or replacing – the filters when necessary. The new subscription-based business model demands the minimisation of filter changes. However, the older business model requires maximising product sales and manufacturing large volumes to get the benefit of economies of scale to reduce the costs of production per filter. These conflicts often prevent firms from adopting new business models enabled by digital technologies.

The third insight of the digital transformation highlighted by the Conference Board report relates to how firms measure and manage digital transformation using a multifaceted approach consisting of input, throughput and output. Input involves measuring the capability and readiness of the organisation for digital transformation. For example, some organisations measure the digital capability of their staff in both soft and hard skills and ensure sufficient diversity among others between the sciences and the humanities. Gurbaxani and Dunkel (2019) proposed a six-dimension framework to measure firms that are gearing up for digital transformation. These six dimensions are: clarity of the strategic vision; the degree of alignment of the vision with investments; the suitability of the culture of innovation; the possession of sufficient intellectual property assets and know-how; the strength of digital capabilities; and the use of digital technologies. Firms can benchmark themselves on these dimensions against other firms in four broad categories: behind, on par, slightly ahead, and significantly ahead. Throughput requires organisations to systematically report on how effectively and efficiently their business model delivers the right customer value. The business model coherence scorecard (BMCS) discussed in Chapter 3 might provide a useful framework to identify and manage the efficiency and effectiveness of business models as part of the digital transformation effort. Finally, digital transformation success should be measured against achieving the business strategy. Such output measures call for a balance between financial and non-financial measures (Kaplan and Norton, 2004; Velu, 2020). Firms should use digital technologies to have real-time scorecard systems with customer-centric metrics across the different levels of the organisation that need to be fully aligned with the overall strategy of the firm.

4.4 The Age of Data and Artificial Intelligence

An increasing number of firms rely less on traditional business processes operated by customer service representatives, engineers and managers and more on algorithms to make decisions (Iansiti and Lakhani, 2020; Bader and Kaiser, 2019: Brock et al., 2019). Artificial intelligence (AI) based algorithms set the prices for Amazon, recommend songs on Spotify, suggest films on Netflix, match cars with passengers on Uber and approve loans on Ant Group. These AI-based algorithms are able to learn and update in order to improve the decisions being made over time (Brynjolfsson and McAfee, 2017). Many traditional firms are also beginning to embrace the use of AI to transform their business models (Cappa et al., 2021; Del Giudice et al., 2020).

One of the implications of liquefaction, the ability of digital technologies to decouple information from its related physical form or device, is the abundance of data that becomes available (Normann, 2001). Data has been defined as sign tokens or marks used to describe, represent or perform reality or index other marks (Alaimo et al., 2020). Studies have claimed that data as sign tokens or marks operates at a far more granular level of reality than higher-order functional entities such as components (Von Krogh, 2018). These sign tokens or marks in the form of data are a key resource used in the digital economy to create value; the value is created from both recombination and reinterpreting through a process of encoding, aggregation and computation of data (Alaimo et al., 2020).

Since John McCarthy coined the term AI (artificial intelligence) in 1956 at a conference in Dartmouth, there has been steady improvement in the techniques used to analyse and compute data. The ability to collect large amounts of data resulting from an increase in computer power has given rise to this era of AI advances. Artificial intelligence describes a set of advanced general-purpose technologies that enable machines to perform highly complex tasks effectively (Hall and Pesenti, 2017; Ransbotham et al., 2019). AI technologies aim to reproduce or surpass abilities (in computational systems) that would require "intelligence" if humans were to perform them – the science and engineering of intelligent machines (McCarthy, 1999). Machine learning is a type of AI in which a machine approaches a problem not by being explicitly programmed but by learning from data; it tackles a task by making data-driven decisions and predictions (Ghahramani, 2015). There are broadly three ways in which machines can learn: supervised learning, unsupervised learning, and reinforcement learning. In the case of supervised learning, algorithms learn to predict the output from the input data where all the observations in the data set are labelled.[3] Unsupervised learning involves observations in the data set that are unlabelled, and the algorithms learn the inherent structure from the input data. Reinforcement learning is based on interactions with the environment whereby the algorithm learns how to optimise based on the presence or absence of some reward.[4]

The application of AI may be classified into a hierarchy of analytical tasks, namely, descriptive, diagnostic, predictive and prescriptive (Davenport and Harris, 2007). Descriptive AI involves the process of gathering and interpreting data to describe what has occurred. Diagnostic AI involves the process of gathering and interpreting data sets to detect patterns and anomalies and determine relationships in order to explain why something has happened. Predictive AI involves the use of descriptive and diagnostic analysis from the past and identifying the likelihood of particular outcomes in the future. Finally, prescriptive AI involves using descriptive analysis for what has happened, diagnostic analysis for why, predictive analysis for timing and a form of reoccurrence in order to infer actions to influence future desired outcomes. For example, in the case of Uber, descriptive relates to understanding the customer profile and the rides that customers have taken in each car. Diagnostic involves understanding why customers have taken those rides, for example, as a result of weather conditions. Predictive involves using historical data to predict which customers are going to need cars, when and for which destinations. Finally, prescriptive informs drivers about which passengers are likely to need cars, and when, and informs drivers to wait at the right time and in the right place for passengers.

---

[3] Data labelling is the process of identifying raw data (images, text files, videos, etc.) and adding one or more meaningful and informative identifiers in order to provide context.
[4] Deep learning is a term used with neural networks where multiple layers (deep) are used to represent the data structures that can be used by structured, unstructured or reinforcement learning-based algorithms.

This could also involve suggesting to passengers that they might want to take an Uber for a particular ride. In the case of industrial applications, such as the use of sensors in manufacturing operations, descriptive might involve understanding the breakdown of machines in terms of type and timing. Diagnostic would include an understanding of why they broke down. Was it due to overheating, stress on the rotating parts or other factors? Predictive involves an analysis of which machines are likely to break down, and when, based on the past pattern of usage. Finally, prescriptive provides information for making suggestions about what should be done to minimise or avoid losses. Most applications of AI are predominantly descriptive, diagnostic and predictive, while the use of prescriptive is still in its infancy. Recent advancement in generative AI (such as Chat GPT) can create novel content from audio, text, images and video which can augment human creativity and potentially complement predictive AI (Eapen et al, 2023).

Many studies have highlighted the notion that AI should be used for augmentation rather than pure automation. Automation implies that machines take over a human task, whereas augmentation implies that humans collaborate closely with machines to perform tasks. However, Raisch and Krakowski (2021), in their review paper, mentioned that augmentation cannot be neatly separated from automation because these dual AI applications are interdependent across time and space, creating a paradoxical tension. They provide two use cases of AI to illustrate their point about time and space. Let us consider the time element first, whereby the use of automation will have an impact on augmentation in the future, and there will be continuous interaction between them. JP Morgan Chase is increasingly using AI to help set the criteria for the selection of candidates to hire. By removing the human element, the idea is to make the system fairer and more efficient in choosing candidates for interview. However, over time it is likely that digitalisation might require employees to have data science skills, which do not play a major role in the extant criteria for selecting candidates. Hence, the initial use of AI for automation would require subsequent human involvement, with a focus on augmentation, which allows humans and machines to work together by altering the context and adjusting their models accordingly.

Let us consider the space element next, whereby the use of automation will have an impact on augmentation in adjacent processes. For example, Symrise, a major global fragrance company, adopted an augmentation approach to generate ideas for new fragrances using a database of 1.7 million fragrances based on customer requirements. This model was reached through a combination of master perfumers' knowledge and customer purchases. The system initially consisted of automated searches for new novel fragrance formulas faster than humans were able to do. However, this use of AI to automate the idea-generation stage has an impact on the preceding objective-setting stage, whereby master perfumers must identify and input customer objectives and constraints in order to allow the automated generation of fragrance formulas matching these requirements in the idea-generation stage. This continuous iterative process of AI for automation and augmentation will enable new business models.

As machines become more intelligent using AI methods, they tend to have feedback systems to continuously improve performance, which in turn affects the organisational design (Galbraith, 1974). This feedback is likely to affect business model design through the content of activities of the organisation, the structure in terms of the relationship between activities, and the governance with respect to the responsibility for decision-making. Studies have highlighted that AI today is particularly focused on machine intelligence, which tries to solve well-defined problems. AI is less suited to defining the problem, as this requires a sense of self, motivation and purpose (Raisch and Krakowski, 2021; Von Krogh, 2018). However, one of the challenges in redesigning the business model, as machines become more intelligent, is to identify the appropriate problems that need to be solved to enable the business model to evolve. Such types of problem identification might require more general or human intelligence (Davenport and Kirby, 2015; Shevlin et al., 2019). Hence, cooperative methods for managers to use AI to enhance general intelligence would be needed for the business model to evolve appropriately to act as a complementary asset to intelligent machines in order to fully benefit from AI. Moreover, AI increases connectivity across the value chain. For example, AI is being used to develop digital twins, the generation or collection of digital data representing a physical object, which enables closer linking of product development, production, distribution and aftersales performance in the automotive industry, which calls for co-evolution of the business models of firms across the ecosystem. Hence, the business model needs to be seen as a complex system that co-evolves with the entire business ecosystem in which the firm is embedded as machines become more intelligent and connected (Burström et al., 2021).

4.5   Next-Generation Digital Technologies – Quantum Technologies

One of the key issues of digital technologies for firms is not just considering technologies that have been commercialised but also looking into the future at emerging technologies. History shows us that the benefits of new technologies can take many years, if not decades, to materialise, as this requires new social, legal and organisational approaches (Geels, 2002). Hence, it is appropriate to look forward in time to see forthcoming technologies that might have a profound effect on productivity and economic growth. One such technology is based on quantum mechanics, which is beginning to show incredible promise as a general-purpose technology that might have profound implications for all walks of life in years to come (Knight and Walmsley, 2019; van Dam, 2020; MacQuarrie et al., 2020; Vedral, 2011). Quantum technologies are expected to enable business model innovations and contribute to productivity growth as well as economic and societal well-being (Velu et al, 2022; Velu and Putra, 2023).

In the early 1980s, Nobel-prize-winning physicist Richard Feynman challenged computer scientists to develop a quantum computer (Cusumano, 2018). Feynman's challenge was based on his intuition that one could not solve problems in physics using classical digital computers with bits or binary digits, which are always either 0 or 1. This is problematic for physicists when representing a particle that could be in multiple states. For example, a particle (e.g., electron or photon) such as a qubit could simultaneously be in two states, both 0 and 1. It would be relatively straightforward to simulate with a single qubit, as it is in state 0 or 1. With two qubits, we have the possibility of having both in state 0, both in 1, one in 0 and the other in 1, or vice versa, which results in a total of four probabilities. This implies that N qubits could be in 2^n states. Therefore, with 10 qubits, 1,024 probabilities are needed, and with 20 qubits, 1,048,576 are needed. The information states required for over 300 qubits would soon surpass the number of particles in the universe. However, the systems that scientists investigate may have a number of particles that is many orders of magnitude larger, and hence the number of probabilities becomes unimaginably large – for example, simulating molecules for drug discovery. Feynman published a paper in 1982, *Simulating Physics with Computers*, where he postulated that to simulate quantum systems one needs to build quantum computers, as the problem cannot be solved by simply scaling or applying principles of parallel processing with classical computers (Feynman, 1982). Feynman went on to remark (1982, p. 486): "Nature isn't classical, dammit, and if you want to make a simulation of nature, you'd better make it quantum mechanical, and by golly it's a wonderful problem, because it doesn't look so easy."

Physicists, computer scientists and engineers have come a long way since 1982 in trying to harness the power of quantum technologies (Pirandola and Braunstein, 2016; Wehner et al., 2018). In particular, there are three properties of quantum technologies that have significant implications for solving some of the most intractable problems of the world and significant societal challenges, such as the need for better medicines and therapies, understanding nitrogen fixation for making ammonia, discovering low-carbon technologies to address climate change and greater security around information, among others (Ball, 2019; Government Office of Science, 2016). First, quantum technologies display *superposition*, where a particle can be in two or more states at once. Second, when two particles could be remotely connected – the *entanglement* principle – their state needs to be described jointly as a system and not according to the components separately which results in a correlation between spatially separated particles. Hence, when a measurement of the state is made on one particle, the outcome of the other entangled particle is known, regardless of the distance between them. Third, there is the *uncertainty* principle, whereby it is not possible to know the state of the particle until it is measured, when it will collapse to one state or the other, nor can an arbitrary quantum state be copied exactly (the "no-cloning principle"). These properties of quantum technologies have significant implications for how they might offer new solutions to problems that existing classical technologies (e.g., digital computers) will be unable to solve. We discuss below each of these properties and their implications for business model innovation in the case of quantum computers, sensing and imaging and communications.

4.5.1 *Quantum Computing and Simulation*

Quantum superposition, as a result of qubits being able to be in many states at once and entanglement enables complex calculations to be done much faster than classical digital computers[5] (Cusumano, 2018).

---

[5] The complex calculations use the properties of quantum entanglement and quantum superposition to perform calculations simultaneously rather than sequentiality which reduces the steps needed and speeds up the computation compared to a digital computer.

Hence, a quantum computer can process many inputs simultaneously instead of going through them one at a time, like a classical computer that can only be in binary states of 0 or 1. For certain classes of problems, this can mean a much faster solution – solving complex combinatorial problems or simulating material at the atomic or molecular structure (Sodhi and Tayur, 2022; Ruane et al., 2022). In order to harness the benefits of quantum computers, the qubits need to be realised and manipulated, which is not easy, as they are not stable. Qubits can be realised and manipulated using several classes of technology, such as superconductors, silicon spins or trapped ions among others, all of which are being developed as possible underlying technologies for quantum computers. Recently, there has been progress in achieving quantum supremacy, whereby a quantum system was able to do a calculation faster than a classical system (Ball, 2020). For example, Google claimed in 2019 that its quantum computer carried out a specific calculation that would have taken a classical supercomputer 10,000 years to compute (Gibney, 2019).[6] A group of scientists based in China were subsequently able to demonstrate this using beams of laser light to perform computations that have been shown to be mathematically impossible for normal computers (Ball, 2020). These are still the very early stages for comprehensive quantum computers. Nonetheless, although quantum computing is unlikely to replace classical computers, it might be very helpful in complementing them to tackle complex problems. The current state of art quantum computing is called noisy intermediate-scale quantum computers, as they experience errors for a particular number of operations and hence are not yet advanced enough for fault-tolerance. The vision is to build a fully fault tolerant quantum computer sometime in the future.

Quantum computers will have an enormous advantage in addressing two major classes of problems, namely, factoring large numbers and optimisation or simulation. We discuss the impact of factoring in the section on communications. Many commercial activities rely on optimisation or simulation; for example, complex products in aeroplanes are optimised using computer models before any real parts are manufactured, drugs are discovered by simulating new molecule

---

[6] This claim was later challenged by IBM, which claimed that its supercomputers could have done the same calculation in just over two days using a different classical technique (Gibney, 2019).

combinations, new materials are created for batteries, financial portfolios are optimised, and routing is managed for logistics operations, among others. Moreover, many of the solutions using artificial intelligence use ever-larger data sets, where quantum computing might play an increasingly critical role in the future in speeding up machine learning capabilities. These optimisation- and simulation-based problems would result in more dynamic personalisation, for example, in the delivery of goods using logistics, where there is a much faster sense of responding to new requirements that are specific to individual preferences or in personalised medicine.

4.5.2 Sensing and Imaging

Quantum entanglement enables particles to be connected to one another, whereby the state of one of them provides information on the other (National Science and Technology Council, 2016). This unique property, which has no classical equivalent, together with the very sensitive nature of quantum mechanical systems can be used for various imaging and sensing applications.

Most cameras and imaging technology today are restricted to visible light and capturing images in two dimensions. However, the real world is three-dimensional and has multiple light spectrums going from radio waves and ultraviolet to infrared. Quantum technologies can leverage these multi-spectrums of light to capture images. Conventional cameras rely on recoding light that bounces back from an illuminated object, which requires the wavelengths of the light illuminating the object and the light captured by the camera to be the same. However, quantum imaging enables the illumination of an object with one type of light, such as infrared, but recording of the image using visible light. This is possible because the two types of light emitted by, say, an ultraviolet laser are entangled. Hence, the camera can build an image of an object based on the visible light, but it is the non-visible light that is projected onto the image because these two types of light are entangled. This type of quantum imaging is called ghost imaging and it is particularly useful for gas-emission detection in hazardous areas or for analysing chemical compositions.

Quantum sensors are being developed to provide more effective and non-invasive health and medical imaging such as brain tumours and cancer detection using entanglement principles. Quantum sensing is also very valuable for surveying hazardous environments such as mineshafts and also more efficient in the maintenance of infrastructure such as rail networks (Stray et al., 2022). Moreover, the use of quantum sensors can improve position, navigation and timing (PNT) systems to much-improved levels of accuracy compared to global positioning systems or global navigation satellite systems. These quantum sensors are particularly helpful for positioning and route navigation for autonomous cars, trains and other vehicles, especially in densely built environments, underwater, underground and in tunnels. Moreover, these PNT applications of quantum technology provides more accurate timing for energy management or financial transactions recording that calls for very fine-grained time stamping.

4.5.3 Communications

One of the most important areas of the application of quantum technologies is in communications (Cacciapuoti et al., 2020; Wehner et al., 2018). The first application relates to the security of communications and the second to the development of the quantum enabled Internet. Networking digital computers to create the original internet helped to transform business models and accelerate growth across many industries, and we believe that a quantum-enabled Internet will spur such new developments.

In order to ensure secure communications, cryptography is built into many communication systems, including commonly used web browsers and mobile phones. Cryptographic keys are analogous to keys in the physical world – they are used to encrypt and decrypt data from sender to receiver. Factoring is very important because it is behind the most common form of cryptography, which is used to protect private and sensitive data. The encryption commonly used today relies on factoring large prime numbers, which a classical computer is unable to do sufficiently quickly. However, a quantum computer could easily break this kind of cryptography, solving large prime number factoring, which could render global communications systems vulnerable to hacking. One possible solution is to use quantum key distribution, where it would not be possible to effectively intercept the message because any tampering would be detected through the principle of uncertainty. This ensures the security of communications.

The quantum-enabled Internet, a network connecting devices through quantum links together with classical ones, is often envisioned as the final stage of the quantum revolution (Cacciapuoti et al., 2020), which could open fundamentally new communications and computing capabilities such as blind quantum computing which allows fully private computation. The quantum-enabled Internet would need to produce entanglement on demand between any two users. This might involve sending photons through both fibre-optic networks and satellite links that can extend the reach of entanglement by relaying it from one user to another along intermediate points. This would require routers and repeaters to transport quantum information to enable communication between distant quantum computers – a phenomenon called quantum teleportation.

Overcoming the class of problems outlined above by leveraging the properties of quantum technologies in the case of computers, sensing, imaging and communications could create new customer value propositions. Making such customer value propositions valuable to society calls for new means of organising the value creation, value capture and value network, and hence the development of new business models. Firms in some industries, such as financial services and healthcare, are already beginning to experiment with quantum technologies to solve problems that existing classical computers are unable to address effectively. The development of new business models to fully benefit from an emerging digital technology, such as quantum technologies, will require new cognitive models and leadership from both start-ups and established firms.

Conclusion

Organisations adopt different approaches to their digital transformation journeys (Hao et al., 2020). For example, in the financial services industry, with a vibrant fintech market and with start-ups disrupting the established ways of banking, some banks, such as Barclays and BBVA, have taken venture capital and incubation approaches to observe promising start-ups and drive innovation from an outside-in perspective. In the healthcare sector, health service providers have been trying to consolidate client data at each point of the life cycle and health journey to enable digital technologies to provide a holistic service and enable new business models. In other sectors, a performance-target-driven approach has been adopted. For example, a target of achieving 80 per cent deployability of aircrafts, which is often achieved by commercial airlines, enabled the US military service to implement digital transformation by adopting more data-driven analytical approaches for aircraft utilisation and maintenance.

Studies on digital transformation show that it is important to maintain customer-centricity and to keep the transformation journey agile by building cross-functional teams, working with external partners and ensuring the development of data proficiency among staff (Hao et al., 2020). Another area that has been emphasised as important in enabling digital transformation is the notion of the digital mindset. The digital mindset relates to employees having the perception that digital technologies are a strategic pillar of the organisation, and hence the firm having structures and processes in place for knowledge sharing, experimentation, continuous improvement, innovation and flexibility (Solberg et al., 2020). Studies show that there could be two major considerations in shaping the digital mindset (Solberg et al., 2020). The first relates to individual personal resources, where individuals see themselves as having either a fixed or a growth mindset. A fixed mindset relates to individuals who believe that their competencies are relatively fixed and who tend less towards embracing new opportunities to learn and grow. A growth mindset relates to individuals who believe that intelligence and ability can grow and hence look for ways to learn and grow. The adoption of digital technologies provides opportunities to experiment, learn and grow and might therefore be conducive to the growth mindset.

The second consideration relates to situational resources and whether people believe that resources are finite or expandable. On the one hand, when resources are finite, gains for one party correspond to losses for others. On the other hand, when resources are expandable, gains are possible for all parties. Therefore, it is important for management to understand the digital mindset of employees across these two dimensions when proposing digital transformation projects in order to position the opportunities and address the challenges appropriately. For example, when the Royal Bank of Scotland, a major British bank, was adopting an advanced data analytics system that could take over the core duties of financial advisors (primarily to sell ad hoc financial products), the bank created a new position of "journey manager" for advisors to take up a new format of customer service. The role entailed facilitating customers' journeys through their major financial moments with the help of data analytics (Solberg et al., 2020). This approach enabled the change to be accepted and the digital transformation to be implemented more efficiently.

The emergence of digital technologies also creates a challenge for firms designing business models that does not provide firms with an unfair advantage over their competitors. Digital technologies could result in unfair practices. For example, there is a practice known as the "last look" in foreign exchange markets (Anderson, 2005). This is where banks have the option to pull prices that they have offered on an electronic trading platform in order to protect them against toxic trade, with faster electronic trading venues being able to trade milliseconds faster because of the latent advantage, to the detriment of the banks. However, it has been known for banks to use this "last look" facility to pull a trade even when the trade is less profitable as a result of regular market price movements, to the detriment of customers. Such a practice could become prevalent in other fast-moving markets that are using ever-more sophisticated artificial intelligence and machine learning algorithms. These practices could result in business model designs that embed unfair advantages for certain firms over others and hence threaten the integrity of the marketplace.

There are several areas in the field of digital technologies and business model innovation that require further study, covering the identification of opportunities, phases of digital transformation and measuring the success of the transformation. First, what processes do firms have in place to identify digital transformation opportunities? We have discussed various ways in which firms seem to identify digital transformation opportunities. The question of whether or not there are certain ways of organising to identify new digital transformation opportunities that work under certain conditions compared to others requires further investigation. Second, do firms need to follow a phased approach to digitisation, and then digitalisation, followed by digital transformation? When does such a phased approach become effective and what should firms do to ensure that they are able to migrate seamlessly from one phase to the next? Third, how should firms measure the success of their digital transformation efforts? Whether or not there are particular metrics that are dependent on the type of digital transformation is an area that could be further explored as part of a research study.

This chapter has provided an overview of the opportunities and challenges of digital technology adoption and business model innovation and proposed some outstanding research issues on this topic.

References

Alaimo, C., Kallinikos, J., and Aaltonen, A. (2020). *Handbook of Digital Innovation*. Edward Elgar Publishing Limited, pp. 162–178.

Andal-Ancion, A., Cartwright, P. A., and Yip, G. S. (2003). The Digital Transformation of Traditional Businesses. *MIT Sloan Management Review* 44(4): 33–41.

Anderson, M. (2015). *Barclays Last Look*. Department of Financial Services Press Release.

Appio, F. P., Frattini, F., Petruzzelli, A. M., and Neirotti, P. (2021). Digital Transformation and Innovation Management: A Synthesis of Existing Research and an Agenda for Future Studies. *Journal of Product Innovation Management* 38(1): 4–20.

Alchian, A. and Demsetz, H. (1972). Production, Information Costs, and Economic Organization. *American Economic Review* 66: 777–795.

Aversa, P., Formentini, M., Iubatti, D., and Lorenzoni, G. (2020). Digital Machines, Space and Time: Towards a Behavioral Perspective of Flexible Manufacturing. *Journal of Product Innovation Management* 38(1): 114–141.

Bader, V. and Kaiser, S. (2019). Algorithmic Decision-Making? The User Interface and Its Role for Human Involvement in Decisions Supported by Artificial Intelligence. *Organization* 26(5): 655–672.

Baines, T. and Lightfoot, H. (2013). *Made to Serve: How Manufacturers can Compete through Servitization and Product Service Systems*. John Wiley & Sons.

Baldwin, C. Y. (2007). Where Do Transactions Come from? Modularity, Transactions, and the Boundaries of Firms. *Industrial and Corporate Change* 17(1): 155–195.

Ball, P. (2019). *Beyond Weird: Why Everything You Thought You Knew About Quantum Physics Is Different*. London, UK: Vintage, Penguin Random House.

Ball, P. (2020). Physicists in China Challenge Google's "Quantum Advantage." *Springer Nature Limited* 588: 380.

Baskerville, R. L., Myers, M. D., and Yoo, Y. (2020). Digital First: The Ontological Reversal and New Challenges for Information Systems Research. *MIS Quarterly* 44(2): 1–15.

Berman, S. J. (2012). Digital Transformation: Opportunities to Create New Business Models. *Strategy & Leadership* 40(2): 16–24.

Berman, S. and Dalzell-Payne, P. (2018). The Interaction of Strategy and Technology in an Era of Business Re-invention. *Strategy & Leadership* 46(1): 10–15.

Bharadwaj, A., El Sawy, O. A., Pavlou, P. A., and Venkatraman, N. (2013). Digital Business Strategy: Toward a Next Generation of Insights. *MIS Quarterly* 37(2): 471–482.

Bjorkdahl, J. (2020). Strategies for Digitalization in Manufacturing Firms. *California Management Review* 62(4): 17–36.

Bloom, N., Garicano, L., Sadun, R., and Van Reenen. J. (2014). The Distinct Effects of Information Technology and Communication Technology on Firm Organization. *Management Science* 60(12): 2859–2885.

Bresciani, S., Huarng, K-H., Malhotra, A., and Ferraris, A. (2021). Digital Transformation as a Springboard for Product, Process and Business Model Innovation. *Journal of Business Research* 128: 204–210.

Brock, J.K.-U. and von Wangenheim, F. (2019). Demystifying AI: What Digital Transformation Leaders Can Teach You about Realistic Artificial Intelligence. *California Management Review* 61(4): 110–134.

Broekhuizen, T. L. J., Broekhuis, M., Gijsenberg, M. J., and Wieringa, J. E. (2020). Introduction to the Special Issue – Digital Business Models: A Multi-Disciplinary and Multi-Stakeholder Perspective. *Journal of Business Research* 122: 847–852.

Brynjolfsson, E. and McAfee, A. (2017). The Business of Artificial Intelligence: What It Can – and Cannot – Do for Your Organization. *Harvard Business Review*: 3–11.

Burström, T., Parida, V., Lahti, T., and Wincent, J. (2021). AI-Enabled Business-Model Innovation and Transformation in Industrial Ecosystems: A Framework, Model and Outline for Further Research. *Journal of Business Research* 127: 85–95.

Cacciapuoti, A. S., Caleffi, M., Tafuri, F., Cataliotti, F. S., Gherardini, S., and Bianchi, G. (2020). Quantum Internet: Networking Challenges in Distributed Quantum Computing. *IEEE Network*, 34(1): 137–143.

Cappa, F., Oriani, R., Peruffo, E., and McCarthy, I. (2021). Big Data for Creating and Capturing Value in the Digitalized Environment: Unpacking the Effects of Volume, Variety, and Veracity on Firm Performance. *Journal of Product Innovation Management* 38(1): 49–67.

Cennamo, C., Dagnino, G. B., Di Minin, A., and Lanzolla, G. (2020). Managing Digital Transformation: Scope of Transformation and Modalities of Value Co-Generation and Delivery. *California Management Review* 62(4): 5–16.

Christensen, C. M., Bartman, T., and van Bever, D. (2016). The Hard Truth about Business Model Innovation. *Sloan Management Review* 58(1): 31–40.

Coase, R. H. (1937). The Nature of the Firm. *Economica*: 386–405.

Correani, A., De Massis, A., Frattini, F., Petruzzelli, A. M., and Natalicchio, A. (2020). Implementing a Digital Strategy: Learning from the Experience of Three Digital Transformation Projects. *California Management Review* 62(4): 37–56.

Cusumano, M. A. (2018). Technology Strategy and Management: The Business of Quantum Computing. *Communications of the ACM* 61(10): 20–22.

Davenport, T. H. and Harris, J. G. (2007). *Competing on Analytics: The New Science of Winning*. Harvard Business School Press.

Davenport, T. H. and Kirby. J. (2015). Beyond Automation. *Harvard Business Review* 93(6): 58–65.

David, P. A. (1990). The Dynamo and the Computer: An Historical Perspective on the Modern Productivity Paradox. *The American Economic Review* 80(2): 355–361.

Del Giudice, M., Scuotto, V., Papa, A., Tarba, S. Y., Bresciani, S., and Warkentin, M. (2020). A Self-Tuning Model for Smart Manufacturing SMEs: Effects on Digital Innovation. *Journal of Product Innovation Management* 38(1): 68–89.

Dosi, G. (1982). Technological Paradigms and Technological Trajectories: A Suggested Interpretation of the Determinants and Directions of Technical Change. *Research Policy* 11: 147–162.

Eapen, T. T., Finkenstadt, D. J., Folk, J., & Venkataswamy, L. (2023). How generative AI can augment human creativity. *Harvard Business Review* 101(7–8): 55–64

Faulkner, P. and Runde, J. (2013). Technological Objects, Social Positions, and the Transformational Model of Social Activity. *MIS Quarterly* 37(3): 803–818.

Feynman, R. P. (1982). Simulating Physics with Computers. *International Journal of Theoretical Physics* 21(6/7): 467–488.

Galbraith, J. R. (1974). Organization Design: An Information Processing View. *Interfaces* 4(3): 28–36.

Geels, F. W. (2002). Technological Transitions as Evolutionary Reconfiguration processes: A Multi-Level Perspective and a Case-Study. *Research Policy* 31: 1257–1274.

Ghahramani, A. (2015). Probabilistic Machine Learning and Artificial Intelligence. *Nature* 521: 452–459.

Gibbons, R. (2005). Four Formal(izable) Theories of the Firm? *Journal of Economic Behavior & Organization* 58: 200–245.

Gibney, E. (2019). Google Publishes Landmark Quantum Supremacy Claim. *Nature* 574: 461–462.

Government Office of Science. (2016). *The Quantum Age: Technology Opportunities*. United Kingdom.

Grossman, S. J. and Hart, O. D. (1986). The Costs and Benefits of Ownership: A Theory of Vertical and Lateral Integration. *Journal of Political Economy* 94(4): 691–719.

Grubic, T. and Jennions, I. (2018). Do Outcome-Based Contracts Exist? The Investigation of Power-by-the-Hour and Similar Result-Orientated Cases. *International Journal of Production Economics* 206: 209–219.

Gurbaxani, V. and Dunkle, D. (2019). Gearing Up for Successful Digital Transformation. *MIS Quarterly Executive* 18(3): 209–220.

Hall, W. and Pesenti, J. (2017). Growing the Artificial Intelligence Industry in the UK. *GOV.UK*: 1–78.

Hao, J., Hicks, S., Popper, C., and Velu, C. (2020). Realizing the Full Potential of Digital Transformation. *The Conference Board*: 1–26.

Hart, O. and Moore, J. (1990). Property Rights and the Nature of the Firm. *The Journal of Political Economy* 98(6): 1119–1158.

Iansiti, M. and Lakhani, K. R. (2014). Digital Ubiquity: How Connections, Sensors, and Data Are Revolutionizing Business. *Harvard Business Review*: 3–11.

Iansiti, M. and Lakhani, K. R. (2020). Competing in the Age of AI. How Machine Intelligence Changes the Rules of Business. *Harvard Business Review*.

Jacobides, M. G. and Billinger, S. (2006). Designing the Boundaries of the Firm: From "Make, Buy, or Ally" to the Dynamic Benefits of Vertical Architecture, *Organization Science* 17(2): 249–261.

Kaplan, R. S. and Norton D. P. (2004). Measuring the Strategic Readiness of Intangible Assets. *Harvard Business Review*: 52–63.

Knight, P. and Walmsley, I. (2019). UK National Quantum Technology Programme. *Quantum Science and Technology* 4: 040502.

Koebnick, P., Velu, C., and McFarlane, D. (2020). Preparing for Industry 4.0: Digital Business Model Innovation in the Food and Beverage Industry. *International Journal of Mechatronics and Manufacturing Systems* 13(1): 59–88.

Kretschmer, T. and Khashabi, P. (2020). Digital Transformation and Organization Design: An Integrated Approach. *California Management Review* 62(4): 86–104.

Langlois, R. N. (2007). The Entrepreneurial Theory of the Firm and the Theory of the Entrepreneurial Firm. *Journal of Management Studies* 44(7): 0022–2380.

Leonard-Barton D. (1992). Core Capabilities and Core Rigidities: A Paradox in Managing New Product Development. *Strategic Management Journal* 13(S1):111–125

MacQuarrie, E. R., Simon, C., Simmons, S., and Maine, E. (2020). The Emerging Commercial Landscape of Quantum Computing. *Nature Reviews* 2: 596–598.

Martinez, V., Neely, A., Velu, C., Leinster-Evans, S., and Bisessar, D. (2017). Exploring the Journey to Services. *International Journal of Production Economics* 192: 66–80.

McCarthy, J. (1999). Concepts of Logical AI. In: *Logic-Based Artificial Intelligence*. New York: Springer, pp. 37–56.

Milgrom, P. and Roberts, J. (1990). The Economics of Modern Manufacturing: Technology, Strategy, and Organization. *The American Economic Review* 80(3): 511–528.

Neely, A. (2008). Exploring the Financial Consequences of the Servitization of Manufacturing. *Operations Management Research* 1(2): 103–118.

Neely, A., Gregory, M., Platts, K., 1995. Performance Measurement System Design: A Literature Review and Research Agenda. *International Journal of Operations and Production Management* 15 (4), 80–116.

Nickerson, J. A., and Zenger, T. R. 2004. A knowledge-based theory of the firm – The problem-solving perspective. *Organization Science*, 15: 617–632.

Normann, R. (2001). Evolution of Strategic Paradigms. In: *Reframing Business: When the Map Changes the Landscape*. Chichester, UK: Wiley, pp. 15–44.

Pagani, M. and Pardo, C. (2017). The Impact of Digital Technology on Relationships in a Business Network. *Industrial Marketing Management* 67: 185–192.

Pirandola, S. and Braunstein, S. L. (2016). Unite to Build a Quantum Internet. *Nature* 532: 169–171.

Porter, M. E. and Heppelmann, J. E. (2014). How Smart, Connected Products Are Transforming Companies. *Harvard Business Review*: 96–114.

Priem, R. L. (2007). A Consumer Perspective on Value Creation. *Academy of Management Review* 32(1): 219–235.

Priem, R. L., Wenzel, M., & Koch, J. (2018). Demand-Side Strategy and Business Models: Putting Value Creation for Consumers Center Stage. *Long Range Planning* 51(2018): 22–31.

Puranam, P., Alexy, O., and Reitzig, M. (2014). What's "New" about New Forms of Organizing? *The Academy of Management Review* 39(2): 162–180.

Raisch, S. and Krakowski, S. (2021). Artificial Intelligence and Management: The Automation-Augmentation Paradox. *Academy of Management Review* 46(1): 192–210.

Ransbotham, S., Khodabandeh, S., Fehling, R., LaFountain, B., and Kiron, D. (2019). Winning with AI. MIT Sloan Management Review and Boston Consulting Group, October.

Rosenberg, N. and Trajtenberg, M. (2004), A General-Purpose Technology at Work: The Corliss Steam Engine in the Late-nineteenth-century United States. *Journal of Economic History* 64(1): 61–99.

Ruane, J., McAfee, A., and Oliver, W. D. (2022). Quantum Computing for Business Leaders. *Harvard. Business Review* 2022 (Jan–Feb).

Shevlin, H., Vold, K., Crosby, M., and Halina, M. (2019). The Limits of Machine Intelligence. EMBO Reports, pp. 1–5.

Smith, D. J. (2013). Power-by-the-Hour: The Role of Technology in Reshaping Business Strategy at Rolls-Royce. *Technology Analysis & Strategic Management* 25(8): 987–1007.

Smith L., Maull R. S., and Ng I. (2011). Servitization and Operations Management: A Service Dominant-Logic Approach. *International Journal of Operations and Production Management*, 34(2), 242–269.

Sodhi, M. and Tayur, S. (2022). Make Your Business Quantum-Ready Today. *Management and Business Review* 2: 78–84.

Solberg, E., Traavik, L. E. M., and Wong, S. I. (2020). Digital Mindsets: Recognizing and Leveraging Individual Beliefs for Digital Transformation. *California Management Review* 62(4): 105–124.

Steinmueller, W. E. (2000). Will New Information and Communication Technologies Improve the "Codificatio" of Knowledge? *Industrial and Corporate Change* 9(2): 361–376.

Stray, B., Lamb, A., Kaushik, A. et al. (2022). Quantum Sensing for Gravity Cartography. *Nature* 602: 590–594.

Tongur, S. and Engwall, M. (2014). The Business Model Dilemma of Technology Shifts. *Technovation* 34: 525–535.

Townsend, D. M. and Busenitz, L. W. (2008). Factor Payments, Resource-Based Bargaining, and the Creation of Firm Wealth in Technology-Based Ventures. *Strategic Entrepreneurship Journal* 2: 339–355.

van Dam, K. K. (2020). From Long Distance Entanglement to Building a Nationwide Quantum Internet: Report of the DOE Quantum Internet Blueprint Workshop. Computation Science Initiative, Brookhaven National Laboratory. US Department of Energy.

Vedral, V. (2011). Living in a Quantum World. *Scientific American* 304(6): 38–43.

Velu, C. (2016). Evolutionary or Revolutionary Business Model Innovation through Coopetition? The Role of Dominance in Network Markets. *Industrial Marketing Management* 53: 124–135.

Velu, C. (2020). Business Model Cohesiveness Scorecard: Implications of Digitization for Business Model Innovation. In: S. Nambisan, K. Lyytinen, and Y. Yoo (eds), *Handbook of Digital Innovation*. UK: Edward Elgar.

Velu, C., Pooya, G., and Dalzell-Payne, P. (2019). Targeting the Full Value of Digital Disruption. Cambridge and IBM Report.

Velu, C. and Putra, F. H. (2023). How to introduce quantum computers without slowing economic growth, *Nature* 619 (7970), 461–464.

Velu, C., Putra, F., Geurtsen, E., Norman, K. and Noble, C. (2022). *Adoption of Quantum Technologies and Business Model Innovation. Institute for Manufacturing*, University of Cambridge, Cambridge UK.

Verhoef, P. C., Broekhuizen, T., Bart, Y., Bhattacharya, A., Dong, J. D., Fabian, N., and Haenlein, M. (2021). Digital Transformation: A Multidisciplinary Reflection and Research Agenda. *Journal of Business Research* 122: 889–901.

Von Krogh, G. (2018). Artificial Intelligence in Organizations: New Opportunities for Phenomenon-Based Theorizing. *Academy of Management Discoveries* 4(4): 404–409.

Wehner, S. Elkouss, D., and Hanson, R. (2018) Quantum Internet: A Vision for the Road Ahead. *Science* 362(6412): eaam9288.

Williamson, O. E. (1985). *The Economic Institutions of Capitalism: Firms, Markets, Relational Contracting*. New York; London: The Free Press.

Yoo, Y., Henfridsson, O., and Lyytinen, K. (2010). The New Organizing Logic of Digital Innovation: An Agenda for Information Systems Research. *Information Systems Research* 21(4): 724–735.

Zittrain, J. L. (2006). The Generative Internet. *Harvard Law Review* 119(7): 1974–2040.

5 | *Digital Platforms and Ecosystems*

It is by logic that we prove, but by intuition that we discover.

Poincairé

Introduction

IBM's System 360 was seen as the first platform-based business model in the computer industry, whereby a bundle of standard components enabled users, buyers, developers or sellers to coordinate their efforts, providing IBM with a dominant position in the mainframe segment from the mid-1960s onwards (Bresnahan and Greenstein, 1999). More recently, there has been a proliferation of platform business models such as Amazon, Uber, Apple iOS, Google Android and Airbnb in the consumer market, as well as Siemens MindSphere and GE Predix in the business-to-business markets. Established firms such as Philips have also adopted platform-based business models for their healthcare proposition. Philips was founded in 1891 as a carbon-filament lamp manufacturer (Lal and Johnson, 2019). From its foundation in lamps, Philips went into X-ray tubes, radios, electric razors, televisions, compact cassette players, video cassette players and compact discs, among others. Philips' expansion into this array of products and services was based on its technological know-how being applied in adjacent markets.

However, in the early 2000s Philips realised that, in the digital world, competitive advantage comes from having a holistic understanding of customer needs in a particular sector and addressing their needs (Quelch and Rodriguez, 2015). In 2013 Philips, under the leadership of the CEO, Frans van Houten, decided to focus exclusively on healthtech – based on its strength in healthcare technology – and to exit all other sectors. However, serving customer needs in healthcare required the launch of a healthcare platform, meaning Philips would have a holistic understanding of customer needs and be able to be innovative in the provision of services across the consumer health journey, from healthy living to prevention, diagnosis, treatment and recovery. In 2014 Philips launched its HealthSuite digital platform in order to support the secure collection and exchange of consumers' health and lifestyle data. Philips partnered with firms such as Salesforce and Amazon Web Services (AWS) to build HealthSuite as an open, cloud-based platform that would enable third parties to develop applications for health systems, care providers and individuals to access data and provide personalised and empowered healthcare services.

The platform-based business model makes it easier for parties to transact between themselves and enables innovations to happen more efficiently. The platform business model facilitates an increase in the variety of the offering and is able to customise the offering to specific customers. This is exemplified by the objective of achieving personalised healthcare for the Philips HealthSuite. However, such platform business models require an ecosystem of partners in order to provide variety on the supply side and a broad set of customers to engage on the demand side (Helfat and Raubitschek, 2018; Gawer, 2021). There are several strategic issues to consider in designing platform-based business models.

The first issue is how to encourage the participation of partners and the design of suitable governance of such models. There need to be sufficient incentives for partner firms to engage, whereby they see the participation of other partners as an asset to help create and capture value. Second, the platform needs to attract enough customers to use the platform, which typically displays demand-side network effects, where customers get value from the participation of other customers on the platform. Third, the product and service proposition are not complete with digital platforms, and they therefore evolve continuously. Hence, the platform needs to decide how open to be to enable third-party firms to provide applications that will increase the variety offered to customers (Hilbolling et al., 2021). The platform faces a trade-off in that the more open it becomes, the more value it creates, but it also makes it less likely to be able to capture that value. Hence, there is an optimal openness for each platform depending on its market and technological characteristics. Related to this is when the integration of the components as part of the product or service should take place: Should it be done by the platform firm or by the customers themselves with a more modular systems-based architecture? This chapter provides an overview of these strategic questions when designing platform-based business models. We first discuss the theory of platforms, which will provide the underlying conceptual framework. We then discuss a number of challenges that firms face when designing and scaling up such digital platforms. In the conclusion section the chapter provides some of the challenges with respect to the power that platform firms wield and the implications for business model design.

5.1 The Types, Theory and Strategic Issues of Digital Platforms

This section outlines the principal types, theories and strategic issues of digital platform business models.

5.1.1 The Types of Digital Platform

The term "platform" has been used in a number of different ways. First, the organisational perspective views a platform as organisational capabilities that enable superior performance; the product family perspective views a platform as a stable centre of a family of products to enable derivative products; the market intermediary perspective views a platform as an intermediary between parties to a market-based exchange; and, lastly, the platform ecosystems perspective views a platform as a system that supports a collection of complementary assets (Thomas et al., 2014).

In order to reconcile these different perspectives, it would be helpful to review the origins of the use of the term in management literature. One of the early scholars used the term "platform" in the context of manufacturing firms providing a product or service that meets the core group of customer needs but which can be modified through the addition, substitution and removal of features (Wheelright and Clark, 1992). Some scholars have highlighted that a platform consists of common elements or assets across a product that enable the development of new products and services (Robertson and Ulrich, 1998). Gawer (2014) highlights that the commonality across these definitions is the systemic reuse of components across a family of products. Early studies of platforms were observed in manufacturing within firms, then across firms within supply chains, and more recently across a network of firms where there is no specific "buyer–supplier" relationship. The latter has often been called the "innovation ecosystem," with firms bringing together assets that can be used to develop complementary products, technologies or services (Gawer, 2014). Innovation ecosystems enable a collection of assets to be leveraged jointly by member firms in order to help stimulate innovation that allows for economies of scope in production, whereby the cost of joint production is less than the cost of producing each output separately (Thomas et al., 2014).

Two primary literature streams have focused on the economics and management of digital platforms: the economics literature; and the design engineering literature (Gawer, 2014). The economics literature has primarily focused on the demand-side network externalities by emphasising pricing and competition. Demand-side network externalities arise from increasing returns from the number of users of a product or service. These consist of direct network effects, whereby the benefit to users of the proposition depends positively on the number of other users. Indirect network effects arise when the benefit to users in one group depends positively on another group and vice versa. The economics literature on platforms focuses on connecting two or more groups through the platform and implementing an appropriate pricing strategy to maximise the value, hence outlining the competitive dynamics of platforms (Rochet and Tirole, 2003). The emphasis of the economics literature stream is on the economies of scope in demand. This could entail studying the cross-price elasticity of demand in determining optimal pricing. Cross-price elasticity captures the extent to which the demand for products on one side of the market increases as a result of cutting the price of the product on the other side and vice versa. At the limit, it is possible to charge a price of zero or to give away the product or service for free because the increase in demand and corresponding profits on the other side more than compensate for the loss of profits from the free proposition (Parker and Van Alstyne, 2006). Sometimes platforms, such as Taobao, allow free sign-ups for sellers and charge for providing complementary services such as obtaining better ranking in its internal search engine (Cusumano et al., 2019). The design engineering literature, on the other hand, has focused primarily on the modularity of the platform (Baldwin and Clark, 2000). The focus is on the design of the platform into a stable core and a variable peripheral component to stimulate innovation and hence the evolution of the platform (Baldwin and Woodard, 2009).

The emphasis of the design engineering literature stream is on economies of scope in supply through innovation.

Platforms deliver products and services by bringing together two or more stakeholders, and they are often referred to as multi-sided (Cusumano et al., 2019; Yoffie and Cusumano, 2015). For example, Facebook began in 2004 by connecting Harvard College students to their classmates; it then added advertisers to its platform as more students and their acquaintances joined. Following this, Facebook opened its platform to a third side – application software developers and game developers – to provide additional services. Finally, it added content providers such as newspapers and magazines, among others. Studies have shown that there are broadly two types of platforms. The first are transaction platforms, which are market intermediaries that make it possible for people and organisations to share and transact goods and services between themselves (Gawer, 2021). Transaction platforms include Alibaba and Amazon Marketplace, which aim to improve the transaction efficiency of the market. Platforms capture value or monetise the platform by collecting transaction fees, charging for advertisements or both. The second is innovation platforms, which have a common technological building block to enable the creation of new complementary products and services that add functionality or access to resources, which make the platform increasingly valuable (Gawer, 2021). Innovation platforms include Apple iOS, Amazon Webservices and Microsoft Azure, which promote innovation efficiency. Firms capture value by directly selling or renting the product or giving the core proposition for free and earning revenue elsewhere, for example, through advertisements. A number of major platforms are a hybrid of both transaction and innovation platforms, as they combine the characteristics of market intermediary and innovation. Examples of such platforms include Salesforce, Apple and Amazon, among others.

Innovation platforms add transaction capabilities in order to facilitate and maintain control over the distribution channel for complements (Cusumano et al., 2019). Transaction capabilities create value for complementors such as application developers, as they offer access to a wider customer base. In addition, platform firms are able to capture value from additional revenue from distribution. For example, Apple added the App Store about eight months after launching the iPhone; similarly, Google added the Google Store about a year after it started licensing Android in order to enhance their distribution capabilities. Transaction platforms tend to add innovation platforms to their business model design to stimulate innovation by third parties (Cusumano et al., 2019). This makes it attractive to both users, as it broadens the products and services, as well as the platform provider, providing additional sources of revenue such as transaction fees or advertisement revenue. For example, Expedia, the travel marketplace, opened a set of APIs in order to allow third-party firms to build applications for payments, hotels, cars, flights and other travel-related services.

5.1.2 The Theory of Digital Platforms

Digital platforms benefit from the liquification and reprogrammability characteristics of digital technology (Yoo et al., 2010; Baskerville et al., 2020, Yoo, 2010; You et al., 2012). Liquification implies data homogenisation, which enables different digital and physical objects that have been digitised to be processed using the same machine, such as a computer. Reprogrammability enables the separation of logical functions from the executing physical components, thus allowing the creation of different kinds of data and functions that permit multiple uses. Moreover, platforms have a layered modular architecture (LMA) (Yoo et al., 2010). The LMA is a set of loosely coupled digital resources brought together in real time through algorithms at, or near, the point of use across multiple layers on a common digital infrastructure. The LMA typically consists of four layers, as shown in Figure 5.1: contents, service, network and hardware layers. The contents layer contains data from various sources; the service layer contains the software used to access and interact with the data; the network layer refers to connectivity to the device, such as the communication protocols; and the hardware layer consists of the physical components of the device.

The combination of data homogeneity and reprogrammability enables recombinations to create new value propositions that are unprompted and not predictable, driven by large, varied and uncoordinated audiences – often called generativity (Zittrain, 2006). The ability of the platform to create new value propositions enables the fine segmentation of customers' unique requirements. Some feature of the product or service proposition is demanded by most customers and needs to be combined with the core platform. However, other

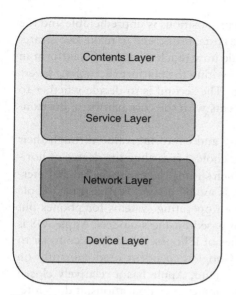

Figure 5.1 Layered modular architecture
Source: Adapted from Yoo et al. (2010)

features that bring different types of value to the customer need to be tailored to each customer's requirements. Such peripheral propositions that provide the value of variety need to be combined differently for each customer and hence brought together later, as and when the customer needs them. For example, Apple's iPhone has certain features embedded as part of the core phone offering, such as the email application. However, there are numerous other applications developed by third-party developers and available to iPhone users for free or by paid download, which enables each phone to be configured differently. The value of variety that is provided creates dynamic complementarity, whereby two assets complement each other with a feedback effect – they display economies of scope in demand. However, the increased variety could contribute to increased costs of complexity in the production and delivery of the proposition. Hence, the objective is to minimise costs by modularising the supply side and standardising as far as possible so that the component parts are compatible. The need to achieve compatibility could result in incurring higher fixed costs through standardisation via the platform. Since the process of generativity to create such value propositions is unpredictable and the value of variety will influence the costs, firms need to make two strategic decisions. The first is to decide how much to open the platform in order to choose what to integrate within the platform across the layers of the LMA: vertical integration. The second is to decide whether to integrate the peripheral components with the core platform: horizontal integration.

Firms need to balance creating and capturing value through their decisions about the two strategic choices regarding the degree of horizontal and vertical integration. Such strategic alternatives will be determined by the appropriate business model design. For example, Apple iOS and Google Android are both operating systems for phones but based on very different platform-based business models. Apple iOS is reliant predominantly on the sales of iPhones, which is in contrast to Google Android phones, with Google dependent predominantly on advertising revenue. On the one hand, Apple has a relatively closed architecture with controlled development of applications; it does integrate some hardware and services to the iPhone, such as Apple Music. On the other hand, Google Android uses open-source architecture with less controlled application development; Google does integrate some hardware and services into the Android-based phones, such as Gmail and Google Chrome. As of April 2021, Android users were able to choose from over 3.1 million applications from the Google Play store, while Apple users could choose from around 2.1 million applications for Apple iOS on the Apple Store (Statista Research, 2021).

In April 2021, Apple removed automatic consent from users of iPhones with iOS 14.5 to provide access to personal information such as location, what other apps are used, the timing of logging into an app, an encrypted version of email addresses, phone numbers and a unique number that identifies iPhones for advertisers: the IDFA (identifier for advertisers) (*Financial Times*, 2021). Such information is critical for advertisers to be able to provide personalised advertisements and generate revenue. The logic is that Apple charges 15–30 per cent commission on all application purchases and subscriptions through its App Store. Hence, Apple is banking on apps turning to charging customers higher fees, as they will lose some of the revenue from targeted advertising. Google, on the other hand, decided to stop using IDFA altogether. Although it is disadvantageous for Google to lose access to data from other apps, it already has a large amount of data from its own suite of apps that it can rely upon. For example, when phone owners use Google Search, Maps, Chrome, Gmail or YouTube, Google can still use that data to build advertising profiles. These examples show how business models need to be carefully designed, as they influence the degree of vertical and horizontal integration, which determines the value-creation and value-capture opportunities of the platform.

The degree of openness across the vertical and horizontal activities is also relevant in the context of business-to-business platforms. We compare and contrast the GE Predix and Siemens MindSphere platforms (Immelt, 2017; IMD, 2019, Case Study no: IMD-7-2011). General Electric (GE) launched Predix as an ingestion and processing platform for industrial operations data; it was developed to provide a standardised way for firms to utilise the information coming from their sensor-equipped industrial machinery. Predix focused initially on a pre-packaged software as a service (SaaS) solution; it was an integrated solution and less developer-friendly. Predix supported many of the vertical businesses of GE, such as aerospace, power and renewable energy, among others. GE initially built its own cloud data centre, which resulted in low take-up because clients were reluctant to have their data on GE servers. For this reason, GE later decided to use Amazon AWS and Microsoft Azure. GE's initial strategy was to target Predix at organisations that were deeply invested in GE products and services. The sales compensation strategy was very different, which created tensions between the industrial vertical sales teams that sold machines and the Predix sales teams that sold intangible digital offerings.

Siemens managed to overcome some of these challenges in launching the MindSphere Internet of Things Industrial Platform, which followed an open architecture model, whereby third parties can bring variety by developing applications – Siemens bought Mendix, a low-code software platform company that provides tools to build, test, deploy and iterate applications. MindSphere was geared not only towards organisations invested in Siemens products and services but also others. Customers own their data, develop their own apps and do not have to have Siemens machines. Hence, the MindSphere platform was much more open, both vertically and horizontally, than the GE Predix platform, at least initially. This gave MindSphere a more successful start compared to the challenges in scaling up faced by GE's Predix.

Gawer (2021) developed these notions of the boundary of the platform further by examining three interrelated choices. The first relates to the platform scope in terms of what is owned and performed in-house. In the digital economy, assets can be enabled without necessarily owning them because of digital connectivity. The second relates to the platform sides in terms of which distinct group of stakeholders have access to the platform. The third choice relates to digital interfaces, namely, the degree of openness and flow of information between different sides of the platform. Studies have argued that platforms need to balance minimising transaction costs, on the one hand, and enabling generativity, on the other. The boundary decisions across these three elements may vary depending on whether it is a transaction platform or an innovation platform and also whether the platform is in a launch or a maturity phase. For example, a transaction platform might be narrow in scope in the launch stage and only have a few sides, while being fairly open to enable increasing transaction and monitoring. However, as the platform matures, it might broaden its scope to exploit the asymmetric data flows between parties and add sides, but it might close its interfaces to prevent competitors from accessing data. Innovation platforms might start with a broad scope and have open interfaces with a few sides. When the innovation platform matures, it might broaden further as it incorporates complements into its core proposition, be more selective about adding sides and start to close its interfaces to prevent competitors from accessing data.

5.1.3 Ecosystem Platform Governance

A digital platform often requires an ecosystem of firms to create and capture value. Jacobides et al. (2018) argued that ecosystems are a different form of governance compared to markets and hierarchically managed organisations such as firms. Platform ecosystems are seen as "semi-regulated marketplaces" that foster interdependence between platform sponsors and their complementors to make them valuable to consumers (Wareham et al., 2014). Ecosystems help to coordinate interrelated organisations that display autonomy. Autonomous organisations arise from the existence of thin crossing points, where transactions costs are minimised by having a boundary between tasks (Baldwin, 2007); these boundaries create the modular architecture of the ecosystem. Some firms have been able to re-architect their conventional business to become more modular. For example, Intel took the lead in investing in a new peripheral component interconnect architecture to be able to better connect the main subsystems and the Universal Serial Bus standard, which enabled innovation to connected devices such as microphones, keyboards, printers and cameras, among others. This, in turn, increased the value of Intel's microprocessors, as their performance doubled over time (Cusumano and Gawer, 2002).

Modular architecture needs to display complementarity that is non-generic and where the complements are either unique or have the property of supermodularity.[1] The combination of modularity and non-generic complementarity gives rise to the emergence of ecosystems. In the context of platforms, there are benefits to group-level coordination of production and joint consumption of the complements, as it results in higher utility. Hence, ecosystem members retain residual claims over their assets and no one party can set all of the terms of operations. Therefore, ecosystems need to be both *de jure* and *de facto*, whereby some of the decision-making needs to be distributed (Jacobides et al., 2018).[2]

The question naturally arises about the optimal governance structure and hence the degree of centralisation of the decision-making. On the one hand, fully centralised governance can be beneficial when making decisions, but it might not take into account the perspectives of the different ecosystem members. On the other hand, a fully decentralised model reduces the likelihood of collective action and slows down decision-making, but it might allow the benefits of federated information to be brought together. Chen et al. (2021) demonstrated that the value of the platform is maximised when there is semi-decentralised governance, whereby members are given freedom and rights to participate in the platform while having some key members sponsor and shape the platform governance.

---

[1] Unique complementarity is where A needs B, and vice versa, to work effectively, where A and B are products, assets or activities. Supermodular complementarity is where A makes B more valuable, and vice versa. Both unique and supermodular complementarities can be applied to production and consumption.

[2] *De facto* means practices that exist even though they are not officially recognised by laws or rules, and *de jure* means recognised by the law or rules.

The acquisition, sharing and utilisation of knowledge is key to stimulating innovation within the platform ecosystem. The role of the lead firm in creating the governance mechanism for platforms is key to an efficient and effective knowledge-management system. By making an analogy of the platform ecosystem as a team (Gebert et al., 2010), Velu (2015) showed that the use of open and closed action strategies to foster innovation highlights three salient forms of tension that need to be managed in ecosystem governance (Wareham et al., 2014). The three tensions are autonomy–control, dissent–consent and uncertainty–certainty. In the case of autonomy–control, autonomy provides decentralisation and empowerment in order to expand the range of possibilities, which – when combined with the need to curtail freedom based on time and budget constraints, centralised control and frequent feedback – provides the right balance in terms of knowledge acquisition. In the case of dissent–consent open communication, debate and disagreement necessitate a variety of views, which – when combined with promoting informal communication, collectivist culture and team homogenising in order to enhance consensus potential – provides the right balance in terms of knowledge sharing. In the case of the uncertainty–certainty tension, fostering knowledge exchange with external entities generates new knowledge and might create uncertainty, which – when combined with promoting internal team communication and utilising existing knowledge – consolidates new and existing knowledge and promotes certainty, hence providing the right balance in terms of knowledge utilisation. In addition, scholars have emphasised the importance of integrative capabilities among lead firms in a platform ecosystem (Helfat and Raubitscheck, 2018). Integrative capability refers to the capability for effective communication and the coordination of activities, knowledge and objectives of firms within the ecosystem in order to achieve alignment across the complementary assets and enhance innovation.

The conventional wisdom is that firms need to own physical assets in order to capture value. However, in the digital economy such conventional wisdom needs to be enhanced to incorporate the notion of orchestrating external assets to help create and capture value (Hagiu and Wright, 2018; Parker et al., 2016). On the one hand, we have seen value being created by delinking assets fully, such as Airbnb and Uber, in sharing-economy business models. On the other hand, firms can orchestrate the right combination of complementary assets within the ecosystem to create and capture value. Such orchestration of the ecosystem implies that platform business models are likely to not only disintermediate or eliminate middlemen, or intermediate layers, but also to reintermediate with new middlemen. For example, in the travel business, TripAdvisor has created a new intermediation role by enabling certification of the quality of products and service providers.

Orchestrating external assets within an ecosystem would naturally result in the tension of when and how to provide products and services in such a way as to encourage partners to join the ecosystem while enhancing the value of the core platform. When Taobao – the Chinese online marketplace – started, it wanted to provide all products and services (Zeng, 2015). As a result of the company's rapid growth, many services were provided. However, Taobao opened itself up to an "ecosystem" mindset because of its inability to provide all of the services itself. However, the ecosystem mindset took time to embed, as there was still a desire by employees to be in control. For example, Taobao had introduced a standard software for store design, which not only could not serve the variety of sellers' requirements but also cannibalised the business for the store-design service providers. Hence, Taobao decided to provide a simple basic module for free and left the premium version to be provided by partner firms.

Governance of platforms becomes challenging when the platform competitors are also complementors. There are occasions when the application or service becomes mainstream and hence the firm embeds it within the core offering (Cusumano et al., 2019). For example, Google Maps was displayed prominently on the first Apple iPhones. However, by 2012, Apple viewed Google as a competitor and therefore developed a competing product, Apple Maps, which was preloaded on iPhones instead of Google Maps, which are available separately via Apple's App Store. Platforms also try to prevent multi-homing among users, as this makes it difficult to create and capture value. Multi-homing occurs when users or service providers use multiple platforms for similar types of interaction. For example, passengers and drivers use both Uber and Lyft. Apple avoided multi-homing by excluding Adobe Flash Player from its iPhone operating system. Apple's claim was that Flash was an inferior option to similar tools provided by Apple; however, the principal reason could be that Flash developer tools would allow content and program porting from Apple iOS to Google Android. Such portability between platforms would have enabled multi-homing and hence made the iPhone less distinct (Parker et al., 2016).

Firms also tend to use platform envelopment as a strategy to overcome competitive threats posed by adjacent platforms providing new features that might enable multi-homing. Platform envelopment is the strategy of one platform absorbing the functions and user base of another adjacent platform. For example, in 1995, RealNetworks invented the streaming audio product, Real Audio. Microsoft wanted to capture this market but was left behind by the initial success of Real Audio. Most of the users of the Real Audio streaming service were probably also users of the MS Windows operating system provided by Microsoft. Hence, Microsoft decided to compete with RealNetworks by developing its own audio streaming application and embedding it within Windows, which then enveloped the platform created by Real Audio, although the latter's software had superior performance (Parker et al., 2016).

5.2 Opportunities and Challenges in Transitioning to Digital Platforms

Traditional firms in value chains have scaled in two ways. The first is to integrate vertically by owning a larger proportion of the value creation and delivery chain of activities. The second is to integrate horizontally by expanding the scope of products and services produced and distributed. Platforms provide a new means by which traditional firms can integrate vertically and horizontally: Philips developing a healthcare platform; and GE and Siemens connecting their machines to the Internet of Things to create industrial platforms. Nike is continuing to build fitness-based application platforms that connect to its shoes and sportswear. However, what are the challenges for traditional firms in developing such platform-based business models? Let us examine digital platform business model adoption across various industries to highlight some of the key issues.

Volvo, the leading Swedish car company, made connected cars a strategic focus area in 2010 (Svahn et al., 2017). Volvo outlined a vision that would "give life" to cars beyond the time of production. The idea is to have an enhanced customer experience while opening new revenue streams for the firm. This initiative involved creating a platform business model that could provide additional connectivity and services to the car. Volvo created a transient initiative, the Connectivity Hub, as a forum for taking forward the Volvo Connected cars initiative. Volvo faced four competing concerns in adopting the digital platform business model (Svahn et al., 2017). The first involved developing the appropriate innovation capability without jeopardising existing product innovation practices. Volvo Cars was used to selecting the technology and functionality early for its next generation of products. However, the features of the connected car required ongoing interplay between the different stakeholders, such as the auto-makers, end-users, developers and public authorities. This required Volvo to develop skills and to be comfortable with delayed decision-making, which is a new type of capability of the firm. The second concern was related to the innovation focus between product and process innovation. The connected car initiative requires Volvo to work with its ecosystem of partners to guide the emergence of new designs and features. Hence, the focus shifts from product to process innovation, which is a new capability for Volvo Cars.

Volvo's third concern relates to the innovation collaboration model, which requires the balancing of internal and external collaboration. Volvo increasingly recognised that the connected car, unlike the traditional car, is not complete when it leaves the plant and will never be complete until it is taken in for scrapping. Hence, the capability of Volvo was predominantly developing new cars with its internal capabilities rather than the aftermarket, which requires collaboration with external partners. This required Volvo to reassign responsibility for business functions such as information technology (IT); the IT department was traditionally seen as a support function without product responsibility. However, to keep pace with the non-linear cloud-based innovation cycle, the IT department was given a new responsibility for end-user functions. Fourth, Volvo needed to consider innovation governance when dealing with partners that were not suppliers in the traditional sense of being contracted to deliver to a specified quality, time and price. Many of the new ecosystem partners for the in-car applications such as Spotify or TuneIn did not consider Volvo to be a customer, as their revenue was generated by selling to the end-user directly or to advertisers. Hence, Volvo needed to balance traditional cost control and requirement validation in a supplier contract with the need to incentivise partners to stimulate innovation.

LEGO, the Danish-based toy production company, shifted its strategy in 2008 from stabilising the organisation, after some challenging years, to focusing on growth under the leadership of the CEO, Jorgen Vig Knudstorp. As part of this growth strategy, LEGO emphasised the need to focus on digitalisation by purposefully evolving its business model to integrate digital into everything that it does. LEGO was looking to build on its digital platform to embrace digitalisation more holistically across the organisation. It used three lenses to leverage digitalisation: products, marketing and enterprise (El Sawy et al., 2016). First, the product lens centred on product innovation and the product ecosystem. LEGO had already built a robotics platform, Mindstorms, in 1998 in order to combine digital and physical experiences. It embraced a more open architecture for its Mindstorms platform after its proprietary operating system was hacked by LEGO fans. The company then launched numerous digital platforms to strengthen its connection to large user communities. These include, among others, LEGO Dimensions, a video game for popular consoles such as Sony PlayStation, Nintendo Wii and Microsoft Xbox, combining the digital and physical by enabling the player to have LEGO figures and a toy pad that can be played within the game itself. LEGO Club and My LEGO Networks allow children to share LEGO creations and to be creative. Second, LEGO shifted its marketing to become a pull activity to engage and interact with customer communities rather than a push activity to deliver product information. Third, it extended its IT skills and architecture in order to build its engagement platform to complement its strength in enterprise platforms.

Traditional enterprise platforms such as ERP and the supply chain management integration paradigm focus on transaction recording and reporting. However, the increased intensive interactive digital connectivity to the outside required integration between outside and within the enterprise; for this reason, LEGO built the engagement platform capability. This requires the IT team to be solution-takers, partners and integrators through a joint collaboration model with the business units rather than the traditional "plan–build–run" requirement-focused approach of the systems development model. This also required staff to have a higher digital quotient, with appropriate digital skills and training provided by LEGO.

One of the major challenges for incumbent firms is to develop a potentially competing digital platform while being involved with an existing platform ecosystem. Cisco, the multinational technology firm based in the United States, faced such a challenge (Khanagha et al., 2022). Cisco develops, manufactures and sells networking hardware, software and other related telecommunications equipment. Cisco was part of a cloud platform ecosystem based on centralised computing architecture using the cloud; it provided complementary products and services to the cloud platform ecosystem. The rapid emergence of the "Internet of Things" created the demand for decentralised data processing closer to machines or devices where the sensors are embedded. Hardware companies spotted an opportunity to lead this fundamental shift in the computing paradigm and to provide a range of services based on edge computing architecture. Cisco leveraged this opportunity to create a decentralised technology platform, where data is managed near the physical devices but between the so-called edge computing and the cloud. Cisco called this fog computing in 2014; fog is a viable complementor to cloud computing, while also being a potential competitor. The firm had to balance between positioning the fog platform as a symbiotic proposition to the cloud computing platform in order to attract the right type of partner in the early stages. Moreover, this approach enabled Cisco to neutralise resistance by powerful players in the existing platform. It then switched to positioning the fog platform in partial competition with the cloud computing platform once it had gathered sufficient momentum. In the initial stage, Cisco combined appropriate symbolic action, such as framing fog computing as a complement to cloud computing, by developing exclusivity. In the subsequent stage, Cisco started to relinquish exclusivity by positioning the fog platform in competition with cloud computing by fostering its own compatibility standards and forming appropriate partners to do so.

Digital platforms often require coopetition, whereby firms compete and cooperate at the same time to create and capture value. Customer adoption dynamics in network markets will influence how and when firms engage in coopetition (Brandenburger and Nalebuff, 1996; Velu, 2016). Demand-side network effects could affect incumbent firms differently as a result of the effect of their installed base of customers. This is because the resource base of the incumbent firms diminishes as customers dis-adopt an existing product or service proposition in order to adopt a new proposition provided by another firm, such as a new entrant. The diminishing customer base of the incumbent firms might provide the incentive for them to cooperate with their competitors. This cooperation with competitors enables incumbent firms to defend and regain market share in order to innovate their business models as a means to retain their leadership position in the industry. For example, in the US corporate bond trading market, it was observed that, with trading volumes exceeding US$400 billion per day in the early 2000s, incumbent firms chose to engage in coopetition in light of the competitive threat and adopted a defensive or offensive strategy when adopting electronic trading platforms to trade corporate bonds (Velu, 2016).

The less dominant firms engaged in coopetition by forming a consortium to innovate their platform business model in an evolutionary manner before the dominant firms; this was a defensive strategy to protect their existing business model. The evolutionary platform business model took the form of replicating the existing telephone-based trading systems but merely migrated the processes to an Internet-based interface, whereby the banks continue to act as market-making intermediaries. On the other hand, the dominant firms engaged in coopetition by forming a separate consortium to innovate their platform business model in a revolutionary manner after the less dominant firms, as an offensive strategy, as they saw their market share eroding fast following the move by the less dominant firms. The revolutionary platform business model took the form of radically altering the existing business model by eliminating the role of the banks as market-making intermediaries and enabling direct trading by buyers and sellers, with the banks acting as credit guarantors.

Amazon also adopted a coopetition-based platform business model (Velu, 2018), launching Amazon Marketplace in 2001 in response to a loss in investor confidence that Amazon would be suitable with its online business model; this was reflected in its share price declining by 80 per cent by the end of 2000. Amazon Marketplace enabled the firm to offset operating expenses while increasing sales. Competitors could list and sell their books and other products alongside Amazon's own propositions by leveraging Amazon's e-commerce platform and customer base. This platform business model enabled the firm to implement its "single store strategy," whereby it becomes the place of choice for customers to buy either new or used books from Amazon or its competitors by comparing them on a single page. In addition, Amazon provided automated tools to third-party retailers to migrate their catalogues of new and used books to the Amazon web page. The economic logic was the marginal cost of enabling competitors to list their products on Amazon.com, which was relatively small compared to the commissions and subscription fees earned. In addition, Amazon needed to hold less inventory of its own. In summary, Amazon built a platform-based business model by linking competitors' activities with its own in order to leverage the combined resources and provide a compelling customer value proposition.

5.3 Sharing-Economy Business Models

The emergence of Uber in transportation and Airbnb in the accommodation rental market has brought to the fore the notion of sharing-economy business models. Sharing is the act and process of distributing what is ours to others, and vice versa (Belk, 2014). A sharing economy is defined as the socio-economic ecosystem that commonly uses information technology to connect different stakeholders to share products and services in order to facilitate collaborative consumption (Belk, 2014; Laamanen et al., 2018). Sharing-economy models could be business-to-consumer (B2C), such as Zipcar, consumer-to-consumer (C2C), such as BlaBlaCar, or business-to-business (B2B), such as Yard Club, owned by Caterpillar, which enables equipment sharing among construction contractors (Chasin et al., 2018; Munoz and Cohen, 2018). The Internet has created new ways of sharing and also widened the access and scale of existing ways of sharing. An example of sharing material goods between consumers facilitated by the Internet is Sharehood, which was started in Melbourne by Michael Green, who knew that there were many washing machines between where he lived and the nearest laundromat that were often idle but which he could not access to do his laundry. Michael started an online sharing service, whereby neighbours could list things that were available (power tools, sewing machines, washing machines, etc.), which others could reserve and use at no cost. This created not only a more efficient use of machines and other items but also a greater sense of community among neighbours. Moreover, studies have shown that the average car in North America and Western Europe is used 8 per cent of the time and the average electric drill is used for between 6 and 13 minutes over its lifetime (Belk, 2014; Sacks, 2011).

A number of trends are encouraging firms to consider looking at sharing-economy-based business models (Kathan et al., 2016). First,

Internet technology and other digital technologies, such as distributed ledger, enable ways to secure trust via screening people, feedback loops and online payment systems. For example, increased peer-based self-regulation and ratings systems provide a check on possible dishonest behaviour. Second is the shift in values, especially among the younger generation, whereby ownership of tangible goods is less central to their identities and they have an increased focus on intangible attributes such as knowledge and reputation. Moreover, the economic pressures arising from uncertainties in the economy make the popularity of ownership less easily attainable, making sharing a viable alternative. Studies have shown that sharing-economy markets are likely to expand consumption as a result of the more efficient allocation of unused capacity in goods and services (Filippas et al., 2020). For example, a study comparing utilisation rates in Los Angeles and Seattle shows that Uber taxis are utilised over 55 per cent of the time compared to regular taxis, which are utilised approximately 40 per cent of the time (Cramer and Krueger, 2016).

The rapid growth of the sharing economy has attracted scholars to examine the performance implications of sharing platforms (Jiang et al., 2021). Studies have shown that up to a quarter of sharing platforms fail fewer than three years after their launch (Chasin et al., 2018). A configurational approach to studying the performance of business models has merit because of the causal complexity of the activity system within business models (Misangyi et al., 2016). This is the result of three features of business models, the first being the conjunction, where outcomes are often the result of interdependence of multiple conditions. The second feature is equifinality, where there could be more than one pathway for a given outcome. And the third is asymmetry, where attributes found to be causally related in one configuration may be less so – or even reversed – in another configuration (Misangyi et al., 2016).

Jiang et al. (2021) use a configurational approach to identify six design elements that are most salient in the sharing economy: (1) the degree of asset lightness, which describes the extent to which the products or services belong to the focal sharing platform itself; (2) the frequency of recurring transactions within a certain amount of time; (3) anonymity, which describes whether or not the actors that transact are anonymous; (4) transferability, which refers to the extent to which the assets being transacted or used on the platform are portable to other locations for use by a different set of users; (5) modularity, which refers to services provided by the platform that can be divided into a set of sequenced activities to be separated or recombined; and (6) the product category, which refers to customers' ability to judge the quality of the products or services before purchasing, which might vary according to the type of goods, such as search goods, experience goods or credence goods. Search goods enable customers to search for product quality before buying (e.g., watches, mobile phones). Experience goods are products for which product evaluation and consumption take place simultaneously (e.g., restaurants, hairdressers). Credence goods are products where evaluation is difficult even after consumption (e.g., management consulting services).

The study identifies four business model configurations that result in high performance. The first is the product-based sharing economy exemplified by the platform Poshmark, the social commerce marketplace where individuals can curate looks for their shoppers in order to buy and sell used clothing, shoes and accessories. The idea is to buy, sell and share personal style. The high performance of Poshmark is the result of it being asset-light, high frequency and having high transferability in terms of fashion goods that might ordinarily be credence goods in order to make them search goods. The second configuration is the rental-based sharing economy exemplified by Zipcar, the car-rental company that enables a business-to-customer sharing network. High performance is associated with it being asset-heavy, high frequency, high anonymity and high modularity in terms of how the service is designed: becoming a member, booking, obtaining and returning the car. Third is the knowledge-based sharing economy exemplified by the Khan Academy, the free peer-to-peer education platform. The Khan Academy considers education to be a credence good: it makes video clips in digestible 5–20-minute sessions available so that students can learn at their own pace in a modular and interactive way rather than a rigidly timetabled format. Hence, high performance is associated with low frequency, low anonymity and high transferability for credence goods. The fourth configuration is the labour-based sharing economy exemplified by Fiverr, an online marketplace for freelance digital services such as graphic design translation and video production, among others. Fiverr is a streamlined service model creating a demand and supply marketplace for these online services, similar to buying goods via Amazon. The high performance of Fiverr is associated with it being asset-light, high frequency, low anonymity and having low transferability and high modularity.

Conclusion

IBM's System 360 platform-based business changed the basis of competition in the computer industry from firms to ecosystems (Bresnahan and Greenstein, 1999). Since then, platform-based business models have become prevalent across many industries and have grown to be very popular and topical in recent years. However, platform business models are not without their challenges, from both theoretical and practical points of view. From a theoretical point of view, one of the main challenges is the conceptualisation of an ecosystem for digital platforms. The literature on ecosystems can be grouped into the structure view and the co-evolution view (Hou and Shi, 2020). On the one hand, the structure view emphasises the modular architecture of multilateral dependencies (Adner, 2017; Jacobides et al., 2018). The structure view focuses on facilitating value co-creation and coordination among actors in order to explain the uniqueness and when and why ecosystems emerge (Hou and Shi, 2020). Such a view pays attention to the role-based dynamics of the ecosystem. On the other hand, the co-evolution view emphasises the community-affiliated and interacting actors that keep an open exchange with the environment (Moore, 2006). The co-evolution view focuses on both the emergence and evolution of the ecosystem, paying attention to the actor-based dynamics of the ecosystem. This process of actor-based dynamics highlights the importance of lead firms developing integrative capabilities to enable the alignment of activities, products, resources, investments and objectives with partners and to facilitate internal coordination within the firm to enable platform evolution (Helfat and Raubitschek, 2018).

One of the other major challenges in platform business models is the ability of platforms to garner massive amounts of data, and hence to create a monopoly – and often an uneven playing field – as a result of the benefits of increasing returns from information. We have seen numerous cases against the major platform businesses, such as Google, Amazon, Airbnb and Uber, around issues ranging from market access and data privacy to pricing and classification of service providers. Google processes around 90 per cent of all online searches in the United States, which is coupled with a massive advertising business that generates a significant portion of its revenue (The United States Department of Justice, 2020). Moreover, Google pays Apple ad revenue to make Google search the default on Apple devices. The data that Google is able to garner from its dominant position in searches and advertisements, and creating exclusive agreements for its services, makes it the focus of anti-trust investigations (The United States Department of Justice, 2020). This dominance is also prevalent in sharing-economy business models. For example, in 2020, the UK Supreme Court decided to classify Uber drivers in the UK as employees rather than contractors (or "gig" economy workers), contrary to the position taken by the firm. This means that Uber's drivers will get certain employment benefits in the UK. The ability of platform business models to gain significant monopoly power through the design of their business models raises questions around welfare and societal issues, which requires further consideration, from an ethics and regulation perspective.

Moreover, the literature so far has focused predominantly on the indirect network effects from the quantity of complements. However, the quality of complements is equally important, as generativity enables the variety of products and services to proliferate on the platform (Hilbolling et al., 2021). As platforms grow, changes to the platform core, the ecosystem elements and the idiosyncrasies of how users connect to the platform could increase the chances of glitches and also contribute to obsolescence (Hilbolling et al., 2021). Therefore, platform owners, complementors and users need to work together to maintain the quality of the platform as it grows. In summary, the operating model of the platform that enables scale, scope and learning effects needs to enhance the variety while maintaining the quality (Iansiti and Lakhani, 2020).

There are a number of areas on platform business models and the sharing economy that require further study, covering aspects of the evolution of platforms, societal and welfare implications and maintaining quality. First, how do platforms evolve over time? We highlighted the role of the focal firm in curating and providing leadership for the platform. One of the key open areas from a theoretical perspective is how the structural characteristics of the ecosystem influence its evolution, and vice versa. The second relates to the societal and welfare implications of platform business model design. Platform business models can gain enormous power through mobilisation of their ecosystem and the accumulation of data. The principles of designing platform business models in order to balance the benefits to society, while not over-penalising some aspects of society, is an important area for further research. The third area that requires further consideration relates to how to maintain quality as platforms scale up, which could result in externalities. For example, when Uber is used extensively in a major city it could result in large traffic jams that reduce the welfare of other residents. In addition, as noted earlier, the increase in the volume of complementary assets on a platform could contribute to glitches and obsolescence. The challenge of how we internalise such externalities in order to build platform business models that maintain quality as they scale up calls for further research.

This chapter has provided an overview of the opportunities and challenges of platform and sharing-economy business models and proposed some outstanding research issues on this topic.

References

Adner, R. (2017). Ecosystem as Structure: An Actionable Construct for Strategy. *Journal of Management* 43(1): 39–58.

Baldwin, C. (2007). Where Do Transactions Come From? Modularity, Transactions, and the Boundaries of the Firms. *Industrial and Corporate Change* 17(1): 155–195.

Baldwin, C. Y. and Clark, K. B. (2000). *Design Rules, Volume 1: The Power of Modularity*. Cambridge, MA: MIT Press

Baldwin, C. Y. and Woodard, C. J. (2009). The Architecture of Platforms: A Unified View. *Research Collection School of Information Systems*: 19–44.

Baskerville, R., Myers, M., and Yoo, Y. (2020). Digital First: The Ontological Reversal and New Challenges for IS Research, *MIS Quarterly* 44(2), 509–523.

Belk, R. (2014). You Are What You Can Access: Sharing and Collaborative Consumption Online. *Journal of Business Research* 67: 1595–1600.

Brandenburger, A. M. and Nalebuff, B. J. (1996) *Coopetition*. Doubleday, New York.

Bresnahan, T. F. and Greenstein, S. (1999). Technological Competition and the Structure of the Computer Industry. *The Journal of Industrial Economics* 47(1): 1–40.

Chasin, F., von Hoffen, M., Hoffmeister, B., and Becker, J. (2018). Reasons for Failures of Sharing Economy Businesses. *MIS Quarterly Executive* 17(3): 185–198.

Chen, Y., Pereira, I., and Patel, P. C. (2021). Decentralized Governance of Digital Platforms. *Journal of Management* 47(5): 1305–1337.

Cramer, J. and Krueger, A. B. (2016). Disruptive Change in the Taxi Business: The Case of Uber. *American Economic Review: Papers & Proceedings* 106(5): 177–182.

Cusumano, M. A. and Gawer, A. (2002). The Elements of Platform Leadership. *MIT Sloan Management Review* 43(3): 50–58.

Cusumano, M. A., Gawer, A., and Yoffie, D. B. (2019). *The Business of Platforms. Strategy in the Age of Digital Competition, Innovation, and Power.* New York: Harper Collins.

El Sawy, O. A, Kraemmergaard, P., Amsinck, H., and Vinther, A. L. (2016). How LEGO Built the Foundations and Enterprise Capabilities for Digital Leadership. *MIS Quarterly Executive* 15(2): 141–166.

Filippas, A., Horton, J. J., and Zeckhauser, R. J. (2020). Owning, Using, and Renting: Some Simple Economics of the "Sharing Economy." *Management Science* 66(9): 4152–4172.

Financial Times. (2021), How Apple's iOS 14.5 Update Is Shaking Up the App Economy, 27 April.

Gawer, A. (2014). Bridging Differing Perspectives on Technological Platforms: Toward an Integrative Framework. *Research Policy* 43: 1239–1249.

Gawer, A. (2021). Digital Plaforms' Boundaries: The Interplay of Firm Scope, Platforms Sides, and Digital Interfaces. *Long Range Planning* 54(5): 102045.

Gebert, D., Boerner, S., and Kearney, E. (2010). Fostering Team Innovation: Why Is It Important to Combine Opposing Action Strategies? *Organization Science* 21(3): 593–608.

Hagiu, A. and Wright, J. (2018). Controlling vs. Enabling. *Management Science* 65(2): 577–595.

Helfat, C. E. and Raubitschek, R. S. (2018). Dynamic and Integrative Capabilities for Profiting from Innovation in Digital Platform-Based Ecosystems. *Research Policy* 47: 1391–1399.

Hilbolling, S., Berends, H., Deken, F., and Tuertscher, P. (2021). Sustaining Complement Quality for Digital Product Platforms: A Case Study of the Philips Hue Ecosystem. *Journal of Product Innovation Management* 38(1): 21–48.

Hou, H. and Shi, Y. (2020). Ecosystem-as-Structure and Ecosystem-as-Coevolution: A Constructive Examination. *Technovation*: 100.

Iansiti, M. and Lakhani, K. R. (2020). Competing in the Age of AI. How Machine Intelligence Changes the Rules of Business. *Harvard Business Review.*

IMD – International Institute for Management Development. (2019). Digital Transformation at GE: Shifting Minds for Agility.

Immelt, J. R. (2017). How I Remade GE and What I Learned along the Way. *Harvard Business Review* 95(5): 42–51.

Jacobides, M. G., Cennamo, C., and Gawer, A. (2018). Towards a Theory of Ecosystems. *Strategic Management Journal* 39: 2255–2276.

Jiang, F., Zheng, X., Fan, D., Zhang, P., and Li, S. (2021). The Sharing Economy and Business Model Design: A Configurational Approach. *Journal of Management Studies*: 1–28.

Kathan, W., Matzler, K., and Veider, V. (2016). The Sharing Economy: Your Business Model's Friend or Foe? *Business Horizons* 59: 663–672.

Khanagha, S., Ansari, S., Paroutis, S., and Oviedo, L. (2022). Mutualism and the Dynamics of New Platform Creation: A Study of Cisco and Fog Computing. *Strategic Management Journal* 43(3): 476–506.

Laamanen, T., Pfeffer, J., Rong, K., and Van de Ven, A. (2018). Editor's Introduction: Business Models, Ecosystems, and Society in the Sharing Economy. *Academy of Management Discoveries* 4(3): 213–219.

Lal, R. and Johnson, S. (2019). *Philips: The Shift to Value*. Boston, MA: Harvard Business School Publishing, Case Number: 9-517-045.

Misangyi, V. F., Greckhamer, T., Furnari, S., Fiss, P. C., Crilly, D., and Aguilera, R. (2016). Embracing Casual Complexity: The Emergence of a Neo-Configurational Perspective. *Journal of Management* 43(1): 255–282.

Moore, J. F. (2006). Business Ecosystems and the View from the Firm. *The Antitrust Bulletin* 51(1): 31–75.

Munoz, P. and Cohen, B. (2018). A Compass for Navigating Sharing Economy Business Models. *California Management Review* 61(1): 114–147.

Parker, G. G. and Van Alstyne, M. W. (2006). Two-Sided Network Effects: A Theory of Information Product Design. *Management Science* 51(10): 1494–1504.

Parker, G. G., Van Alstyne, M. W., and Choudary, S. P. (2016). *Platform Revolution. How Networked Markets Are Transforming the Economy and How to Make Them Work for You*. New York, NY: W.W. Norton & Company.

Quelch, J. A. and Rodriguez, M. L. (2015). *Philips Healthcare: Marketing the HealthSuite Digital Platform*. Boston, MA: Harvard Business School Publishing, Case Number: 9-515-052.

Robertson, D. and Ulrich, K. (1998). Planning for Product Platforms. *Sloan Management Review* 39(4): 19–31.D

Rochet, J-C. and Tirole, J. (2003). Platform Competition in Two-Sided Markets. *Journal of the European Economic Association* 1(4): 990–1029.

Sacks, D. (2011). The Sharing Economy: Fast Company (April 18, online edition). Available at: www.fastcompany.com/1747551/sharing-economy (accessed 8 May 2022).

Statista Research. (2021). Number of Apps Available in Leading App Stores as of 1st Quarter 2021.

Svahn, F., Mathiassen, L., and Lindgren, R. (2017). Embracing Digital Innovation in Incumbent Firms: How Volvo Cars Managed Competing Concerns. *MIS Quarterly* 41(1): 239–253.

The United States Department of Justice. (2020). Justice Department Sues Monopolist Google for Violating Antitrust Laws.

Thomas, L. D. W., Autio, E., and Gann, D. M. (2014). Architectural Leverage: Putting Platforms in Context. *The Academy of Management Perspectives* 28(2): 198–219.

Velu, C. (2015). Knowledge Management Capabilities of Lead Firms in Innovation Ecosystems. *AMS Review*.

Velu, C. (2016). Evolutionary or Revolutionary Business Model Innovation through Coopetition? The Role of Dominance in Network Markets. *Industrial Marketing Management* 53: 124–135.

Velu, C. (2018). Coopetition and Business Models. In: P. Chiambaretto, W. Czakon, A. Anne-Sophie Fernandez, and F. Le Roy (eds), *Handbook of Coopetition Strategies in the Routledge Companion on Coopetition Strategy*. Routledge.

Wareham, J., Fox, P. B., and Giner, J. L. C. (2014). Technology Ecosystem Governance. *Organization Science* 25(4): 1195–1215.

Wheelwright, S. C. and Clark, K. B. (1992). *Revolutionizing Product Development: Quantum Leaps in Speed, Efficiency, and Quality*. New York: Free Press.

Yoffie. D. B. and Cusumano, M. A. (2015). *Strategy Rules: Five Timeless Lessons from Bill Gates, Andy Grove and Steve Jobs*. New York: Harper Collins.

Yoo, Y. (2010). Computing in Everyday Life: A Call for Research on Experimental Computing. *MIS Quarterly* 34(2): 213–231.

Yoo, Y., Henfridsson, O., and Lyytinen, K. (2010). The New Organizing Logic of Digital Innovation: An Agenda for Information Systems Research. *Information Systems Research* 21(4): 724–735.

Yoo, Y., Boland, R. J., Lyytinen, K., and Majchrzak, A. (2012). Organizing for Innovation in the Digitized World. *Organization Science* 23(5): 1398–1408.

Zeng, M. (2015). Economic and Business Dimensions: Three Paradoxes of Building Platforms. *Communications of ACM*, 58(2): 27–29.

Zittrain, J. L. (2006). The Generative Internet. *Harvard Law Review* 119(7): 1974–2040.

6 | Small- and Medium-Sized Enterprises and Start-Up Business Models

When the time comes in which one could, the time has passed in which one can.

Marie Ebner Eschenbach

Introduction

Small- and medium-sized enterprises (SMEs) play a key role in most national economies around the world by generating significant employment and value added (OECD, 2017a). SMEs contribute to over 70 and 45 per cent of jobs in OECD countries and emerging economies, respectively. In addition, they contribute up to 50–60 and 33 per cent of GDP in OECD and emerging economies, respectively. Hence, improving the productivity of the SME sector could enhance economic growth and create jobs. However, there is ample evidence that productivity growth among SMEs lags behind large firms across major economies (Llinas and Abad, 2020; OECD, 2017a, 2017b). Such productivity differences could be gleaned from the lack of adoption of digital technologies and opportunities to reshape business models. For instance, across OECD countries, enterprise resource planning (ERP) software applications to manage business information flows are popular among large firms, with more than 75 per cent adoption rate, but less than 20 per cent by SMEs (OECD, 2017a). Despite the prevalence of digital technologies, SMEs face challenges in adopting these technologies as a result of the lack of investment in complementary assets, particularly knowledge assets and organisational changes such as process innovation and business models. This might be due to limited management and leadership capabilities, a narrow focus on specialised products and services, with a dependence on a small number of customers, limited opportunities for scale economies, constraints in terms of internal and external knowledge capabilities, and resource limitations such as finance (Miller et al., 2021).

Studies have shown that for large firms, the main challenge regarding innovation is reducing inertia, while for SMEs, the challenge is to increase cooperative capacity (see Cosenz and Bivona, 2021; Miller and Friesen, 1980). However, start-up firms might also face a form of inertia because of the influence of their founding members. For example, in biotechnology, where firms need to continuously come up with new drugs, the experience of a firm's founder can be detrimental to performance in terms of growth, perhaps as a result of the lack of new knowledge (Patzelt et al., 2008). Research also shows that partnering with third-party firms with complementary assets reduces the survival of new firms as the degree of business model innovation increases (Velu, 2015). The conjecture is that, as the degree of business model innovation increases, relying on partners for appropriability via complementary assets increases the new firm's exposure to coordination costs and asset-specific investments, which prevents the benefits of collaboration from materialising (Bock et al., 2012).

Start-up firms face enormous challenges in overcoming the liability of newness. This is particularly evident in science-based start-up firms in the early stages of product development, where the market for the product might not exist; hence, there are significant technological and market uncertainties to overcome (Bigdeli et al., 2016; Coombes and Nicholson, 2013; Lubik and Garnsey, 2016). The business model design of such science-based start-ups is challenging because of the long lead time between scientific development and technology commercialisation (Mason et al., 2019).

This chapter provides an overview of the opportunities and challenges of business model innovation among SMEs and science-based start-ups. We first discuss SMEs within complex supply chains, followed by a discussion of some of the challenges inherent in the adoption of digital technologies among SMEs in order to innovate their business models. We then discuss the challenges of business model innovation among family-owned SMEs, followed by an exploration of some of the frameworks for the development of SME business models. Next, we look at the challenges for science-based start-ups in designing and innovating their business models to enable the commercialisation of new technologies. In the conclusion section, the chapter looks at some of the opportunities and challenges faced by SMEs and start-ups when innovating their business models in order to enhance productivity and stimulate economic growth.

6.1 Supply Chains and Small- and Medium-Sized Enterprises

SMEs can be part of a supply chain to manufacture and deliver products and services to customers, as in the aerospace industry (Greenwood and Hinings, 1993; Smith and Tranfield, 2005). Some of these supply chains are tiered, with a large firm often the prime contractor or the original equipment manufacturer (OEM), which outsources part of the manufacturing and assembly of the product to other firms, which then sub-contract to SMEs (Godsell et al., 2010; Lee et al., 2020). We examine below the business model implications of SMEs in these supply chains.

Firms that supply customised high-volume products, such as automobiles, electronics and clothing, will be incentivised to push finished goods into the market in order to cover their high production and operating costs (Holweg and Pil, 2001). Such a made-to-stock (MTS) model needs to forecast demand and manufacture products, holding them in inventory ahead of sales. Often the MTS model results in a mismatch between the forecast demand and the actual sales. For example, in the automobile industry, dealers might need to give discounts to sell the inventory of cars in their showrooms. Customers might be persuaded to buy a pink Chevrolet, as a result of the discount offered by the dealer, rather than the blue one that they were keen to acquire. However, if the family does not like the pink Chevrolet, the car is then sold in the second-hand market after less than a year. The demand forecasting system in the meantime has predicted the demand for pink Chevrolets; hence, more of them are made under the MTS model. Moreover, firms need to increase volume because of the eroding margins created by the discounts. Hence, the MTS model could result in an inadequate supply of the desired product and an oversupply of undesired variants (Holweg and Pil, 2001). The US car market was particularly prone to low profitability in the late 1990s and early 2000s; for the average of 17 million vehicles sold, up to 2 million vehicles were held in inventory for between 40 and 60 days. Such high inventory results in significant costs in terms of interest and logistics, among others. In order to overcome some of these challenges and meet customer requirements, European car manufacturers, followed by American car manufacturers, moved to a made-to-order (MTO) model, which helped them to improve their profitability significantly. This is a result of the MTO model enabling process, product and volume flexibility to meet customer requirements.

Dell is well known for pioneering a variant of the MTO model, the assemble-to-order model, to customise personal computers (Gunasekaran and Ngai, 2005). Moreover, in the retail clothing industry, Zara, which is owned by Inditex, has adopted a "sense and respond" model known as "pronto moda" or "rapid fire fulfilment," where the aim is to turn over its inventory every two weeks, as opposed to the much longer lead times based on forecasting sales among other major retailers such as H&M (Martinez et al., 2015).

Most clothes retail chains sell fashion items where stock is held for several weeks or months. Prices are generally set higher when the items are first brought out for sale. These clothing retail chains often provide discounts to clear inventory of slow-moving items when the season is over or coming to an end. Most clothes retailers do not have their own manufacturing facilities but tend to outsource manufacturing, some of which are SMEs, to help reduce costs. In addition, retailers hold a large inventory of items, as the design and delivery of stock from manufacturers involve time lags of several months. The clothes are transported to retail outlets from low-cost countries, where the outsourced manufacturers are typically located.

The Zara model effectively tries to come closer to mimicking the MTO model by reducing the time between detecting fashion trends and bringing products to market. Zara has a fast stock rotation: it rotates its stock every two weeks, enticing customers to make frequent visits and purchases (Girotra and Netessine, 2011). It has a more vertically integrated supply chain with respect to designers and manufacturers of its clothing, where more of the activities are done in-house than externally sourced, in the case of conventional clothing retailers. Zara manufactures most of its lines in Europe, using fully owned or closely controlled plants. Therefore, it has higher manufacturing costs for equivalent products than its other retail clothing competitors. However, Zara is able to adjust quickly to fashion trends, reduce mark-downs and cut inventory costs, which has significant implications for SMEs, who are often involved in supplying material and products to the major retail firms in the supply chain.

SMEs across the manufacturing continuum between MTS and MTO need to have different business models to serve the supply chain efficiently and effectively. The MTS system is based on building to forecast, while the MTO system is based on building after receiving the customer order.[1] The customer order point (COP) is the point in the manufacturing system where the product is assigned to a customer order. In MTS the COP is at the finished inventory, while in MTO it could be earlier, at the material inventory stage (Olhager and Ostlund, 1990). Hence, MTS is a push system, while MTO is a pull system, with materials and production being pulled through the system based on customer orders (Gunasekaran and Ngai, 2005). MTS meets customer requirements from stock and relies on a stable production schedule with a relatively deterministic demand. MTO relies on supply chain flexibility to meet customised product requirements. The MTO system relies on tight integration of the supply chain with the upstream supplier of materials, midstream manufacturer and assembly of components and downstream distributor of finished goods. Demand management techniques such as marketing and promotions, as well as flexible arrangements with suppliers, are often adopted to balance supply and demand.

SMEs need to design their business models to determine the scope of the firm in terms of the degree of vertical integration across the supply chain. In particular, firms that have access to key information and material flow control the bottlenecks in the supply chain, which determines the competitive advantage – and therefore profitability (Jacobides and Tae, 2015). Hence, the industry architecture and the role of SME business models could determine their competitive position and performance, respectively. For example, OEMs in the automotive sector in the late 1990s and early 2000s decided to vertically unbundle and adopt a modular architecture based on an analogy from the evolution of the computer sector. However, once the OEMs began to outsource their production to SMEs in the supply chain, they realised that the computer sector – where outsourcing led to vertical unbundling and the creation of modular open access components – is different to the automobile sector. In particular, in the automobile sector the components are proprietary in nature; hence, outsourcing still required a degree of hierarchical control in order for the OEMs to create and capture value and not lose control to the tier 1

---

[1] There are variations to the MTO such as build-to-order (BTO), assemble-to-order (ATO) or engineer-to-order (ETO), which are principally based on manufacturing or assembling the product after the customer order has been received (Gunasekaran and Ngai, 2005).

supplier and SMEs that provide specialised components (Jacobides et al., 2016). Therefore, the OEMs changed course in the mid-2000s onwards to maintain the outsourcing but regain control of the design element. This approach was adopted to retain the systems integration role in order to maintain differentiation and hence guarantee the quality of the automobiles. This, in turn, contributes to the changes needed among the SMEs in the supply chain to adapt their respective business models.

The creation and development of complex products and systems (CoPS), such as aircraft carriers, battleships and nuclear power plants, often require supply chains to consist of both large firms and SMEs. The complexity of products can be defined by some principal features such as the novelty of the technology, the quantity of subsystems, the degree of customisation and the intensity of regulatory involvement, among others (Hobday, 1998). As the complexity of products increases, so does the number of feedback loops in the design and production process from the later to the earlier stages of production. There has been a continuous increase in specialisation and production artefacts and knowledge, coupled with advances in information and communications technology (ICT). Such developments provide the impetus for the continued disintegration of the value chain for product development and manufacturing of CoPS (Hobday et al., 2005). This results in increasing outsourcing of the development and manufacturing function. For example, Airbus, a major civil aircraft manufacturer, has increased the outsourcing of its planes from around 30–70 per cent over several years. Firms that outsource also need the capability to provide systems integration, which is the ability to define and combine the necessary input for a system and agree on a path for future development (Hobday et al., 2005).

These trends in CoPS result in SME firms adopting a "made-to-print" business model, which requires SMEs to deliver the parts to the design specification provided by the firm above them in the supply chain or the OEM. Studies show that SMEs might under-invest in intangible capital, such as human, information and organisational capital, as these are less measurable, and over time they become less able to innovate their products and processes and their business models (Said et al., 2022). This might partly explain the increasing disparity in the productivity of large firms and SMEs. On the one hand, vertical disintegration contributes to specialisation that might improve productivity; and, on the other hand, effective systems integration also leads to productivity improvements. SMEs need to develop dynamic capabilities to reinvent their business models so as not to be caught between the specialisation and systems integration roles of changing technological systems.

6.2 Industrial Digital Technologies and Small- and Medium-Sized Enterprises

SMEs tend to digitise general administration and marketing functions first (Ehret and Wirtz, 2017; OECD, 2021). Therefore, the gap between SMEs and larger firms tends to be smaller in terms of online government interactions, social media, selling online and electronic invoicing. However, the gap increases when the digital technology becomes more sophisticated, such as data analytics, ERP, cloud computing and other production technologies. Government-funded technology extension programmes have expanded across the world to help SMEs adopt digital technologies and enable digital transformation (OECD, 2021; Shapira et al., 2011). These include financial and non-financial support in consultancy and advice, for example, the Industry 4.0 Voucher (Portugal), SME Digital (Denmark), Capital Investment for Revolutionising SME Productivity (Japan), Digital Economy Corporation (Malaysia), Robo-Lift (Sweden), Digital India (India) and the Manufacturing Extension Partnership[2] programme (USA), among others.

The Made Smarter Review (2017) identified poor levels of adoption of industrial digital technologies (IDT)[3] in the UK among SMEs and under-leveraged innovation assets to help support start-ups and

---

[2] The Manufacturing Extension Partnership (MEP) programme was initially established with the goal of transferring technology developed in federal laboratories to SMEs in the manufacturing sector. However, MEP changed its strategic focus in the early 1990s to respond to needs identified by SMEs, including off-the-shelf technologies and business advice, which includes digital transformation (Voytek et al., 2004).

[3] The Made Smarter Review (2017) defines IDT, which includes the application of digital tools and technologies to the value chain of businesses involved in the production of things or which are operationally asset-intensive, such as power grids and wind farms. These include technologies at different levels of maturity, such as robotics, additive manufacturing, the Internet of Things (IoT) and artificial intelligence (AI), among others.

scaling up. These factors – together with the lack of effective leadership on a clear narrative about the opportunities of adopting IDT – hamper productivity growth in the UK. One of the Made Smarter Review (2017) recommendations was to set up a pilot programme to help SMEs in the North West of England adopt IDTs. The *Made Smarter Pilot Report* highlighted that, although 75 per cent of SME manufacturers in the North West of England had invested in new technologies in the last three years, most were larger SMEs, with one in eight smaller SMEs never having invested in new technologies over that period (Made Smarter, 2019). Moreover, most of the SMEs that have invested in new technologies have done so without a clear plan for implementation, resulting in disparate and disconnected equipment. Therefore, many of the IDT pilot programmes have focused on data and systems integration to ensure a more holistic view of operations and performance before adopting other digital technologies. The pilot report also identified that the major barriers to the adoption of IDTs among SMEs were insufficient capital, gaps in skills and knowledge and the need for guidance.

There are four reasons for a lack of digitalisation among SMEs: (a) less need resulting from specific foci; (b) a lack of resources and managerial vision; (c) taking a gradual approach compared to larger firms; and (d) heavily relying on financial performance and therefore having limited resources in this area (Gruber, 2018; Suppatvech et al., 2019). SMEs tend to perform better in digital transformation if they allocate more resources for business model implementation and also engage more in strategy implementation (Bouwman et al., 2019). Moreover, research shows that SMEs that adopt the notion of the self-tuning model are better able to execute digital innovation (Del Giudice et al., 2021). Such self-tuning organisations display the following: agility – the dynamic capability to integrate new processes and expertise using advanced technologies; adaptation – which refers to the learning curve of the enterprise due to change in the business model brought about by the transfer of organisational capabilities; and ambidexterity – which comprises exploration and exploitation in new forms of advanced technologies. Moreover, it is managers' lack of perceiving Industry 4.0 drivers, and not their perceptions of high Industry 4.0 barriers, that obstructs SMEs' development of digital readiness and their application of digital technologies (Stentoft et al., 2021). The study shows that among SMEs the main drivers of digital technology adoption are cost reduction and speed to market, while the main barriers are a lack of knowledge, as well as operational applications. The case studies based on four Danish SMEs show that the combination of digital technologies such as robotics with technologies that provide better systems integration between the shopfloor and business intelligence enables cost reduction and improves time to market.

The internationalisation of SMEs has been shown to affect business models and hence performance, as these firms need to compete for business in a more globalised setting with increased competition (Rissanen et al., 2020). Moreover, internationalisation could also act as an impetus for the adoption of digital technologies. For example, Li et al. (2018) showed how SME firms based in China, with little experience in international e-commerce, were able to do business internationally. This was because Alibaba, the major Chinese e-commerce platform, provided mentoring, facilitating and rule-making to help SMEs build managerial and organisational capabilities to facilitate digital transformation, thereby enabling business to be conducted on their platform for international e-commerce.

6.3 Family Firms

Family firms account for 85 per cent of firms worldwide (Chirico et al., 2011). For example, in the United States it is estimated that family firms employ more than 80 per cent of the workforce, producing more than 50 per cent of the output and contributing to a significant level of innovation (Chirico et al., 2011). Family firms differ in their approach to product and process innovation, and therefore business model innovation, compared to non-family firms, because of the resources and non-financial goals of family firms (Soluk et al., 2021). The difference between family and non-family firms results from the strong attachment between the family and the business, distinct knowledge management capabilities and the concentration of the family's wealth in the business, which can lead to risk aversion (Chirico et al., 2011). Family involvement often means business decisions can be overlaid with complex emotional relationships such as sibling rivalry or discord among family members (Jones and Girodano, 2021).

For example, *ECessori* is an electronic trading company that buys and sells goods on an e-commerce platform, which was started by two brothers (Jones and Girodano, 2021). The brothers started the business based on their activities selling sweets and pens to school-mates, which eventually grew to be a successful e-commerce trading business that bought and sold goods from China to the UK and other European markets. The business model was initially based on trading in its own avenue but it expanded to include Amazon Marketplace. One of the reasons for scaling up their hobby business was that the brothers wanted to generate enough revenue for their father – who normally travelled for work – to work from home. The business grew from selling various third-party accessories, such as smartphone accessories and memory cards, until a new business model was launched by one of the brothers and the business became very successful, selling own-brand e-cigarettes, Ez Cig, via Amazon Marketplace. However, Amazon then decided to ban the sale of these e-cigarettes, which created significant tension among the brothers, with the one who had started Ez Cig wanting to continue this line of business and the other brother having misgivings. The sibling rivalry had to be mediated by the boys' parents, who were intimately involved with the family business, in order to ensure its continued growth and success.

Family ownership has been shown to positively influence the ability to innovate business models using digital technologies (Soluk et al., 2021). Moreover, this positive relationship is mediated by dynamic capabilities such as knowledge exploitation, risk management and marketing capabilities. Family ownership might result in building specific capabilities in how knowledge is shared because of strong family ties. However, there is a management risk because of the stake of family members and their marketing capabilities that could be prone to being selective in customer partnerships to protect the family reputation. Family involvement can be both a favourable influence and a liability if there is a tendency to avoid risk or delay change. Hence, the involvement of families across generations in a participatory manner has been shown to positively influence family firms' performance (Chirico et al., 2011).

Family businesses often face two opposing forces: the first drives them to grow and expand beyond traditional markets; and the second encourages stability and the development of low-risk avenues in traditional markets (Casillas et al., 2010). Hence, the internationalisation of the business model of family firms is one way to seek growth, which requires risk-taking. Studies have shown that family businesses that are able to develop the know-how, desire and commitment for internationalisation are able to demonstrate profitable growth. This is because exposure to global competition enables these firms to innovate their business models and hence introduce competitive products at low cost (Calia et al., 2007).

For example, a Brazilian metal company, Metallurgy, was a leading provider of metallic chrome powder for the Brazilian market using a process called aluminothermy (Calia et al., 2007). This was a successful business between its founding in 1978 and 1986, serving the growing maritime platform of the Brazilian oil company when the Brazilian market was protected from international competition. However, after 1986 Metallurgy faced stiff international competition and a period of challenging financial conditions. The founder passed the baton to the second generation, consisting of his son and daughter, respectively. The firm decided to build a new product line by relying on recycled iron and aluminium alloys as raw materials and a new atomisation process to obtain metal powder. This desire to internationalise required the acquisition of know-how by partnering with a local institute for technological research in order to do the requisite R&D together. The innovation was required based on technological development, procurement via a joint venture with an aluminium recycling company and also a partnership for operational development of the atomisation technology. The combination of these capabilities and the transformation of the business model enabled Metallurgy to thrive and compete in a global market.

Family ownership and management have been shown to have a negative impact on innovation input but a positive effect on innovation output (Matzler et al., 2014). Innovation input relates to a firm's investment in research and development. Innovation output relates to a firm's different strategic considerations, activities and capabilities, including intellectual property. On the one hand, based on the principles of agency theory, there is a tendency for family firms to be more risk-averse than non-family firms, as there is often less separation between principal and agent. Since the family's wealth is at stake, in terms of investment in risky innovation-related input, family firms tend to display risk aversion to protect their personal investment value. On the other hand, human and relational capital are rich among family members and constitute important intangible capital. Family-owned firms are less concerned with short-term returns and more concerned with long-term performance. This longer-term orientation puts the family firm in a better position to more easily make adjustments to the structures, processes and strategic orientation of the firm.

An example of this was evident in the case of Cimber, a Denmark-based family-owned airline (Bogers et al., 2015). Initially, the founder–owner set up the airline business as a partner to other airline firms such as SAS and Lufthansa because of the close relationship with their senior executives. The focus was on serving a small set of business customers. However, later on, bringing external members into the business meant that its complexity increased through the adoption of a hybrid model, that is, by moving into the consumer and holiday market space, while still serving the business customer market. This created complexities in the business, which the family members had to reverse in order to become a more simplified customer-based business model while relying on the relationship with SAS to bail them out of financial trouble.

6.4 Early-Stage Science-Based Start-Ups

Early-stage technologies often face the challenge of novel applications for markets that do not yet exist and which therefore need to be created (George and Bock, 2011; Pisano, 2006; Shane, 2004). In such early-stage technologies, there is significant market ambiguity. The focus of start-ups in avoiding such ambiguity by primarily focusing downstream on end-users might lead to technology commercialisation failure (Molner et al., 2019). This market ambiguity calls for a wide search for the application of technology across different domains. In such settings partnering firms that are willing to jointly learn and explore the possible landscape of applications of the technology is more important than a focus on any immediate end product (Molner et al., 2019). Hence, the creation of such markets, with the development of appropriate business models, is often the challenge for science-based start-ups, where the market for the product is not readily available (Pisano, 2010).

During the twentieth century, large-scale incumbent firms such as DuPont, GE, Westinghouse, IBM, Kodak, Xerox (PARC) and AT&T (Bell Laboratories) created in-house labs to perform scientific research in order to commercialise products (Pisano, 2010). More recently, the connection between science and business has begun to change as a result of the highly risky nature of some of the scientific research and the increasingly long time needed to convert this into viable products, often between five to ten years or more. The investment in in-house scientific labs declined among incumbent firms and was replaced by new "science-based businesses"; start-ups in sectors such as bio-tech, nanotech and energy emerged, with an increasing role played by universities in enabling such technology transfer from their labs (Gumusay and Bohne, 2018; Pisano, 2010). It is becoming increasingly common for incumbent firms to acquire these science-based start-ups. For example, Japanese incumbent Sumitomo Chemical acquired Cambridge Display Technology (CDT), which had developed the P-OLED (polymer-organic light-emitting diode) technology for over a decade; and Medigene AG acquired Oxford biotech spin-out Avidex, which went on to integrate Avidex T-cell protein technology with Medigene's own offering (Lubik and Garnsey, 2016).

Science-based start-ups need to be considered in relation to whether the technology has a clear market where they are targeted to help solve a problem. This depends on the technology. Often in areas such as biotechnology and pharmaceuticals the breakthroughs are targeted at solving specific problems (Lubik and Garnsey, 2016). However, in other areas, such as new energy or material, the technology is often generic and could be used for a wide variety of applications. Such generic technologies are often known as general-purpose technologies, which display general applicability across a number of products or production systems, display technological dynamism with continual innovation, and prompt innovation in complementary technologies in the application sectors (Goldfarb, 2005; Rosenberg and Trantenberg, 2004). These properties of generic technologies make it challenging for start-up firms to develop their business models. Two case examples of start-ups – Cambridge Display Technology (CDT) and Metalysis in the advanced materials sector – illustrate these challenges.

CDT was founded in 1992 following 10 years of science-based research at the Cavendish Laboratory, the University of Cambridge, following the invention of polymer transistors (Maine and Garnsey, 2006).[4] Light-emitting polymers (LEPs) were seen as having the potential to replace cathode ray technologies, which were still the standard for electronic display applications. CDT created intellectual property on LEP technology platforms, as well as the production process for

---

[4] This case study is from Maine and Garnsey (2006).

the flat-panel organic light-emitting diode (OLED). LEP and OLED technologies had new attributes for display design such as flexible screens, efficiency and weight compared to existing technologies such as cathode ray displays and LCD displays. Initially, CDT licensed its technology to incumbent firms involved in materials supplies, as well as displaying manufacturers such as Philips, Hoechst and Uniax as a means to develop the market through manufacturing partnerships. Moreover, a joint venture partnership was formed with Seiko Epson Corporation, resulting in the first video display LEP. However, CDT needed more funds to conduct R&D for materials and devices surrounding its OLED patents: it sold out to a New York private equity fund, Kelso and Hillman, in 2000. In order to increase the value of the licensing agreements, CDT decided to re-enter small-scale manufacturing to demonstrate the viability of its pioneering technology. To this end, it developed its own manufacturing facilities in Cambridge. CDT's first commercial product was the OLED electronic shaver display, which was launched in 2002. Following this, CDT's LEP display was incorporated into mobile phones through various partnership agreements. However, the cost of manufacturing was too high, as the volume was still relatively low; hence, CDT decided to scale back its manufacturing by selling its facilities. Despite the slow growth, CDT positioned itself at the centre of the network of companies developing technologies using LEP displays and was successful in listing on the Nasdaq in December 2004. As mentioned earlier, CDT was acquired by the Japanese firm Sumitomo Capital in 2007.

CDT faced significant market and technological uncertainties, the latter because its technology was competing with existing technologies. For this reason, it needed to invest in reducing costs in the upstream, as well as downstream, process to enable component suppliers and OEM manufacturers to utilise the products in existing product applications. CDT focused exclusively on the consumer electronics market but examined several applications. It faced the challenge of acquiring an accurate picture of consumer needs because it did not have direct contact with consumers. Hence, CDT initially decided to pursue in-house manufacturing in order to demonstrate the benefits of its technology. However, the combination of market and technological uncertainty resulted in CDT iterating between manufacturing and licensing business models before finally settling on licensing as its core business model.

Metalysis (called FCC Ltd until 2003) was a spin-out of the University of Cambridge whose aim was to commercialise the Cambridge FCC process, which is an electrochemical method of producing metals from metal oxides through electrolysis in molten calcium salts (Lubik and Garnsey, 2016).[5] The process could be applied to various metals such as chromium, tungsten, cobalt, tantalum and titanium. The Cambridge FCC process has significant benefits, as it allows for the production of metal powders directly from metal oxides, lowers processing costs and removes the need for machining, among others. Moreover, the technology was seen to be green, as it significantly reduces environmental impact by lowering temperature and using fewer toxic chemicals. The founders approached Cambridge Enterprise, the technology-transfer office of the University of Cambridge, in order to license the patent to a number of firms. Metalysis built a small-scale pilot plant in one of the science parks in Cambridge to develop the process further. It originally targeted tantalum, which was costly to produce, but the tantalum market did not prove to be a success.

In 2006, Metalysis decided to focus on titanium as a result of a partnership with Rolls-Royce, which provided funding for R&D activities and scale-up facilities as part of its tax off-set programme in Malaysia. Initially, the rights for the use of titanium were licensed to another firm but this was overcome through a transfer of the licensing rights by Cambridge Enterprise, which was followed by a legal battle. Moreover, BHP Billiton joined Metalysis to jointly develop the method for processing titanium. Initially, Metalysis adopted the pure licensing model and demonstrated the benefits of the technology using tantalum. However, it needed a market with a high-value-added metal with a sufficient market size; for this reason, it split to enter scale-up production in the titanium market despite the existence of large dominant players. Metalysis was able to collaborate to produce metal powders, which were very valuable to this segment. This strategy overturns the conventional wisdom of serving the niche market first, as it protects start-ups from stiff competition and enables them to build a bridge for future growth. As this case illustrates, Metalysis began by focusing on the high-end segment of a large market such as titanium and added value to the existing players by reducing the costs for them.

[5] This case study is from Lubik and Garnsey (2016).

Ambos and Birkinshaw (2010) discussed the process of the evolution of new science-based ventures. The authors highlighted three distinct venture archetypes. The first is a capability-driven venture, in which the primary driver of action is the development of an internal technology or capability. The second is a market-driven venture, where the primary driver is the development of sales and the relationship with customers or alliance partners. The third archetype is the aspiration-driven venture, where the primary driver of action is the growth aspiration of the venture's leaders and legitimising the business among stakeholders. The study shows that often new science-based ventures start with one of these three types of focus and over time transition to another focus. For example, a venture could start with an aspiration-driven venture, with the founder wanting to build a company almost for its own sake. The aspiration-driven orientation shifts to capability orientation when the technology needs to be developed and then a market-driven orientation when the emphasis shifts to finding a customer for the proposition.

This idea draws upon the cognitive view of strategy that emphasises what preoccupies the senior management team the most, whereby strategy is defined as an "enabler of action," as the viewpoint about the future, which people cluster in order to mobilise a set of actions (Weick, 1987). In science-based ventures the focus often shifts between the three archetypes, which defines the focus of management or founders on one set of issues, while keeping the other two on the backburner. This is often a result of the highly constrained resources of science-based new ventures, unlike large firms, where there are often functional heads to manage different areas and priorities. Often, the emphasis shifts from one archetype to another because of the cognitive dissonance between management's understanding of one cognitive schema and another because of changes triggered by internal events, such as a change in personnel or new technological breakthroughs, or external events such as regulatory changes or customer needs. Such transitions could be either sustaining, building on existing capabilities, or disruptive, which requires dropping some capabilities and building new ones. Therefore, the chances of success are as much a function of decisive and committed action to pivot between the different archetypes as they are about identifying objective actions. Such intrinsic ambiguity means that the importance of ensuring the shared interpretive scheme can act as an enabler or an inhibitor of action, which could eventually determine the design of appropriate business models, contributing to success or failure, respectively (Leonard-Barton, 1992).

6.5 Business Model Design of Start-Up Ventures

One of the major challenges for start-up firms during the early stages of the venture is designing their business models. Various studies have proposed principles for founders and managers of start-up firms facing significant uncertainty in designing and evolving their business models. We review some of the principles in this section.

Amit and Zott (2015) highlighted the design thinking approach in crafting the business model architecture. They proposed goals, templates, stakeholder activities and environmental constraints as the antecedents for business model design. They highlighted how these antecedents affect business model design themes of novelty – the provision of new value propositions; lock-in – the ability to lock in customers and partners; complementarity – the bundling of activities to promote synergies; and efficiency – linking activities to reduce costs. The first antecedent is for the start-up to identify its goals to create and capture value in broad open-ended terms rather than being too specific. This approach allows the design of the business model to evolve and create value for various stakeholders. The objectives of the stakeholders will not all be aligned; hence, there is a need to balance managing the tension with the appropriate judgement that arises from conflicting objectives in creating and capturing value. Such a process creates and captures value for the new venture while enhancing the lock-in of the stakeholders. For example, in designing person-to-person (P2P) lending the objectives are defined as overcoming social injustice as a result of the lack of transparency in the existing lending model (Amit and Zott, 2015).

The second antecedent is the use of the template from other existing businesses in designing the business model of the new venture. Here, being mindful of the similarities and differences is important in terms of the ability to graft the relevant aspects to the new start-up firm. Mindless copying could result in a sub-optimally designed business model. For example, in the P2P lending market, one of the start-ups combined the template from the corporate bond market and the match-making model of eBay. The idea of the servicing-type match-making platform was built on the principles of people having the power and democracy to decide on borrowing and lending rather than institutionalised players dictating the terms.

The third antecedent is based on the design concept of collaboration among partners to bring complementary assets together, to create either novelty or efficiency of both, and hence create appropriate lock-ins. The idea of a highly reputable anchor partner is important in terms of enhancing the attractiveness of less committed stakeholders. Partners can help to increase revenue or reduce costs (Kesting and Gunzel-Jensen, 2015). An example of increasing revenue is Google in its early days adding Google AdWords, a pay-per-click advertising service; the founders of Google realised that appearing high on search results holds tremendous value for stakeholders with a willingness to pay for this service. An example of engaging with partners in reducing costs is TripAdvisor utilising social media to collect and display user evaluations.

The final antecedent is the environmental constraint, which can serve as a stimulus for the invention of new approaches to adopting practices from other domains. These constraints can be external or internal. External constraints are imposed on the business from the outside, such as regulation, culture or socio-politics, while internal constraints are due to limited resources and capabilities within the firm. Therefore, focusing on constraints can enable creativity and hence the design of novelty in the business model of the new firm. For example, in the case of the P2P business model design, one of the firms felt that, if they pooled risks, the regulators would consider them a collection investment scheme with a significant regulatory burden. Hence, the start-up firm decided to set up individual contracts directly between borrower and lender, which resulted in further novel business model designs.

Studies have also emphasised the need for start-up firms to adopt the principles of parallel play or simultaneous experiments to overcome business model development challenges due to uncertainty. McDonald and Eisenhardt (2020) borrowed from the child development literature, whereby pre-schoolers play near one another but not together, taking an interest in what their peers are doing and often mimicking them. They tend to build objects and might even pause and consider their progress before continuing. Parallel play refers to children playing in a space, borrowing from peers, testing assumptions and pausing before elaborating on the activity system. Such a process of parallel play among start-up firms might enable them to achieve "optimal distinctiveness," where there are similarities that enable them to conform to the established rules in the market but enough differences to highlight their differentiation (Zhao et al., 2017). The study observes that entrepreneurs often borrow from their peers. In addition, similar to pre-schoolers, these entrepreneurs tend to test major assumptions to reduce uncertainty about which template to choose. Finally, entrepreneurs who design effective business models tend to pause and reflect before completing their activity system.

Andries et al. (2013) highlight the need for start-up firms to conduct simultaneous experiments as a learning strategy. They contrast simultaneous experiments with focused commitments, which might be instrumental in acquiring dedicated resources but reduce the ability to conduct experiments to learn, and hence they might be detrimental to long-term survival. The authors borrow from the effectuation literature to make an analogy to causation and effectuation (Sarasvathy, 2001). Causation is where entrepreneurs choose specific means, such as technology and employee skills, to create a desired effect, such as a specific business model design. Effectuation implies that the venture draws upon its knowledge and networks and selects between possible effects that can be created with this set of means. Simultaneous experimentation is seen as representing effectual logic, as it takes a set of means as a given; for example, investment decisions involve a commitment limit in terms of affordable loss, in order to focus on selecting between possible effects that can be created from this set of means. The focused commitment follows causal logic, where the venture chooses a specific means to create a desired effect, such as an *ex ante* chosen business model.

Conclusion

SMEs are a significant part of most developed and developing economies in terms of their contribution to both output and employment; however, their productivity often lags behind larger incumbent firms. Therefore, SMEs are a major source of opportunities to increase jobs and stimulate economic growth. Nonetheless, they do face major hurdles in innovating their business models as the result of a combination of a lack of resources, knowledge and capabilities (Masood and Sonntag, 2020). Recent studies also show that, because of such constraints, SMEs might want to adopt a "shoestring" approach to off-the-shelf simple digital technology solutions rather than complex industrial solutions, which are often designed for larger firms (Hawkridge et al., 2021). Moreover, when SMEs are part of larger, more complex supply chains, they are often tied to the requirements of larger prime firms, which can result in a lack of incentives to invest in the intangible capital that is often required to innovate business models, especially when new technologies come on board (Made Smarter Review, 2017; Said et al., 2022).

The above issues are particularly challenging, as the evolution of digital technologies enables more distributed production architecture, which will call upon SMEs to be more involved in local production and distribution (Klockner et al., 2020). In addition, the emergence of platform architecture business models increasingly relies on generative principles to create new products and services, which might rely on a plethora of SMEs to develop such a proposition (De Marco et al., 2019). Moreover, it is possible that the emergence of radically new general-purpose technologies will rely on start-ups and SMEs to develop the new propositions, which might be less interesting to established firms that do not want to cannibalise the status quo.

Governments around the world have instituted various programmes to overcome some of these challenges. For example, in the United States the Manufacturing Extension Partnership (MEP) programme helps SMEs to improve their performance by providing a combination of advice and help on various aspects of business, including the adoption of digital technologies. In the United Kingdom the Sharing in Growth (SiG) programme is designed to help SME firms in the aerospace sector address the shortcoming of not being able to invest sufficiently in intangible capital, as this is the less measurable part of the business (Said et al., 2022). The immediate objective of the SIG programme is to help SMEs navigate the challenges posed by an increasingly competitive global aerospace supply chain. However, the resulting improved performance helps SME firms to innovate their business model as a result of the changing market and technological conditions in the aerospace sector. Moreover, there are also initiatives to help educate SMEs on the benefits of digital technologies by building demonstrators or model factories using the latest digital technologies, such as the ModelFactory@SIMTech in Singapore (Tay et al., 2021).

These initiatives help SME firms not only to learn about the benefits – and hence be able to de-risk investment in new technologies – but also to build capabilities to transform their business models through a sense and response manufacturing approach. Studies show that start-ups and SMEs need to play their part by being open to such learning, being able to partner with other firms to acquire skills and capabilities, and also keeping their business models agile in order to pivot to new opportunities as they arise.

There are a number of areas for further investigation of business model design among start-ups and SMEs. The first major area of research is to better understand how intangible capital plays a role in the digital transformation of SMEs. The resources, knowledge and capabilities constraints of SMEs might tilt them towards low-cost digital technology solutions to improve efficiency and productivity. More in-depth research is needed to better understand how to provide a systematic roadmap for SMEs to transition from low-cost digital solutions to the digital transformation of their business models as their industrial ecosystem transforms as a result of new digital technologies.

The second major area of research is to better understand how the dynamics of family businesses influence the decision-making and implementation of business model innovation. The complex interplay of family relations and senior management decision-making needs to be better understood to enable family businesses to transition from niche players to more major firms in the national and international landscape. Such growth and the ability to compete on a global scale require business model innovation. However, the right balance needs to be struck between family involvement and professional management, which requires further research and in-depth understanding.

The third key area concerns how new markets come about in science-based start-up propositions. An increasing amount of work has been done in understanding the emergence of new markets. However, more insights are needed to understand the links between technology transition (TT) literature that highlights the socio-technical changes and the incentives provided by business models. Studies in technological transitions have emphasised the importance of examining different levels, such as the multi-level perspective, which have argued that technological breakthrough and replacing an existing technological regime arise from dynamics across different levels; or they have emphasised how system builders are key to enabling alignment across technical and non-technical (such as laws and regulations) artefacts that create unity among the actors to enable technological transitions (Bolton and Hanan, 2016; Hughes, 1979). These approaches to TT highlight the socio-technical nature of change but de-emphasise the activity system inherent in the BM approach, which comprises transactions between firms. Hence, further work is needed to understand the role of the business model designs of start-ups in science-based ventures in order to enable major technological transitions.

This chapter has provided an overview of the opportunities and challenges of SMEs and start-up firms in transforming their business models; it has also proposed some outstanding research issues on this topic.

References

Ambos, T. C. and Birkinshaw, J. (2010). How Do New Ventures Evolve? An Inductive Study of Archetype Changes in Science-Based Ventures. *Organization Science* 21(6): 1125–1140.

Amit, R. and Zott, C. (2015). Crafting Business Architecture: The Antecedents of Business Model Design. *Strategic Entrepreneurship Journal* 9: 331–350.

Andries, P., Debackere, K., and Van Looy, B. (2013). Simultaneous Experimentation as a Learning Strategy: Business Model Development under Uncertainty. *Strategic Entrepreneurship Journal* 7: 288–310.

Bigdeli, A. Z., Li, F., and Shi, X. (2016). Sustainability and Scalability of University Spinouts: A Business Model Perspective. *R&D Management* 46(3): 504–518.

Bock, A. J., Opsahl, T., George, G., and Gann, D. M. (2012). The Effects of Culture and Structure on Strategic Flexibility during Business Model Innovation. *Journal of Management Studies* 49(2): 279–305.

Bogers, M., Boyd, B., and Hollensen, S. (2015). Managing Turbulence: Business Models Development in a Family-Owned Airline. *California Management Review* 58(1): 41–64.

Bolton, R. and Hannon, M. (2016). Governing Sustainability Transitions through Business Model Innovation: Towards a Systems Understanding. *Research Policy* 45(9): 1731–1742.

Bouwman, H., Nikou, S., and de Reuver, M. (2019). Digitalization, Business Models, and SMEs: How Do Business Model Innovation Practices Improve Performance of Digitizing SMEs? *Telecommunication Policy* 43: 1–18.

Calia, R. C., Guerrini, F. M., and Moura, G. L. (2007). Innovation Networks: From Technological Development to Business Model Reconfiguration. *Technovation* 27: 426–432.

Casillas, J. C., Moreno, A. M., and Acedo, F. J. (2010). Internationalization of Family Businesses: A Theoretical Model Based on International Entrepreneurship Perspective. *Global Management Journal* 2(2):16–33.

Chirico, F., Sirmon, D. G., Sciascia, S., and Mazzola, P. (2011). Resource Orchestration in Family Firms: Investigating How Entrepreneurial Orientation, Generational Involvement, and Participative Strategy Affect Performance. *Strategic Entrepreneurship Journal* 5: 307–326.

Coombes, P. H. and Nicholson, J. D. (2013). Business Models and Their Relationship with Marketing: A Systematic Literature Review. *Industrial Marketing Management* 42: 656–664.

Cosenz, F. and Bivona, E. (2021). Fostering Growth Patterns of SMEs Through Business Model Innovation. A Tailored Dynamic Business Modelling Approach. *Journal of Business Research* 130: 658–669.

Del Giudice, M., Scuotto, V., Papa, A., Tarba, S. Y., Bresciani, S., and Warkentin, M. (2021). A Self-Tuning Model for Smart Manufacturing SMEs: Effects on Digital Innovation. *Journal of Product Innovation Management* 38(1): 68–89.

De Marco, C. E., Di Minin, A. D., Marullo, C., and Nepelski, D. (2019). *Digital Platform Innovation in European SMEs. An Analysis of SME Instrument Business Proposals and Case Studies*. Luxembourg: Publications Office of the European Union, pp. 1–71.

Ehret, M. and Wirtz, J. (2017). Unlocking Value from Machines: Business Models and the Industrial Internet of Things. *Journal of Marketing Management* 33(1–2): 111–130.

George, G. and Bock, A. J. (2011). The Business Model in Practice and Its Implications for Entrepreneurship Research. *Entrepreneurship Theory and Practice* 35(1): 83–111.

Girotra, K. and Netessine, S. (2011). How to build risk into your business model. *Harvard Business Review* 89(5): 100–105.

Godsell, J., Birtwistle, A., and van Hoek, R. (2010). Building the Supply Chain to Enable Business Alignment: Lessons from British American Tobacco (BAT). *Supply Chain Management: An International Journal* 15(1): 10–15.

Goldfarb, B. (2005). Diffusion of General-Purpose Technologies: Understanding Patterns in the Electrification of US Manufacturing 1880–1930. *Industrial and Corporate Change* 14(5): 745–773.

Greenwood, R. and Hinings, C. R. (1993). Understanding Strategic Change: The Contribution of Archetypes. *The Academy of Management Journal* 36(5): 1052–1081.

Gruber, H. (2018). Proposals for a Digital Industrial Policy for Europe. *Telecommunications Policy* 43(2): 116–127.

Gumusay, A. A. and Bohne, T. M. (2018). Individual and Organizational Inhibitors to the Development of Entrepreneurial Competencies in Universities. *Research Policy* 47: 363–378.

Gunasekaran, A. and Ngai, E. W. T. (2005). Build-to-Order Supply Chain Management: A Literature Review and Framework for Development. *Journal of Operations Management* 23: 423–451.

Hawkridge, G., Mukherjee, A., McFarlane, D., Tlegenov, Y., Parlikad, A. K., Reyner, N. J., and Thorne, A. (2021). Monitoring on a Shoestring: Low-Cost Solutions for Digital Manufacturing. *Annual Reviews in Control* 51: 374–391.

Hobday, M. (1998). Product Complexity, Innovation and Industrial Organisation. *Research Policy* 26: 689–710.

Hobday, M., Davies, A., and Prencipe, A. (2005). Systems Integration: A Core Capability of the Modern Corporation. *Industrial and Corporate Change* 14(6): 1109–1143.

Holweg, M. and Pil, F. K. (2001). Successful Build-to-Order Strategies Start with the Customer. *MIT Sloan Management Review* 43(1): 73–83.

Hughes, T. P. (1979). The Electrification of America: The System Builders. *Technology and Culture* 20(1): 124–161.

Jacobides, M. G. and Tae, C. J. (2015). Kingpins, Bottlenecks, and Value Dynamics along a Sector. *Organization Science* 26(3): 889–907.

Jacobides, M. G., MacDuffie, J. P., and Tae, C. J. (2016). Agency, Structure and the Dominance of OEMS: Change and Stability in the Automotive Sector. *Strategic Management Journal* 37: 1942–1967.

Jones, O. and Giordano, B. (2021). Family Entrepreneurial Teams: The Role of Learning in Business Model Evolution. *Management Learning* 52(3): 267–293.

Kesting, P. and Gunzel-Jensen, F. (2015). SMEs and New Ventures Need Business Model Sophistication. *Business Horizons* 58: 285–293.

Klöckner, M., Kurpjuweit, S., Velu, C., and Wagner., S (2020). Does Blockchain for 3D Printing Offer Opportunities for Business Model Innovation. *Research Technology Management* 2020 (July–August): 18–27.

Lee, J., Krishnan, V., and Shin, H. (2020). Business Models for Technology-Intensive Supply Chains. *Management Science* 66(5): 2120–2139.

Leonard-Barton, D. (1992). Core Capabilities and Core Rigidities: A Paradox in Managing New Product Development. *Strategic Management Journal* 13: 111–125.

Li, L., Su, F., Zhang, W., and Mao, J. Y. (2018). Digital Transformation by SME Entrepreneurs: A Capability Perspective. *Information Systems Journal* 28(6): 1129–1157.

Llinas, D. and Abad, J. (2019). The Role of High-Performance People Management Practices in Industry 4.0: The Case of Medium-Sized Spanish Firms. *Intangible Capital* 15(3): 190–207.

Lubik, S. and Garnsey, E. (2016). Early Business Model Evolution in Science-Based Ventures: The Case of Advanced Materials. *Long Range Planning* 49: 393–408.

Made Smarter Review. (2017). www.madesmarter.uk

Made Smarter. (2019). *Made Smarter Technology Adoption Pilot Report 2019*. www.madesmarter.uk

Maine, E. and Garnsey, E. (2006). Commercializing Generic Technology: The Case of Advanced Materials Ventures. *Research Policy* 35: 375–393.

Mason, K., Friesl, M. and Ford, C. J. (2019). Markets under the Microscope: Making Scientific Discoveries Valuable through Choreographed Contestations. *Journal of Management Studies*, 56(5), 966–99

Martinez, S., Errasti, A., and Rudberg, M. (2015). Adapting Zara's "Pronto Moda" to a Value Brand Retailer. *Production Planning & Control* 26(9): 723–737.

Masood, T. and Sonntag, P. (2020). Industry 4.0: Adoption Challenges and Benefits for SMEs. *Computers in Industry* 121: 1–12.

Matzler, K., Veider, V., Hautz, J., and Stadler C. (2014). The Impact of Family Ownership, Management, and Governance on Innovation. *Journal of Product Innovation Management* 32(3): 319–333.

McDonald, R. M. and Eisenhardt, K. M. (2020). Parallel Play: Startups, Nascent Markets, and Effective Business-Model Design. *Administrative Science Quarterly* 65(2): 483–523.

Miller, D. and Friesen, P. H. (1980). Momentum and Revolution in Organizational Adaptation. *The Academy of Management Journal* 23(4): 591–614.

Miller, K., McAdam, M., Spieth, P., and Brady, M. (2021). Business Models Big and Small: Review of Conceptualisations and Constructs and Future Directions for SME Business Model Research. *Journal of Business Research* 131: 619–626.

Molner, S., Prabhu, J. C., and Yadav, M. S. (2019). Lost in a Universe of Markets: Toward a Theory of Market Scoping for Early-Stage Technologies. *Journal of Marketing* 83(2): 37–61.

OECD. (2017a). *Enhancing the Contributions of SMEs in a Global and Digitalised Economy*. Paris: OECD Publishing.

OECD. (2017b). *Small, Medium, Strong. Trends in SME Performance and Business Conditions*. Paris: OECD Publishing.

OECD. (2021). *The Digital Transformation of SMEs, OECD Studies on SMEs and Entrepreneurship*. Paris: OECD Publishing.

Olhager, J. and Ostlund, B. (1990). An Integrated Push-Pull Manufacturing Strategy. *European Journal of Operational Research* 45: 135–142.

Patzelt, H., Zu Knyphausen-Aufseb, D., and Nikol, P. (2008). Top Management Teams, Business Models, and Performance of Biotechnology Ventures: An Upper Echelon Perspective. *British Journal of Management* 19: 205–221.

Pisano, G. P. (2006). *Science Business: The Promise, the Reality, and the Future of Biotech*. Boston, MA: Harvard Business School Press.

Pisano, G. P. (2010). The Evolution of Science-Based Business: Innovating How We Innovate. *Industrial and Corporate Change* 19(2): 465–482.

Rissanen, T., Ermolaeva, L., Torkkeli, L., Ahi, A., and Saarenketo, S. (2020). The Role of Home Market Context in Business Model Change in Internationalizing SMEs. *European Business Review* 32(2): 257–275.

Rosenberg, N. and Trajtenberg, M. (2004). A General-Purpose Technology at Work: The Corliss Steam Engine in the Late-Nineteenth-Century United States. *The Journal of Economic History* 64(1): 61–99.

Said, F., Page, A., Salter, L., and Velu, C. (2022). Intangible Capital and Reorientation of Manufacturing during a Pandemic. In: E. Gallitto, M. Massi, and P. Harrison. (eds), *Consumption, Production, and Entrepreneurship in the Time of Coronavirus*. Cham: Palgrave Macmillan.

Sarasvathy, S. D. (2001). Causation and Effectuation: Toward a Theoretical Shift from Economic Inevitability to Entrepreneurial Contingency. *Academy of Management Review* 26(2): 243–263.

Shane, S. (2004). *Academic Entrepreneurship: University Spinoffs and Wealth Creation*. Cheltenham, UK: Edward Elgar.

Shapira, P., Youtie, J., and Kay, L. (2011). National Innovation Systems and the Globalization of Nanotechnology Innovation. *The Journal of Technology Transfer* 36(6): 587–604.

Smith, D. J. and Tranfield, D. (2005). Talented Suppliers? Strategic Change and Innovation in the UK Aerospace Industry. *R&D Management* 35(1): 37–49.

Soluk, J., Miroshnychenko, I., Kammerlander, N., and De Massis, A. (2021). Family Influence and Digital Business Model Innovation: The Enabling Role of Dynamic Capabilities. *Entrepreneurship Theory and Practice* 45(4): 867–905.

Stentoft, J., Wickstrom, K. A., Philpsen, K., and Haug, A. (2021). Drivers and Barriers for Industry 4.0 Readiness and Practice: Empirical Evidence from Small and Medium-Sized Manufacturers. *Production Planning and Control* 32(10): 811–828.

Suppatvech, C., Godsell, J., and Day, S. (2019). The Roles of Internet of Things Technology in Enabling Servitized Business Models: A Systematic Literature Review. *Industrial Marketing Management* 82: 70–86.

Tay, J. W. E., Ng, H. Y., and Tan, P. S. (2021). Model Factory@SIMTech – Sense and Response Manufacturing for Industry 4.0. In: C. Toro, W. Wang, and H. Akhtar (eds), *Implementing Industry 4.0*. Intelligent Systems Reference Library, vol. 202. Cham: Springer.

Velu, C. (2015). Business Model Innovation and Third-party Alliance on the Survival of New Firms. *Tecnhnovation* 35: 1–11.

Voytek, K. P., Lellock, K. L., and Schmit, M. A. (2004). Developing Performance Metrics for Science and Technology Programs: The Case of the

Manufacturing Extension Partnership Program. *Economic Development Quarterly* 18(2): 174–185.

Weick, K. E. (1987). Substitute for Strategy. In: D. E. Teece (ed), *The Competitive Challenge*. Cambridge, MA: Ballinger.

Zhao, E. Y., Fisher, G., Lounsbury, M., and Miller, D. (2017). Optimal Distinctiveness: Broadening the Interface between Institutional Theory and Strategic Management. *Strategic Management Journal* 38: 93–113.

7 | *Sustainability and Business Models*

Earth provides enough to satisfy every man's needs but not every man's greed.

Mahatma Gandhi

Introduction

Business as usual is not an option for a sustainable future because of the rising global population, accelerating global development and increasing resource use and environmental impact (Bocken et al., 2014; Crowley et al., 2017). The world is using the equivalent of 1.5 planets to support human activities (WWF, 2012). In other words, the world will take 1.5 years to regenerate the renewable resources consumed in one year, which is an unsustainable rate of consumption. Firms have a role to play in achieving sustainability by designing sustainable business models. Sustainable business models need to value natural assets that are often "free," internalise externalities and encompass the triple bottom line of economic, social and environmental goals (Bocken et al., 2014). Scholars have called for a more critical assessment of the purpose of the organisation beyond merely profit maximisation, which requires a radical rethink of innovation and industrial systems to address the sustainability challenges facing our world today (Ciulli and Kolk, 2019; Henderson, 2021; Lehoux et al., 2021; Markard et al., 2012).

The need for a sustainable world is not new but has built momentum as a result of its urgency in recent years (Rendtorff, 2019). The Brutland Commission report in 1987 was the original report on sustainability, which was then extended by the Sustainable Development Goals (SDGs) of the United Nations (United Nations, 2020). The SDGs aim to combine economic development, environmental development and social inclusion (Sachs, 2012, 2015). They were meant to be a follow-up from the Millennium Development Goals (MDGs), which focused primarily on poverty, hunger, disease, unmet schooling, gender inequality and environmental degradation. The MDGs, which ran for 15 years, from 2000 to 2015, were seen to be achieved by some countries and not others (Sachs, 2012). Hence, policy-makers and civil society felt the need to continue the poverty reduction goals of the MDGs and enhance them with challenges around climate change and other environmental ills (Sachs, 2012). There was a recognition that human activity might push the global ecosystem past a threshold, which might have devasting and non-linear outcomes for human well-being. Hence, under the leadership of the UN Secretary-General, in June 2012, a high-level global sustainability panel issued a report recommending the adoption of SDGs following the MDGs. The MDG targets were mainly for poor countries, with rich countries helping to provide finance and technology. However, the SDGs pose challenges for all countries, rich and poor; moreover, they embrace a wider set of goals for sustainability by adding prosperity, peace and partnership to people, the planet and profit (Rendtorff, 2019).

Achieving the SDGs would require good governance at all levels within the public and private sectors. These include appropriate economic institutions and firms acting responsibly to a wide range of stakeholders. Private-sector firms are often the main driver of the productive sector of the economy and own many of the advanced technologies and management systems (Sachs, 2012). Therefore, firms in the private sector need to embrace new business models by adopting new technologies and enabling new ways of organising human activities in order to contribute to achieving the SDGs.

There are continued pressures from human activity on different crucial earth systems, including carbon, nitrogen and water cycles (Sachs, 2012), and there are anthropogenic challenges due to climate change and biodiversity.[1] The challenges to climate change are a result of human-created emissions of greenhouse gases, such as carbon dioxide and methane; and increased acidification of the oceans, caused by a greater concentration of atmospheric carbon dioxide. Moreover, there is a growing loss of biodiversity from unsustainable demands on forests and significant environmental pollution from run-off of nitrogen and phosphorus-based fertilisers, among others.

[1] Anthropogenic is used to refer to environmental changes that are caused or influenced, either directly or indirectly, by humans (Chakrabarty, 2020).

Governments agreed to develop voluntary action plans to cut greenhouse-gas emissions under the terms of the Paris Agreement, or COP21 summit, which was signed by 197 countries in 2015 (IPCC, 2018).[2] The objective of the voluntary cutting of greenhouse-gas emissions was to keep the world's average temperature well below rising to 2 °C above what it was before the Industrial Revolution – and preferably keeping it below 1.5 °C (IPCC, 2018). Moreover, during the COP26 summit in Glasgow, in 2021, some countries made collective commitments to curb methane emissions, to halt and reverse forest loss and to encourage the finance sector with a net-zero target by 2050, including the end of international financing of fossil fuels and accelerating the phasing out of coal (*The Economist*, 2021c). Addressing these targets and challenges calls for innovative solutions such as a circular economy to create a closed-loop system that minimises the use of resource input and the creation of waste and pollution. Such a closed-loop system calls for the design of new business models – the focus of this chapter – which provides an overview of the opportunities and challenges associated with addressing one of society's greatest challenges – sustainability issues related to climate change – as well as biodiversity, through business model innovation.

7.1 Sustainable Business Models for a Circular Economy

Sustainability based on a circular economy would be built on some core principles (Bocken et al., 2019). First, it would include a system that encourages the minimisation of consumption or which imposes personal and institutional caps or quotas on energy, goods, water, and so on. Second, the system would be designed to maximise societal and environmental benefit, rather than prioritising economic growth. Third, it would be a closed-loop system where nothing is allowed to be wasted or discarded into the environment, which reuses, repairs and remakes in preference to recycling. Fourth, the system would emphasise the delivery of functionality rather than product ownership; and,

---

[2] The UNFCCC is the United Nations Framework Convention on Climate Change. In the 1990s, the UNFCCC was agreed upon by virtually every nation in the world in order to stabilise greenhouse-gas concentrations that would prevent dangerous human-induced causes of change to the climate system. COP21 means the Conference of the Parties that were signatories to the UNFCCC meeting for the 21st time.

fifth, it would provide fulfilling, rewarding work experiences for all that enhances human creativity/skills. Finally, it would be a system built on collaboration and sharing rather than aggressive competition.[3]

The types of business model design for sustainability could be classified using three broad groupings, namely, technological, social and organisational (Bocken et al., 2014). First, the technological grouping could be due to technical innovations such as manufacturing processes or new materials. Technological-grouping-based business model innovation includes maximising material and energy efficiency, creating value from waste and substituting with renewables and natural processes. Maximising material and energy efficiency involves deploying products or services that deliver similar levels of functionality but use fewer resources and generate less waste and emissions, such as dematerialisation, low-carbon solutions and lean manufacturing processes. Creating value from waste involves thinking creatively about transforming existing waste products into valuable input for other processes.

For example, the British Sugar factory in Norfolk, in the United Kingdom, is one of the major producers of tomatoes in the UK because much of the carbon dioxide produced as part of its beet-based sugar production is recycled for growing its tomatoes in controlled greenhouses (Short et al., 2014). Another example of a holistic waste management system is the Kalundborg Industrial Symbiosis System (KISS) in Denmark, which is the world's first working industrial symbiosis ecosystem. The KISS production firms are located close to one another so as to be able to transfer by-products between parties via a network of pipes and by road to make them useful. The results are impressive, with yearly carbon dioxide (CO_2) emissions reduced by 240,000 tonnes, 3 million m^3 of water saved through recycling and reuse, 30,000 tonnes of straw converted to 5.4 million litres of ethanol, 150,000 tons of yeast replacing 70 per cent of soy protein in traditional feed mix for more than 800,000 pigs and recycling of 150,000 tonnes of gypsum from the desulphurisation of flue gas, which replaces the importation of natural gypsum ($CaSO_4$) (Chopra and Khanna, 2014; Team Gemini, 2015). Substituting with renewable energy solutions and natural processes, such as hydrogen and wind energy, involves reducing the environmental impact associated with non-renewable resources.

---

[3] Although these principles seem reasonable, as we will see later there are conditions whereby some of them could create adverse incentives.

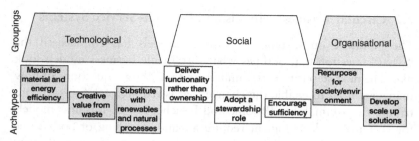

Figure 7.1 Sustainable business model archetypes
Source: Adapted from Bocken et al. (2014)

Second, the social grouping is due to changes driven predominantly by social innovation, such as changes in consumer behaviour. Social-grouping-based business model innovation includes delivering functionality rather than ownership, adopting a stewardship role and encouraging sufficiency. Delivering functionality rather than ownership involves providing services to customers such as pay-per-use-based product–service systems, without customers necessarily owning the product, which might reduce the number of products that need to be manufactured. Adopting a stewardship role involves stewarding assets in such a way as to engage with stakeholders to ensure that their long-term well-being and productive assets are protected, such as ethical fair-trade initiatives. Encouraging sufficiency involves changing demand patterns by, say, educating customers to reduce consumption. This could be achieved, for example, by energy companies providing transparent and clear data on usage patterns in order to encourage savings by reducing consumption.

Third, the organisational grouping is driven primarily by an organisational design change component, such as changing the fiduciary responsibility of the firm. Organisational-grouping-based business model innovation includes repurposing for society and the environment and also developing scale-up solutions. Repurposing for society includes reorganising businesses in such a way as to prioritise the delivery of social and environmental benefits rather than being purely profit-driven. Developing scale-up solutions involves scaling sustainability initiatives to benefit society, which can take a myriad of forms, such as standardising processes and other business practices, including licensing, franchising and openly sharing appropriate knowledge and business processes (Bigdeli et al., 2015). A summary of the grouping of the different business model archetypes is listed in Figure 7.1.

7.2 Circular Business Models and Product–Service Systems

The literature on sustainable business models has emphasised the "what" question that outlines what sustainable business models look like. The next step is to better understand the "how" questions of how managers need to enable the change that is required for firms to contribute to sustainability (Roome and Louche, 2016). Business models for sustainable development require an understanding of both value creation and value destruction across the ecosystem of actors (Batista et al., 2018; Hawken et al., 1999; Parry et al., 2016). Hence, the design and implementation of sustainable business models call for both a system- and firm-level perspective on value creation and an avoidance of value destruction. Research has shown that the process model of change might consist of four phases: identifying the need for change; translating, which involves how the firm adapts new concepts to the organisation; embedding, which focuses on the way the firm adopts new concepts and develops internal routines; and, finally, sharing, which outlines the learning process that goes beyond the boundary of the firm to the ecosystem of partners. We examine some of the enablers and barriers of the process model of change in firms adopting circular business models and product–service systems (PSS).

The aim of sustainability is to benefit the environment, the economy and society at large (Elkington, 1997). More recently, scholars have emphasised the concept of the circular economy, the aim of which is a closed-loop system of eliminating resource input, waste and emissions. This was influenced by Boulding (1966), who described the earth as a closed and circular system with limited assimilative capacity – hence, the need for the economy and the environment to co-exist. A circular economy can be seen as one means of achieving sustainability by emphasising how resources can be better used and waste emissions reduced with a circular, rather than linear, make–use–dispose system[4] (Bounding 1945, 1949; Geissdoefer et al., 2017). An industrial system that is restorative and regenerative by intention and design is called

---

[4] Germany was a pioneer in introducing the concept of the circular economy into national law in 1996 with the "Closed substance cycle and waste management act," which was followed by other countries, for example, Japan's 2002 "Basic Law of Establishing a Recycling-Based Society," China's 2009 "Circular Economy Promotion Law of the People's Republic of China" and the EU's 2015 "Circular Economy Strategy" (Geissdoefer et al., 2017).

a circular economy (Ellen MacArthur Foundation, 2013, 2015). The Ellen MacArthur Foundation circularity analysis focuses on five key areas of economic and environmental impact: material input, labour input, energy input, carbon emissions and balance of trade (Ellen MacArthur Foundation, 2013). The traditional economy is based on the "take, make and dispose" industrial model, which increases the demand for raw materials. For example, the prices of raw materials increased from the turn of the century and there has been an increase in price volatility in recent decades (Ellen Macarthur Foundation, 2013). Hence, firms face higher supply disruptions and higher prices, prompting them to look at circular-economy-based industrial systems with sustainable business models.

The circular economy works on three principles (Ellen MacArthur Foundation, 2013). The first principle needs to design out waste in the system, while the second is to manage the distinction between consumables and durables. Consumables are largely made up of biological nutrients and are non-toxic: the biological nutrients cycle is designed to re-enter the biosphere safely. Durables are made up of technical nutrients and are unsuitable for the biosphere: the technical cycle is designed to circulate without entering the biosphere through end-of-life. Third, the energy required to fuel the cycle needs to be renewable by nature. These principles drive the value-creation opportunities of material through the following: the power of the inner circle – minimising material use; the power of circling longer – maximising the number of consecutive cycles; the power of cascade use – diversifying reuse along the value chain for different purposes as the material changes properties; and the power of pure circles – the use of uncontaminated materials to increase the efficiency of material productivity. A summary of the four sources of value creation for circularity is shown in Figure 7.2.

An example of a change in business model from such circular principles was evident in the case of Rohner, a successful manufacturer of high-end upholstery fabrics based in Switzerland (Roome and Louche, 2016). Between 1981 and 2004, Rohner transformed itself from selling textile products that resulted in a high risk of pollution and generated waste to adopting a closed-loop production–consumption-based circular economy for textiles (Roome and Louche, 2016). Rohner's senior management first identified the need to change when they faced intense competition from non-European textile manufacturers,

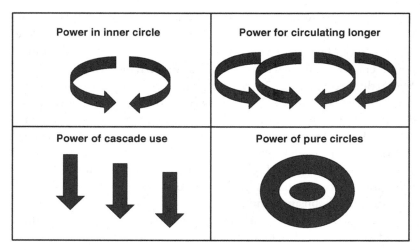

Figure 7.2 Four sources of value creation for circularity
Source: Adapted from Ellen McArthur Foundation (2013)

combined with increased regulation of environmental issues. The regulatory issue was particularly compelling, as Rohner was located near the source of the Rhine River and Lake Constance, where pollution was a major issue.

Hence, the CEO and the management team decided to develop a vision for Rohner for high-quality, well-designed products and manufacturing processes encompassing the highest standards of environmental and social responsibility. The company decided to work closely with Michael Braungart, the founder of the German Greenpeace Chemical Division, and the American architect William McDonough, who were known for the cradle-to-cradle concept, which challenged the way things were made in order to be sustainable (McDonough and Braungart, 2002). This required the firm to work with its employees and suppliers of, for example, dyestuffs to develop and test ideas related to sustainable production. The first period was a process redesign in the textile mill, followed by product innovation and then a product–process redesign. The next stage involved embedding the new concepts within the firm by building appropriate management information systems and tools to support employees by providing information and performance guidelines to reinforce the new products and processes.

Next, they worked with external partners and regulators to transfer knowledge to the agricultural sector, which, for example, provided the wool used in the textiles. Rohner had to radically change its products and production processes, and hence its business model, which resulted in a significant change in the way the firm was governed, organised and managed. In fact, Rohner first developed a vision to contribute to its economic success, while also contributing to sustainable development by reducing the damage to resources from its activities. This vision preceded the development of the new business model; therefore, the revised business model was the outcome of the process. Such a transformation required a move away from a focus on products to a higher level of the system to better understand the sources of value creation and destruction. This required both a problematic and an aspirational search (Cyert and March, 1963).[5]

The closed-loop value chain comprises the production stage, the consumption stage and the subsequent circulation stage (Kortmann and Piller, 2016). The production stage can be conceptualised as what is produced by the firm or its ecosystem. The consumption stage is in the domain of the consumer in terms of how the product is used. Finally, the circulation stage involves the product's end-of-life stage. There are two major forces that focus firms' attention on the circular economy. First, there is an increased cost of product returns such as electronic goods. Second, stakeholders are increasingly willing to participate in firm activities with regards to the circular economy, especially when enabled by emerging information and communications technologies (Kortmann and Piller, 2016). These two developments fundamentally redefine the relationship between the firm and the customer, and hence the business models, by changing the traditionally separated tasks into new forms of horizontal collaboration. Firms are increasingly opening their business models to enable third-party organisations to participate in the end-to-end life cycle of the product. For example, Dell is increasingly cooperating with asset resale and recycling partners to develop products with the end in mind (Kortmann and Piller, 2006). This involves emphasising the use of recyclable and renewable materials, standardising components, replacing glues with adhesives and

---

[5] Firms are likely to search for solutions and change when they are either facing problems or have an excess of resources, which could result in a problematic search or an aspirational search (Cyert and March, 1963)

snapfits, as well as new types of paint and coating. These initiatives require more open business models through alliances or engagement with firms with platform-based business models that enable multi-parties to transact efficiently to achieve closed-loop objectives.

Ricoh, a provider of production, printing and office solutions, developed "GreenLine" as part of its Green Office Solutions Programme. Copiers and printers returning from its leasing programme were refurbished and updated with new software and rented to the market under a similar warranty scheme to its new products (Ellen MacArthur Foundation, 2013). Ricoh was able to launch the GreenLine label because of its adoption of the "Comet Circle" programme, whereby the firm builds its products on the basis that all product parts should be recycled or reused. Moreover, the transition to a circular economy shows that adopting a circular economy business model requires not only manufacturing and operations but also marketing to do its share in changing the culture of consumers and business users (Hopkinson et al., 2018).

The closed-loop principle requires firms to extend their value-added services to not only the consultation stage but also developing propositions around product returns. The consumer becomes more engaged in the activities traditionally associated with the firm. Moreover, external stakeholders increase their participation in the creation and capture of value. Because of the possibility of returning products and exchanging them for state-of-the-art devices, consumers may become less prone to product ownership and more willing to lease or rent, which might include complementary services (Kortmann and Piller, 2006). Hence, there could be increased use of product–service system (PSS) business models. For example, Moovel, a subsidiary of Daimler Benz, is a platform app that fully integrates various service providers, such as car2go and MyTaxi, railway firms, public transport authorities, as well as bike rental firms, to enable customers to find – and then book – the best way to get from one place to another. In launching the Moovel platform, Daimler has essentially created a mobility service by working closely with an alliance of partners within an ecosystem in order to jointly create and capture value by providing a service based on systems of products (Kortmann and Piller, 2006).

PSS could be product-oriented, where the product is still owned by the customer; use-oriented, where the product is owned by a third party and the customer pays for specific use; and outcome-oriented, where the customer pays for a particular outcome[6] (Pardo et al., 2012; Yang and Evans, 2019). PSS could combine different elements of product, use and outcome-oriented mechanisms to create the customer offering. Pay-per-use business models could contribute to sustainable consumption; for example, in the case of washing-machine implementation, when customers started paying after a period of free consumption, the total number of washes and the washing temperatures reduced significantly (Bocken et al., 2018). Recent studies have shown that, although PSS that provide a service from a set of product offerings could contribute to sustainable initiatives, they are not inherently sustainable (Amasawa et al., 2020; Yang and Evans, 2019). For example, the ownership balance might influence the degree to which the customer uses the product with care. Customers might use products less carefully when they do not own them, and hence they could contribute to a decrease in product life (Yang and Evans, 2019). In addition, there are transportation costs in moving the product to where the customer is in the case of peer-to-peer sharing of products such as books, bicycles and automobiles, among others, which might contribute to greenhouse-gas emissions (Amasawa et al., 2020).

Moreover, there are barriers to adopting a PSS business model because of conflicts between sales and service, for example, in terms of compensation systems, pricing of services and balancing performance with social/ecological issues (Pacheo et al., 2013). For example, research shows that, with PSS, business models tend to focus primarily on value that brings economic benefits in terms of profits and financial returns (Yang and Evans, 2019). The environmental or social value might be created only because it was combined with economic value. For example, in the case of a firm selling gas-generation services, energy consumption was the main cost for air-separation units in the generation of gases. Hence, the firm was incentivised to reduce energy consumption in order to reduce costs, but this also reduced

---

[6] Cusumano et al. (2015) classified product-related services into three types, namely, smoothing, adapting and substituting services. Smoothing relates to services that do not change the product's functionality, such as maintenance and financing. Adapting relates to changing the functionality of the product, such as making it more customised. Substituting services relates to services that replace the purchases of the product, such as leasing or renting. One can posit that adapting and smoothing are related to product-oriented PSS, and substituting relates to use-oriented and result-oriented services (Yang et al., 2018).

carbon emissions. This need to balance economic with environmental and social issues makes it challenging for firms, especially SMEs, to transition to sustainable business models. Moreover, ownership of the underlying equipment could influence the type of source of value creation for sustainability (Yang et al., 2018).

Yang et al. (2018) studied the case of power generation of a firm across three business model archetypes – product, use and results, or outcome-oriented business models – in order to better understand the emphasis of different sources of value. In the case of use and outcome-oriented business models, the firm owns the product and might therefore be incentivised to adopt the inner circle by minimising material use and circling longer by maximising the number of consecutive cycles more than the product-oriented business model. This is because the firm owns the product in the case of use and outcome-oriented business models, which incentivises the firm to create value from the whole product life cycle. The firm has the economic incentive to reduce the environmental impact of products that are in use. In the product-oriented business model the customer owns the product and the firm might have less detailed information about use patterns. Moreover, in the case of the outcome-oriented business model, the firm might also be more incentivised to adopt the power of cascades through the use of co-products and by-products in other value chains – for example, the application of co-produced gases for new applications. In addition, outcome-oriented business models might also be more prone to using the power of pure circles by, for example, the use of uncontaminated materials to increase the efficiency of material productivity.

7.3 Net Zero and Energy Transition

The energy sector accounted for approximately three-quarters of greenhouse-gas emissions in 2021, which means it is important in terms of helping to avoid the negative consequences of climate change[7]

---

[7] Moreover, there are health benefits from reducing greenhouse gases, as they contribute to energy-related emissions of major air pollutants such as sulphur dioxide, nitrogen dioxides and fine particulate matter (IEA, 2021). More than 90 per cent of people around the world are exposed to air pollution, which led to around 5.4 million premature deaths in 2020, mostly in developing countries, which undermines productivity and puts an enormous burden on the healthcare system.

(IEA, 2021). Efforts to limit the long-term increase in average global temperatures to 1.5 °C are consistent with the initiative to reduce carbon-dioxide emissions to net zero[8] by 2050 (IPCC, 2018).[9] This will require a significant transformation of how energy is produced, transported and consumed, which will have major implications for the design of new business models. Such a transformation will require the use of different energy sources and carbon capture, as well as behavioural changes. The estimated global emission of CO_2 was around 33 billion tonnes in 2021. The International Energy Agency (IEA, 2021) believes that most of the reduction of CO_2 emissions through to 2030 could be achieved by technologies that are ready – or almost ready – today, but in 2050, almost half of the reductions will need to come from technologies that are in the demonstration phase or yet to be discovered. Some of the most promising technologies include advanced batteries, hydrogen electrolysers and direct air capture and storage. For example, low-carbon hydrogen could be produced via electrolysis using surplus renewable energy, sometimes termed "green hydrogen"; alternatively, it could be obtained from natural gas, with the carbon emissions reduced via the use of carbon capture utilisation and storage (CCUS) facilities, termed "blue hydrogen"[10] (Nuttall and Bakenne, 2019). Such CCUS facilities demand new business model solutions based on the degree of vertical integration with the generation facilities and the type of services being delivered.

---

[8] Net zero implies that the fossil-fuel usage that will remain in 2050 will be in products where the carbon is embodied in the product, such as plastics, which does not imply emissions; where the fuel is not combusted, such as lubricants; or in sectors where low-emission technologies are limited, such as aviation.

[9] Some countries have made meeting their net-zero target a legal obligation, while others have made pledges in official documents (Branca et al., 2021). For example, the European Green Deal is a combination of policy initiatives and laws to make the economy and the EU climate-neutral by 2050. Moreover, a net-zero pledge could be achieved in the energy sector, where energy-related emissions could be offset by the absorption of emissions from forestry or negative emissions from bioenergy or the direct capture of CO_2.

[10] Carbon capture, utilisation and storage (CCUS) includes methods and technologies to remove CO_2 from fossil fuels and the atmosphere, followed by recycling the CO_2 for possible utilisation in other valuable substances or products and determining safe and permanent storage options. Demand for CCUS facilities could increase, which requires major shared investments by industry in pipeline and shipping infrastructure to link the facilities where CO_2 is captured and the storage sites (IEA, 2021).

Moreover, one of the major challenges is being able to design business models to overcome the cost gap between the deployment of low-carbon hydrogen supply and higher-carbon fuels. This involves addressing the market price – the price for hydrogen is lower than the cost of production and volume risk – with the risk that sales fall below the economically viable level for producers to recover their production costs (BEIS, 2021). Some countries, such as the UK, are considering policy interventions to provide price and volume support mechanisms to enable the transition to a hydrogen-based economy (BEIS, 2021). Moreover, a range of policy interventions might be needed across the hydrogen value chain to help overcome other related barriers such as the high capital costs of investments, a lack of distribution and storage facilities, demand uncertainty, and policy and regulatory uncertainties around standards for low-carbon hydrogen (BEIS, 2021).

The energy sector consists of a large number of long-lived and capital-intensive assets such as pipelines, refineries and coal-powered power plants with lifespans of over fifty years.[11] The key principles for decarbonisation of the global energy system are energy efficiency, behavioural changes, electrification,[12] renewables, hydrogen-based fuels and bioenergy, as well as the use of CCUS facilities, which can enable the transition to net-zero emissions by providing a cost-effective pathway to scale up hydrogen production rapidly and also address CO_2 emissions from some of the challenging sectors, such as cement manufacturing.[13] Modern bioenergy will come from sustainable sources and avoid a negative impact on biodiversity, freshwater systems and processes of agricultural produce for food. An advantage of bioenergy is the ability to use the existing infrastructure; for example, biomethane could use existing natural gas pipelines and end-user equipment (IEA, 2021).

The electricity sector alone accounts for more than 50 per cent of emissions from existing assets, industrial sectors such as chemical,

---

[11] Advanced economies tend to have older capital stock compared to emerging economies (IEA, 2021).

[12] The rapid electrification of all sectors could put electricity at the cornerstone of energy security globally, as electricity infrastructure is more vulnerable to extreme weather events, compared to pipelines and underground storage facilities, and could also be subject to cyber-security risks (IEA, 2021).

[13] The current technology for the production of one tonne of cement creates around 0.6 tonnes of CO_2.

steel and cement account for around 30 per cent, transport accounts for 10 per cent and the building sector just under 5 per cent (IEA, 2021). In 2020, oil provided 30 per cent of the total energy supply, followed by 26 per cent from coal and 23 per cent from natural gas (IEA, 2021). Renewables are likely to provide a significant proportion of energy use in the future, such as hydrogen, bioenergy, wind, solar, hydroelectricity and geothermal. Transportation relied on 90 per cent of carbon-based fuel use in 2020. This is likely to change to electricity for low-duty transportation, hydrogen for long-haul heavy-duty trucks, advanced biofuels and hydrogen-based fuels such as ammonia for shipping and synthetic liquids, and advanced biofuels for aviation. Moreover, buildings need to increasingly decarbonise by using renewable energy, electricity or district heat, which provides heat to homes and businesses generated at a local energy centre.

Renewables such as hydropower, wind and solar will increasingly contribute to energy production in the future.[14] Innovative business models based on electrical-energy storage (EES) would be needed to help balance the demand and supply of these less controllable renewable-based power sources in order to help decarbonise the market (Anaya and Pollitt, 2019). Anaya and Pollitt (2019) provided an analysis comparing the storage business models of cloud data storage, frozen food storage and natural gas storage, as they display increasing maturity in the product life cycle, in order to draw lessons for business model design for the emerging EES market. These include considerations such as regulation, the ability to share capacity via consolidation, product bundling, response times, accessibility and green initiatives, among others. Moreover, start-up firms such as Highview Power are developing new technologies for energy storage, for example, the CRYOBattery, whereby low-cost electricity is used to cool air to reduce it to liquid form (*The Sunday Times*, 2022). The liquid form is then expanded again using turbines to generate electricity when needed, with the resultant process being free of combustion and emissions or the use of rare minerals.

There is also an increasing move towards distributed generation, whereby customers produce their own electricity, for example, with

[14] There could be major demand for critical minerals such as copper, lithium, nickel, cobalt and rare earth elements that are essential for many clean-energy technologies (IEA, 2021).

solar panels. Hence, there is a trend to shift away from centralised conventional electricity generation towards decentralisation that enables customers to generate, store, share and sell energy to the grid (Bryant et al., 2019). Such a trend presents a competitive threat to the business models of electric utilities operating under the traditional structure of selling electricity to customers.[15] There has been increasing interest in analysing future energy utility business models to become energy-solutions providers, including: the provision of services beyond energy sales, such as installation, financing, operations, maintenance and warranty for a fee; energy as a service – the customer pays a flat fee for a certain amount of energy and avoids peak-load pricing uncertainty, which incentivises the utility to promote energy efficiency; and building a platform model – to connect the distributed generation capacity with consumers (Bryant et al., 2019). However, these digitally based smart decentralised energy systems could contribute to the business models of incumbent utility firms being challenged by new entrants trying to disintermediate them using digital platforms to aggregate demand and enabling trading among consumers or providing energy-saving-based demand management propositions (Nillesen and Pollitt, 2016). Hence, utility firms need to rethink "where to play," "how to play" and "how to win" in the emerging net-zero energy industry (Nillesen and Pollitt, 2016).

7.4 Biodiversity and Crafting Business Models

Nature provides us with food, water and shelter, which contributes to our health and well-being. Therefore, nature should be treated as an asset, just like produced capital (such as building and machinery) and human capital (such as knowledge and skills). There has been increasing attention by firms on acknowledging their dependence on nature; the cost to firms from the loss of biodiversity could be enormous. For example, Unilever, a global consumer goods company, faced significantly higher prices for cod in the 1990s as a result of overfishing in the western North Atlantic. Cod is the main fish species, used for

---

[15] Customers under the decentralised model could potentially avoid the joint grid costs of maintaining the network. Some countries are introducing tariffs for their own consumption of domestically generated electricity (Nillesen and Pollitt, 2016).

its fish stick, a premium frozen food product. The replacement of cod with New Zealand hoki fish was not accepted by UK consumers because of its taste and quality, and hence it was delisted as a product by a number of retailers in 2004 (Winn and Pogutz, 2013).

Just as diversity within a portfolio of financial assets reduces risks and uncertainty, biodiversity – the diversity within a portfolio of natural assets – increases nature's resilience to shocks and hence maintains the ability to continue to provide services to humankind and other species[16] (Dasgupta, 2021). Biodiversity enables nature to be productive, resilient and adaptable. In doing so, nature's ecosystem provides two types of service (Cardinale et al., 2012): provisioning services that enable the production of renewable resources (e.g., food); and regulating services (e.g., pest and disease control). Biodiversity is defined as the variety of life forms, including variation among species and their functional traits (Cardinale et al., 2012). The concept of biodiversity is a multi-level construct that captures more than just the variation in species (Cardinale et al., 2012; Winn and Pogutz, 2013). Biodiversity also includes functional diversity and response diversity: functional diversity refers to the number of species that can perform different ecological functions in an ecosystem (e.g., pollination); and response diversity refers to the number of ways in which a specific function, such as pollination, can be performed (e.g., bees or birds).

The Dasgupta Review (Dasgupta, 2021) highlights that, collectively, we have failed to manage the global portfolio of natural assets in a sustainable manner. This is evidenced by estimates showing that, between 1992 and 2014, the capital produced per person globally increased by about 13 per cent, while the stock of natural capital per person declined by 14 per cent. Biodiversity loss is due to a combination of factors such as climate change, pollution, human exploitation of natural resources and the displacement of some species into new territories away from their natural habitat, which causes instability in the existing ecosystem (*The Economist*, 2021a). Firms are increasingly addressing biodiversity

---

[16] There are instances where increasing biodiversity might be detrimental (Cardinale et al., 2012). For example, diverse assemblage of natural enemies (such as predators, pathogens, etc.) can be beneficial in the control of herbivorous pests, but this can also inhibit biocontrol because the enemies attack one another. Another example relates to human health, where a more diverse pathogen population could increase infectious disease (for example, variants of SARS-CoV-2 or COVID-19).

as part of their overall strategic initiatives (Bishop et al., 2009; Winn and Pogutz, 2013). For example, ArcelorMittal, a leading firm in the steel and mining industry, has implemented a biodiversity compensation programme to minimise the impact of iron mining activities in Liberia's Nimba Mountains. Another example is Syngenta, a Swiss agribusiness in the seeds and pesticide market, which launched an initiative to increase farm productivity, with the goal of restoring native pollinators in the agricultural landscape in some major European countries and the United States.

The Intergovernmental Science-Policy Platform on Biodiversity and Ecosystem Services, a body created to bridge the gap between biodiversity science and policy, stated in its 2020 report that the health of natural ecosystems is deteriorating rapidly. This was further supported by the *Living Planet Report 2020*, produced by the World Wildlife Fund and the Zoological Society of London, two conservation and research groups, who stated that the loss of populations of animals such as mammals, birds and fish is accelerating (*The Economist*, 2021b). Moreover, significant deforestation – for example, of the Amazon – beyond a certain point could cause an abrupt transformation of the landscape into a savannah and make it irreversible.

There has been a significant loss of animals that perform important functions within the natural ecosystem. Nearly three billion birds have been lost in North America since 1970 (Paulson, 2021). More than 75 per cent of the global food crop, including coffee, cocoa and almonds, is pollinated by animals (*The Economist*, 2021a). Hence, the loss of birds affects the efficiency of food-crop pollination. Moreover, climate change and biodiversity loss are locked in tandem in a cycle of destruction. For example, scientists predict that 70–90 per cent of coral reefs will disappear over the next 20 years as a result of warming sea temperatures, acidic water and pollution (Paulson, 2021). This will affect 4,000 species of fish, and approximately half a billion people dependent on these coral reef ecosystems for food and employment. There has been an increasing call to finance initiatives to protect the most important biodiversity, and the services it provides, through initiatives such as the UN Convention on Biodiversity. It is likely that low-income countries, which are more dependent than high-income countries on nature's goods and services, will be most affected, contributing to increased inequality.

The goods and services that nature provides to society, and hence its worth or value, are often not reflected in market prices, as many of them are freely available.[17] This pricing distortion leads to under-investment and overconsumption relative to other forms of capital such as produced capital (Dasgupta, 2021). This is a market failure and an institutional failure, with institutions incentivised to exploit, rather than protect, nature. *The Dasgupta Review* (Dasgupta, 2021) recommends three broad transitions to address these issues. The first is to ensure that our demands on nature do not exceed supply. This could take the form of pricing for the use of natural resources, as well as quantity restrictions on the use of such resources. The second suggested transition is the need to change the measure of economic activity in terms of simply output, such as GDP, to a wider concept that incorporates depreciation of the stock of natural assets. This could include natural capital in national accounting systems, as well as at firm level (Haskel and Westlake, 2017). For example, the Integrated Reporting Framework (IRF) might be a broad step in that direction, with members' firms encouraged to report the impact of natural capital and other forms of intangible capital together with the manufactured capital (Flower, 2015; Thomson, 2015).[18] The third recommendation is to reform the institutions and governance system to support the management of such diversity. Such institutions need to be polycentric by consolidating knowledge and perspectives at global, national and local levels. These institutions need to include business and financial institutions by incorporating the impact of their activities on biodiversity. This calls for new business models.

Some firms have taken the opportunity to reinvent their business models, whose core value proposition is, in essence, a contribution

---

[17] Estimating the value of biodiversity loss is not trivial, as it requires a better understanding of the complexity of the ecosystem, which often delivers multiple services and involves trade-offs (Cardinale et al., 2012). For example, carbon sequestration through afforestation might increase the production of timber but reduce the supply of water. Hence, the value of biodiversity needs to factor in both the marginal benefit in terms of services gained and the marginal costs in terms of services lost. A systems thinking approach would be needed to address these types of complexity in valuing nature's services (Lovins et al., 1999).

[18] However, studies have criticised the IRF for focusing on reporting and not going far enough with the changes needed in terms of the power structure of stakeholders (Flower, 2015; Thomson, 2015).

to the management of a given environmental problem. For example, Lyonnaise des Eaux transformed itself from a "small water-cycle" firm to an "extended water-cycle" firm (Feger and Merhmet, 2020). A small water cycle involves providing services for water-treatment plants, pipes and other man-made infrastructures. However, the emergence of digital technologies with sensors enabled Lyonnaise des Eaux to provide extended water-cycle services that cover water-related ecosystem management such as flood risks, green infrastructure for rainwater management, groundwater protection and wetland and ecosystem services, and related biodiversity protection. This was partly driven by the change in perception of the "concessions" management system of public services in France, which was developed in the nineteenth century. The concession-based approach allowed public authorities in France to delegate the financing, construction and management of public services and utilities to private operators while still owning the infrastructure.

In the 1990s and early 2000s, there was a change in perception that this concession-based approach was seen to accelerate the privatisation and commodification of common goods. In particular, there were increasing concerns about the costs of managing environmental and water-resource preservation issues such as less water availability due to climate change, more pollution caused by farming and so on. Moreover, there was a reduction in the amount of water sold although the billing was based on volume. This caused Lyonnaise des Eaux to rethink its customer value proposition based on the extended water-cycle business model. These extended water-cycle services include management of the inland water body as a natural bathing pool, pollution-reduction plans for groundwater and quality monitoring of nearby water streams for construction firms in order to alert them in advance of any damage to fish populations.

There were several challenges that Lyonnaise des Eaux had to overcome in transitioning its business model to incorporate extended water-cycle management. First, there was no predefined customer for the wider ecosystem management of the water system. Second, there was resistance from managers attached to the small water-cycle culture, where there was certainty in terms of billing based on the volume of consumption compared to the less certain, but potentially lucrative, service model. The third challenge was the need to gain legitimacy to intervene in biodiversity management, where there was no single metric to demonstrate ecological performance. These are the types of challenges that firms will need to manage as the maintenance of biodiversity objectives is incorporated into business model design.

7.5 Methane Abatement and Business Model Design

Methane emissions from human activities are the second largest contributor to global warming after carbon dioxide (McKinsey, 2021). Human activity emits less methane than carbon dioxide, which stays in the atmosphere for a long time – often centuries – making it hard to reduce its atmospheric concentrations. In contrast, methane has a half-life of roughly a decade, which implies that it degrades quickly. However, methane has a larger impact on global warming. Over the course of a 20-year period, a tonne of methane (CH_4) will warm the atmosphere 86 times more than carbon dioxide (CO_2). Hence, methane is said to be responsible for 23 per cent of the rise in temperatures since pre-industrial times. The main reasons for the rise in methane emissions are livestock farming, where animals such as cows belch it, rice cultivation, where soggy environments could harbour microorganisms that produce it, and the fossil-fuel industry, whereby pipelines and rigs could leak methane (*The Economist*, 2021a).

Methane emissions and their contribution to climate change have been discussed less frequently among policymakers, corporate decision-makers and society because of the more sporadic nature of its emission compared to carbon dioxide (McKinsey, 2021). These sporadic emissions create a number of problems. First, they are difficult to quantify, making it difficult to take abatement actions. Second, abatement costs vary significantly between one type of asset and another (methane recovery in coal mining has higher costs than gas leaks in the oil and gas industry). Third, often there are trade-offs in the solutions; for example, dry seeding in rice farming might reduce emissions from flooding but increase emissions from nitrous oxide, another greenhouse gas (McKinsey, 2021).

Five industries are responsible for 98 per cent of human emissions of methane, namely, agriculture, oil and gas, coal mining, solid waste management and wastewater management (McKinsey, 2021). Agriculture accounts for 40–50 per cent of anthropogenic methane emissions. Ruminant animals such as cows and sheep create methane during digestion, among other gasses such as carbon dioxide.

Moreover, the mechanical flooding of rice farms to manage pests is also responsible for methane emissions (*The Economist*, 2021b). Firms are already commercialising feed additives for cattle that reduce methane production, while new approaches to water, soil-carbon, nitrogen and land-management systems for rice production are reducing methane emissions. Leakage from the oil and gas industry, for example, from natural gas, accounts for around 20–25 per cent of methane emissions (McKinsey, 2021). Similarly, the leakage from methane trapped in coal that is emitted when the coal is mined accounts for 10–15 per cent of emissions. For example, some countries are beginning to mandate requirements to monitor the intensity of natural gas leakage using more sophisticated sensing equipment. Such extra-sensitive sensing equipment might be provided by quantum-technology-based firms with the opportunity for new business model development. The solid waste and wastewater management industries account for about 7–10 per cent of methane emissions (McKinsey, 2021). Anaerobic organic material, or the breakdown of organic material in wastewater streams, generates methane. There might be opportunities to capture these methane emissions and sell them as renewable natural gas or use them in the production of fertiliser. Alternatively, there are opportunities for the application of microalgae to prevent methane formation (McKinsey, 2021). The above-mentioned management of methane emissions in the relevant key industries requires new business models in order to deliver the solutions effectively and efficiently.

7.6 Discussion

An increasing number of firms are creating purpose-driven strategies to take into account sustainability objectives alongside commercial objectives (Henderson, 2021; Rozentale and van Baalen, 2021). Pursuing conflicting goals inevitably creates ongoing tactical conflicts within the business model when deciding which objective to prioritise and hence which stakeholders to satisfy. Firms need to be cognisant of these tensions and accommodate them when pursuing sustainability goals. This is one of the key challenges in defining value when pursuing multiple objectives. The notion of value based on philosophical pragmatism is neither purely objective nor subjective but rather the result of the social process of action (Painter et al., 2019). In this context, value can be seen as prizing and appraising that comes about from the continuous design and engineering of social activity (Dewey, 1944). Hence, if a sustainable future is prized, valuation should enact and serve this objective. This value is achieved by examining the past problem, for example, environmental degradation, and generating a new imagination of the future to test, amend and modify previous beliefs through a process of participatory involvement by the relevant stakeholders.

Cafédirect, a farmer-owned social enterprise, experienced this tension in defining value and responding to changes and challenges in the market and societal environment with different business models, with varying degrees of success (Davies and Doherty, 2019). The firm initially started with the objective of the core economic activity of selling coffee and tea as a means to serve the social goals of empowering smallholder farmers and pulling them out of poverty. Farmers are not just suppliers but partners in the Cafédirect venture. Cafédirect tried to guarantee a minimum price for coffee to the farmers following the significant reduction in prices that came about after the dismantling of the International Coffee Agreement in 1989; it also tried to provide farmers with welfare protection to promote poverty alleviation. Cafédirect was focused on marketing and sales of the products to consumers and had an agreement with an NGO, Twin Trading, to provide producer-support and development initiatives. By the early 2000s, the fair-trade coffee that it sold had become a commodity, with many suppliers selling to supermarkets at lower prices. Cafédirect's unique position was therefore eroded. Moreover, the period coincided with concerns about the environment such as climate change, and crop dependence was becoming increasingly important. Hence, Cafédirect started to reposition its brand from being a fair-trade producer to a sustainable coffee and producer-advocacy organisation.

In order to achieve this new strategic positioning, the company decided to bring the producer-support and development activities in-house rather than relying on Twin Trading. Such a move required a more complex set of activities to be managed internally around logistics, supply chain management and the related producer-support and development activities. These added complexity and tensions – such as the value proposition, workers, customer communication and branding – to Cafédirect's business model, and this conflict resulted in poor financial performance. Eventually, around 2011, a separate entity, the Cafédirect Producers' Foundation, was set up, which was run independently in order to manage the producer-support and development activities. This model enabled Cafédirect to refocus on its sustainable enterprise business model without creating an overly complex bureaucratic organisation to manage the tensions arising from hybrid business objectives.

7.6.1 Sustainability Transition Challenges

Sustainability initiatives often require the adoption of new technologies and transformation of the socio-technical systems (Köhler et al., 2019). Studies have been critical of the view that transition challenges are merely about overcoming market failure with appropriate pricing of externalities (Rosenbloom et al., 2020). The market failure approach underestimates the fundamental systems problem and focuses on efficiency as opposed to effectiveness, hence stimulating optimisation of the existing system rather than transformation. To envisage how green technologies transform our socio-technical system, one may refer to the research on technological transitions, whereby scholars have aimed to understand the phenomena of technological transitions and their impact on industry and society. In particular, the literature on socio-technology transitions has described how technological transitions come about. Studies of the multi-level perspective have argued that technological breakthrough and replacing an existing technological regime arise as a result of dynamics across three levels: the micro level, which involves *niche* experimentation by firms; the meso level, where regimes maintain stability through a semi-coherent set of rules that orient and coordinate the activities of social groups and determine the institutional interaction; and the macro level, where the external *landscape*, such as deep structural trends, social values and worldviews, largely beyond the control of the system actors, take place, for example, policies on climate change (Elzen et al., 2004; Geels and Schot, 2007).

Given the right landscape conditions, radical niche innovations can overthrow dominant regimes to enable transition pathways for new technologies. The focus of the multi-level perspective is on the evolutionary mechanism of change and less explicit recognition of the agency and politics of change. The large technical systems (LTS) literature has studied the transition of electricity infrastructure. In LTS, system builders are key to enabling alignment across technical and non-technical (such as laws and regulations) artefacts that create unity among the actors to enable technological transitions (Hughes, 1983). Such alignment is often achieved by system builders, who construct the system by breaking down demarcated boundaries between scientific knowledge, technologies, institutions and users, among others, to create a seamless web. Such system builders could be inventors–entrepreneurs, financiers and managers, who might play different roles during the phases of the technical system transition. These approaches to technological transitions highlight the socio-technical nature of change but de-emphasise the activity system inherent in the business model approach, which is composed of transactions between firms (Bolton and Hannon, 2016).

Moreover, recent research suggests that business models can both facilitate and hamper technological transitions (Bidmon and Knab, 2018). For example, DuPont (of the United States) and Imperial Chemical Industries (of the United Kingdom) were both major multinationals whose business models were dependent on chlorofluorocarbon (CFC) production. For this reason, they both played an important role in influencing their respective governments on their initial positions in the 1970s, which entailed a reluctance to support policies to ban CFCs (Rajan, 1997). Subsequently, in the 1980s, the European firm alleged that the US wanted to ban CFCs to open up vast markets for Du Pont, which had a head start in developing CFC substitutes. Therefore, existing theories lack the business model perspective, despite firms being regarded as key performative actors in technology transitions (Sarasini and Linder, 2018). During the transition, firms need to align the content, structure and governance of their business models with the evolving socio-technological context (Bolton and Hannona, 2016).

For example, there were multiple approaches in the transition to combined power and heat (CHP) systems with district-level localised heating in the UK. In the first approach the local authority owns part of a start-up energy service firm and promotes the council's sustainability objectives. The energy service firm might compete with other incumbents in providing energy services based on decentralised energy solutions. The second model consists of the local authority contracting to buy energy services from third-party incumbent energy firms and providing the anchor loads, such as large municipal buildings and residential schemes, as the principal customer. The local authority enters into a long-term contract with the incumbent energy service provider to encourage the large capital investment needed for the local CHP schemes. These two models might be driven by different political considerations, such as whether a local authority should own an energy service firm. In addition, the transition could be driven by a start-up or an incumbent firm. Moreover, these two models of transition to a sustainable energy supply framework show that the business model design needs to be incorporated within the technology transition systems.

It is helpful to contextualise the business model design space to describe the options available for new business model designs and hence how actors need to either "fit and conform" or try to "stretch and transform" the space (Wesseling et al., 2020). The design spaces that firms need to consider include: regulatory – rules and regulations; science and technology – the technology and knowledge to create and capture value; industry – the presence and willingness of firms in the ecosystem to collaborate or compete; cultural – the cultural value of the stakeholders; and the market dimension – which determines user preferences (Wesseling et al., 2020). Stakeholder firms would need to assess which are the softer dimensions, which are malleable, and the order in which to adopt a "fit and conform" or "stretch and transform" strategy. Thus, understanding the firm-level dynamics with a business model lens can shed light on the drivers and barriers of transitioning to a new socio-technical system.

An in-depth examination of firm-level dynamics and their business models can provide deeper insights into the adoption challenges of green technologies and their impact on the systemic process of technological transition to enable sustainability. Both the large technical systems and business model approaches forefront the agency of actors in building systems, while the multi-level perspective emphasises the evolutionary aspects across different levels (Bolton and Hannon, 2016). The large technical systems approach emphasises system builders engaging in political processes, and the business model approach emphasises entrepreneurs and managers entering market transactions to shape the content, structure and governance of business models to drive economic value. All three approaches of technology transition are needed to better understand how green technologies can move towards a sustainable economy and the role that business model design plays. Moreover, the economic system is important, whereby the relationship between the state and the private sector could drive how such technological transitions unfold and the associated policy implications. For example, liberal market economies, whereby the state limits its role to rule setting and conflict settlement (e.g., the United States), coordinated market economies, enabling state arbitration among economic actors to facilitate cooperative relationships (e.g., Germany), state-influenced market economies, where the state plays an active interventionist role (e.g., France, Japan, South Korea), and state capitalism (e.g., China and Russia), where the state or state-owned enterprises undertake commercial activities, could influence the policy and business model design implications (Geels, 2018).

7.6.2 Degrowth Economics

The conventional paradigm in economics and politics is the green growth model to address the issue of climate change. The green growth model assumes that the economy can continue to grow while addressing the threat of climate change through market-led action and technological innovation (Bokat-Lindell, 2021; Paulson, 2021). An alternative perspective is the degrowth paradigm, whereby humanity does not have the capacity to reduce the use of fossil fuels and meet the ever-growing demand for economic growth (Hickel, 2017; Ripple et al., 2020). Hence, the proponents of degrowth emphasise the need to curtail consumption and accept a reduction in the growth rate of the economy to address climate change (Keyber and Lenzen, 2021).

The degrowth paradigm is based on two main premises (Hickel, 2017): the first is that GDP growth cannot be decoupled from material resource use and the second is that GDP can be decoupled from greenhouse gas emissions by replacing fossil fuel with renewal energy, but this replacement is not taking place quickly enough. This might be the result of technological advances not being able to cope with such rapid change or the challenge of technological transitions. Therefore, the degrowth proponents argue that the solution is to reduce resource and energy consumption, which will make it easier to transition to renewable energy. Some have argued that the responsibility to reduce consumption should lie disproportionately with the richer countries in order to allow the poorer countries to catch up and their population to be brought out of poverty (Hickel, 2017). The proponents of such economies that are regenerative and distributive by design have argued that the objective is to find ways to achieve tempered economic growth as a means to reach social goals within ecological limits – and not a goal in itself (Raworth, 2018).

There are proponents of the green growth paradigm that reject calls for a degrowth strategy, as they believe that GDP growth is already being decoupled from material resource use. For example, some richer countries have grown while using fewer of the planet's most important resources. For example, the United States has seen a decline in the use of freshwater withdrawals per day, various metals and trade-adjusted carbon emissions (Smith, 2021). Moreover, they argue that technological developments will enable a faster transition to renewable energy. In addition, the degrowth recommendation of tempered growth might not be politically or socially palatable – and hence less acceptable in practice. In any case, even a partial adoption of the degrowth model could imply significant changes in production and consumption activities. For example, the model could entail a substantial reduction in the use of carbon-based fuel, which might have implications for global transportation such as shipping and air transport. In addition, the reduced use of cement-based mortar or concrete, which is heavy in carbon emissions, could mean changes to the construction industry. The reduction of ruminant meat-based products to curtail methane emissions could imply a greater demand for vegan or vegetarian diets, which has significant implications for the food industry. These factors could change business models in industries such as transportation, construction and food, among others, and hence the ecosystems of firms supplying to these industries. Such a business model change requires firms to internalise negative externalities and generate positive externalities such as securing stable employment, social capital, food security and non-market capital in order to embrace the idea of operating within the carrying capacity of the environment and equitable distribution of wealth (Khmara and Kroneberg, 2018).

Conclusion

Firms in the private sector need to embrace new business models by adopting new technologies that enable novel ways to organise human activities in order to contribute to achieving the Sustainable Development Goals. The pressure on crucial earth systems such as carbon, nitrogen and water cycles is creating anthropogenic-driven challenges as a result of climate change and the impact on biodiversity. However, in order for firms to innovate their business models, major technological transitions are required that call for public policy interventions, as purely market-based systems might fail to achieve such changes quickly enough (Bryant et al., 2019). Modern governments need to think about not just fixing market failures but also acting as transformers and shapers to address societal issues (Rosenbloom et al., 2020). This would include policy initiatives that identify the type of business models needed to achieve the desired outcome – and also the barriers to achieve the outcome. The policy stance of governments could be driven by their political and economic orientations, respectively (Dryzek and Stevenson, 2011). On the political dimension, they could be either conservative – strategies will be executed within existing institutions and power structures; or progressive – where existing institutions and power structures are seen to be inadequate and in need of reform. On the economic orientation, they could be either reformist – they accept that the existing economic objectives and values are sufficient to address the changes needed; or radical – where the existing economic objectives and values are implicated in the problem and require radical change. Most of the policy agenda on climate-change initiatives has focused on the economic orientation, with little emphasis on changing the political dimension, such as institutions or power structures (Bryant et al., 2019).

Studies show that merely focusing on the technological aspects of the transition challenges involved in addressing climate-change issues might not be adequate. Some of the barriers to transition might be related to institutional aspects (Bakker and Konnings, 2018). Hence, these institutional barriers need to be addressed concurrently with the technological issues, such as high component costs and systems integration challenges. For example, in the case of the transition to the use of zero-emission buses (ZEBs), such as electric and hydrogen fuel-cell buses to replace diesel buses in the Netherlands, the institutional barriers were an important hurdle to overcome in order to enable new business models to emerge (Bakker and Konnings, 2018). In order to incentivise new actors to provide refuelling and recharging infrastructure for the ZEBs, it might be necessary to build these facilities to cater not only for buses but also for other users such as rubbish trucks and taxis. Hence, the installation of refuelling and recharging infrastructure in strategic locations that are not necessarily optimised for ZEBs could affect the punctuality of buses. The locations of such infrastructure, together with the longer time required for ZEB recharging, call for a different approach to schedule planning. Moreover, the longer time period needed to depreciate ZEB assets could mean that the local authorities need either to buy the buses and lease them to the operators or to provide a guaranteed residual value for the ZEBs. These measures shift the risks to the local authorities, which requires new institutional arrangements and governance structures in order to stimulate ZEB adoption. Moreover, the conventional approach of focusing on the costs and timeliness of the schedules as the basis for offering contracts might need to be altered to explicitly include ZEBs and provide concessions to overcome the higher initial costs. This case illustrates the need for institutional changes to calibrate the economic incentives for new business models to complement technological developments in order to encourage technological transition to address sustainability issues.

There are a number of areas where further investigation of business model innovation for sustainability could take place. The first major area of research is how to position sustainability issues as gains rather than losses (Solberg et al., 2020). Sustainability can often be seen as a cost to doing business to address climate or biodiversity issues if viewed with a short-term lens. However, from a longer-term perspective, addressing sustainability issues maintains the natural environment upon which firms rely in order to conduct business. Therefore, further research needs to explore the cognitive dimension of how to position sustainability issues as gains. One promising avenue is the development of sustainability measures for different business model design configurations that internalise externalities related to sustainability. The second major area of research is to address the design of business models to enable, and be congruent with, the institutional changes that are needed to address sustainability issues. As discussed, addressing major sustainability issues involves technology-transition challenges. Hence, understanding business model design, and how they interact with institutional changes, is an important aspect of better understanding how to enable such technology-transition challenges to address sustainability issues.

The third major area of research is how to conceptualise business model design to address both climate change and biodiversity simultaneously. As we have discussed, there are some instances where addressing climate change might exacerbate biodiversity issues, and perhaps vice versa. Hence, more research on how business model design and innovation can help to address these two challenges simultaneously, as opposed to individually, is an important area of further research. The fourth area of research is to better understand financial business models to enable sustainability transitions, particularly how the business models of financial institutions need to change and to what extent firms in other sectors in the process of transitioning to sustainable business models might need to internalise the financing of such transitions within existing business models.

This chapter has provided an overview of the opportunities and challenges involved in addressing sustainability issues related to climate change, as well as biodiversity through business model innovation. Sustainability issues address one of the major challenges of our generation, and business model innovation could act as a crucial lever to align the interests of various stakeholders to make a significant change to the status quo. In this context, we propose some outstanding research issues on this topic.

References

Amasawa, E., Shibata, T., Sugiyama, H., and Hirao, M. (2020). Environmental Potential of Reusing, Renting, and Sharing Consumer Products: Systematic Analysis Approach. *Journal of Cleaner Production* 242: 1–11.

Anaya, K. L. and Pollitt, M. G. (2019). Storage Business Models: Lessons for Electricity from Cloud Data, Frozen Food and Natural Gas. *The Energy Journal* 40: 409–432.

Bakker, S. and Konings, R. (2018). The Transition to Zero-Emission Buses in Public Transport – The Need for Institutional Innovation. *Transportation Research Part D* 64: 204–215.

Batista L, Bourlakis M., Smart P., and Maull R. (2018). In Search of a Circular Supply Chain Archetype – A Content-Analysis-Based Literature Review. *Production Planning & Control* 29(6): 438-451

BEIS. (2021). Low Carbon Hydrogen Business Model: Consultation on a Business Model for Low Carbon Hydrogen. Department of Business, Energy & Industrial Strategy: 1–90.

Bidmon, C. M. and Knab, S. F. (2018). The Three Roles of Business Models in Societal Transitions: New Linkages between Business Model and Transition Research. *Journal of Cleaner Production* 178: 903–916.

Bigdeli, A. Z., Li, F., and Shi, X. (2015). Sustainability and Scalability of University Spinouts: A Business Model Perspective. *R & D Management* 46(3): 504–518.

Bishop, J., Kapila, S., Hicks, F., Mitchell, P., and Vorhies, F. (2009). New Business Models for Biodiversity Conservation. *Journal of Sustainable Forestry* 28: 282–303.

Bocken, N. M. P., Short, S. W., Rana, P., and Evans, S. (2014). A Literature and Practice Review to Develop Sustainable Business Model Archetypes. *Journal of Cleaner Production* 65: 42–56.

Bocken, N. M. P., Mugge, R., Bom, C. A., and Lemstra, H-J. (2018). Pay-per-Use Business Models as a Driver for Sustainable Consumption: Evidence from the Case of HOMIE. *Journal of Cleaner Production* 198: 498–510.

Bocken, N. M. P., Boons, F., and Baldassarre, B. (2019). Sustainable Business Model Experimentation by Understanding Ecologies of Business Models. *Journal of Cleaner Production* 208: 1498–1512.

Bokat-Lindell, S. (2021). Do We Need to Shrink the Economy to Stop Climate Change? *International New York Times*, 16 September 2021.

Bolton, R. and Hannon, M. (2016). Governing Sustainability Transitions through Business Model Innovation: Towards a Systems Understanding. *Research Policy* 45(9): 1731–1742.

Boulding, K. E. (1945). The Consumption Concept in Economic Theory. *The American Economic Review* 35(2): 1–14.

Boulding, K. E. (1949). Income or Welfare. *The Review of Economic Studies* 17(2): 77–86.

Boulding, K. E. (1966). The Economics of the Coming Spaceship Earth. *Resources for the Future*: 1–14.

Branca, T. A., Fornai, B., Colla, V., Pistelli, M. I., Faraci, E. L., Cirilli, F., and Schroder, J. (2021). Industrial Symbiosis and Energy Efficiency in European Process Industries: A Review. *Sustainability* 13: 1–37.

Bryant, S. T., Straker, K., and Wrigley, C. (2019). The Discourses of Power – Governmental Approaches to Business Models in the Renewable Energy Transition. *Energy Policy* 130: 41–59.

Cardinale, B. J., Duffy, J. E., Gonzalez, A., Hooper, D. U., Perrings, C., Venail, P., Narwani, A., Mace, G. M., Tilman, D., Wardle, D. A., Kinzig, A. P., Daily, G. C., Loreau, M., Grace, J. B., Larigauderie, A., Srivastava, D. S., and Naeem, S. (2012). Biodiversity Loss and Its Impact on Humanity. *Nature* 486: 59–68.

Chakrabarty, D. (2020). The Human Sciences and Climate Change: A Crisis of Anthropocentrism. *Science and Culture* 86(1–2): 46–48.

Chopra, S. S. and Khanna, V. (2014). Understanding Resilience in Industrial Symbiosis Networks: Insights from Network Analysis. *Journal of Environmental Management* 141: 86–94.

Ciulli, F. and Kolk, A. (2019). Incumbents and Business Model Innovation for the Sharing Economy: Implications for Sustainability. *Journal of Cleaner Production* 214: 995–1010.

Crowley, H., DeKoszmovszky, J., Firbank, L. G., Fulford, B., Gardner, T. A., Hails, R. S., Halvorson, S., Jack, M., Kerrison, B., Koh, L. S. C., Lang, S. C., McKenzie, E. J., Monsivais, P., O'Riordan, T., Osborn, J., Oswald, S., Price Thomas, E., Raffaelli, D., Reyers, B., Srai, J.S., Strassburg, B. B. N., Webster, D., Welters, R., Whiteman, G., Wilsdon, J., and Vira, B. (2017). Research Priorities for Managing the Impacts and Dependencies of Business upon Food, Energy, Water and the Environment. *Sustainability Science* 12: 319–331.

Cusumano, M. A., Kahl, S. J. and Suarez, F. F. (2015). Services, Industry Evolution, and the Competitive Strategies of Product Firms. *Strategic Management Journal* 36(4): 559–575.

Cyert, R. M. and March, J. G. (1963). *A Behavioral Theory of the Firm.* Englewood Cliffs, NJ: Prentice Hall.

Dasgupta, P. (2021). *The Economics of Biodiversity: The Dasgupta Review.* London: HM Treasury.

Davies, I. A. and Doherty, B. (2019). Balancing a Hybrid Business Model: The Search for Equilibrium at Cafédirect. *Journal of Business Ethics* 157: 1043–1066.

Dewey, J. (1944). Some Questions about Value. *The Journal of Philosophy* 41(17): 449–455.

Dryzek, J. S. and Stevenson, H. (2011). Global Democracy and Earth System Governance. *Ecological Economics* 70: 1865–1874.

Elkington, J. (1997). *Cannibals with Forks: The Triple Bottom Line of 21st Century.* Oxford: Capstone.

Ellen MacArthur Foundation. (2013). *Towards the Circular Economy: Economic and Business Rationale for an Accelerated Transition.*

Ellen MacArthur Foundation. (2015). *Delivering the Circular Economy: A Toolkit for Policymakers.*

Elzen, B., Geels, F., and Green, K. (2004). System Innovation and the Transition to Sustainability.

Feger, C. and Mermet, L. (2020). New Business Models for Biodiversity and Ecosystem Management Services: An Action Research with a Large Environmental Sector Company. *Organization & Environment* 35(2): 1–30.

Flower, J. (2015). The International Integrated Reporting Council: A Story of Failure. *Critical Perspectives on Accounting* 27: 1–17.

Geels, F. W. (2018). Socio-Technical Transitions to Sustainability. *Oxford Research Encyclopaedia of Environmental Science.* 39: 187–201

Geels, F. W. and Schot, J. (2007). Typology of Sociotechnical Transition Pathways. *Research Policy* 36(3): 399–417.

Geissdoerfer, M., Savaget, P., Bocken, N. M. P., and Hultink, E. J. (2017). The Circular Economy – A New Sustainability Paradigm? *Journal of Cleaner Production* 143: 757–768.

Haskel, J. and Westlake, S. (2017). *Capitalism without Capital: The Rise of the Intangible Economy*. Princeton, NJ: Princeton University Press.

Hawken, P., Lovins, A. B., and Lovins, L. H. (1999). *Natural Capitalism: The Next Industrial Revolution*. Washington, DC: Island Press.

Henderson, R. (2021). Innovation in the 21st Century: Architectural Change, Purpose, and the Challenges of Our Time. *Management Science* 67(9): 1–10.

Hickel. (2017). *The Divide: A Brief Guide to Global Inequality and Its Solutions*. London: William Heinemann.

Hopkinson, P., Zils, M., Hawkins, P., and Roper, S. (2018). Managing a Complex Global Circular Economy Business Model: Opportunities and Challenges. *California Management Review* 60(3): 71–94.

Hughes, T. (1983). *Networks of Power: Electrification in Western Society 1880–1930*. Baltimore: John Hopkins University Press.

International Energy Agency. (2021). Net Zero by 2050: A Roadmap for the Global Energy Sector. *International Energy Agency Special Report*, IEA Publications, Paris, France.

IPCC (Intergovernmental Panel on Climate Change). (2018). Global Warming of 1.5 °C. An IPCC Special Report on the Impacts of Global Warming of 1.5 °C above Pre-industrial Levels and Related Global Greenhouse Gas Emission Pathways, in the Context of Strengthening the Global Response to the Threat of Climate Change, Sustainable Development and Efforts to Eradicate Poverty. www.ipcc.ch/sr15/.

Keyber, L. T. and Lenzen, M. (2021). 1.5 °C Degrowth Scenarios Suggest the Need for New Mitigation Pathways. *Nature Communications* 12: 1–16.

Khmara, Y. and Kronenberg, J. (2018). Degrowth in Business: An Oxymoron or a Viable Business Model for Sustainability? *Journal of Cleaner Production* 177: 721–731.

Köhler, J., Geels, F. W., Kern, F., Markard, J., Wieczorek, A., Alkemade, F., Avelino, F., Bergek, A., Boons, F., Fünfschilling, L., Hess, D., Holtz, G., Hyysalo, S., Jenkins, K., Kivimaa, P., Martiskainen, M., McMeekin, A., Mühlemeier, M. S., Nykvist, B., Onsongo, E., Pel, B., Raven, R., Rohracher, H., Sandén, B., Schot, J., Sovacool, B., Turnheim, B., Welch, D., and Wells, P. (2019). An Agenda for Sustainability Transitions Research: State of the Art and Future Directions. *Environmental Innovation and Societal Transitions* 31: 1–32.

Kortmann, S. and Piller, F. (2016). Open Business Models and Closed-Loop Value Chains: Redefining the Firm-Consumer Relationship. *California Management Review* 58(3): 88–108.

Lehoux, P., Silva, H. P., Denis, J-L., Miller, F. A., Sabio, R. P., and Mendell, M. (2021). Moving toward Responsible Value Creation: Business Model

Challenges Faced by Organizations Producing Responsible Health Innovations. *Journal of Product Innovation Management* 38: 548–573.

Lovins, A. B., Lovins, L. H., and Hawken, P. (1999). A Road Map for Natural Capitalism. *Harvard Business Review* 77(3): 145–158.

Markard, J., Raven, R., and Truffer, B. (2012). Sustainability Transitions: An Emerging Field of Research and Its Prospects. *Research Policy* 41: 955–967.

McDonough, W. and Braungart, M. (2002). *Cradle to Cradle: Remaking the Way We Make Things.* New York, NY: North Point Press.

McKinsey. (2021). Curbing Methane Emissions: How Five Industries Can Counter a Major Climate Threat, September.

Nillesen P. and Pollitt, M. (2016). New Business Models for Utilities to Meet the Challenge of the Energy Transition Chapter 15. In: F. P. Sioshansi (ed.), *Future of Utilities – Utilities of the Future: How Technological Innovations in Distributed Energy Resources Will Reshape the Electric Power Sector.* London: Academic Press, 283–301.

Nuttall, W. J. and Bakenne, A. T. (2019). *Fossil Fuel Hydrogen – Technical, Economic and Environmental Potential.* Gewerbestrasse, Switzerland: Springer.

Pacheco, D.A. de J., ten Caten, C.S., Jung, C.F., Sassanelli, C., Terzi, S. (2019). Overcoming Barriers towards Sustainable Product-Service Systems In: Small and Medium-Sized Enterprises. *Journal of Cleaner Production.* 222: 903–921

Painter, M., Hibbert, S., and Cooper, T. (2019). The Development of Responsible and Sustainable Business Practice: Value, Mind-Sets, Business-Models. *Journal of Business Ethics* 157: 885–891.

Pardo, R. J. H, Bhamra, T., and Bhamra, R. (2012). Sustainable Product Service Systems in Small and Medium Enterprises (SMEs): Opportunities in the Leather Manufacturing Industry. *Sustainability* 4: 175–192.

Parry, G. C., Brax, S. A., Maull, R. S., and Ng, I. C. L. (2016). Operationalising IoT for Reverse Supply: The Development of Use-Visibility Measures. *Supply Chain Management* 21(2): 228–244.

Paulson, H. (2021). The World's Biodiversity Peril. *The New York Times,* 23 October.

Rajan, M. (1997). *Global Environment Politics: India and North-South Politics of Global Environment Issues.* Delhi: Oxford University Press.

Raworth, K. (2018). *Doughnut Economics. Seven Ways to Think Like a 21st-Century Economist.* White River Junction, VT: Chelsea Green Publishing.

Rendtorff, J. D. (2019). Sustainable Development Goals and Progressive Business Models for Economic Transformation. *Local Economy* 34(6): 510–524.

Ripple, W. J., Wolf, C., Newsome, T. M., Barnard, P., and Moomaw, W. R. (2020). World Scientists' Warning of a Climate Emergency. *BioScience* 70(1): 8–12.

Roome, N. and Louche, C. (2016). Journeying Toward Business Models for Sustainability: A Conceptual Model Found Inside the Black Box of Organisational Transformation. *Organization & Environment* 29(1): 11–35.

Rosenbloom, D., Markard, J., Geels, F. W., and Fuenfschilling, L. (2020). Why Carbon Pricing Is Not Sufficient to Mitigate Climate Change – and How "Sustainability Transition Policy" Can Help. *PNAS* 117(16): 8664–8668.

Rozentale, I. and van Baalen, P. J. (2021). Crafting Business Models for Conflicting Goals: Lessons from Creative Service Firms. *Long Range Planning* 54(2-3): 1–17.

Sachs J. D. (2012). From Millennium Development to Sustainable Development Goals. *The Lancet* 379: 2206–2211.

Sachs J. D. (2015). *The Age of Sustainable Development.* New York: Columbia University Press.

Sarasini, S. and Linder, M. (2018). Integrating a Business Model Perspective into Transition Theory: The Example of New Mobility Services. *Environmental Innovation and Societal Transitions* 27: 16–31.

Short, S. W., Bocken, N. M. P., Barlow, C. Y., and Chertow, M. R. (2014). From Refining Sugar to Growing Tomatoes Industrial Ecology and Business Model Evolution. *Journal of Industrial Ecology* 18(5): 603–618.

Smith, N. (2021). People Are Realizing that Degrowth Is Bad. *Noahpinion.* https://noahpinion.substack.com/p/people-are-realizing-that-degrowth (accessed 29 November 2021).

Solberg, E., Traavik, L. E. M., and Wong, S. I. (2020). Digital Mindsets: Recognizing and Leveraging Individual Beliefs for Digital Transformation. *California Management Review* 62(4): 105–124.

Team Gemini. (2015). Danish Town of Kalundborg Implements Valuable Industrial Resource Management Model. *Sustainable Development.* http://teamgemini.us/danish-town-of-kalundborg-implements-valuable-industrial-resource-management-model/ (accessed 14 January 2022).

The Economist. (2021). Technology Can Help Conserve Biodiversity.

The Economist. (2021a). Put a Plug in It. Governments Should Set Targets to Reduce Methane Emissions. It Would Rapidly Make a Difference to Climate Change, 31 March.

The Economist. (2021b). Global Warming: Those Who Worry about CO_2 Should Worry about Methane, Too, 3 April.

The Economist. (2021c). What Happened at COP26? 11 November.

The Sunday Times. (2022). Highview Chief Rupert Pearce on the Cold Batteries that Could Save the Planet, 24 April.

Thomson, I. (2015). "But Does Sustainability Need Capitalism or an Integrated Report," A Commentary on "The International Integrated Reporting Council: A Story of Failure," by J. Flower. *Critical Perspectives on Accounting* 27: 18–22.

United Nations. (2020). *The Sustainable Development Goals Report.* New York: United Nations Publications.

Wesseling, J. H., Bidmon, C., and Bohnsack, R. (2020). Business Model Design Spaces in Socio-Technical Transitions: The Case of Electric Driving in the Netherlands. *Technological Forecasting & Social Change* 154: 1–11.

Winn, M. I. and Pogutz, S. (2013). Business, Ecosystems, and Biodiversity: New Horizons for Management Research. *Organization & Environment* 26(2): 203–229.

WWF. (2012). *The Living Planet Report 2012.*

Yang, M., Smart, P., Kumar, M., Jolly, M., and Evans, S. (2018). Product–Service Systems Business Models for Circular Supply Chains. *Production Planning & Control* 29(6): 498–508.

Yang, M. and Evans, S. (2019). Product–Service System Business Model Archetypes and Sustainability. *Journal of Cleaner Production* 220: 1156–1166.

8 Business Models for Socio-economic Development

Service to others is the rent you pay for your room here on earth.

Muhammad Ali

Introduction

The increasing environmental, social and economic challenges faced by the world led to 193 of the United Nations (UN) member countries agreeing, at the beginning of 2016, upon 17 Sustainable Development Goals (SDGs) as a common global agenda to be achieved by the year 2030 (United Nations, 2020). The SDGs relate to social targets, the eradication of poverty, zero hunger, good health and well-being, quality education, gender equality and reduced inequalities (Raith and Seabold, 2018). Achieving these targets requires transformation of the financial, economic and political systems that govern our societies (United Nations, 2020). Moreover, the COVID-19 pandemic has exposed and exacerbated existing inequalities and injustice, as the effects have adversely affected the marginalised groups. This calls for even more urgent attention to the 2030 SDG agenda.

The share of the world's workers living in extreme poverty on less than $1.90 a day declined from 14.3 per cent in 2010 to 7.1 per cent in 2019 but the pace of progress has slowed down since 2013. The global prevalence of undernourishment (chronic food insecurity) has remained almost unchanged, at slightly below 9 per cent, but given the growth in population, this translated into 690 million people in 2019, which was up by about 60 million since 2014. Universal health coverage, whereby all people have access to suitable healthcare without unnecessary financial hardship, was about 30–50 per cent of the global population, but only between 12 and 27 per cent in low-income countries. Although the proportion of children out of primary and secondary schools declined from 19 per cent in 2010 to 17 per cent in 2018, there were still over 258 million people out of school in 2018, with three-quarters of these living in sub-Saharan Africa or Southern Asia. Although there have been advances in gender equality in some areas, inequality persists. For example, there are 28 per cent more girls than boys out of school in Africa. Moreover, according to estimates in over 89 countries between 2001 and 2018, women spend about three times as many hours in unpaid domestic and care work as men. Between 2010 and 2017, income inequality, although improving in many countries, increased in 25 of the 89 countries with available data.[1] The existing structures and policies are inadequate to solve such major issues and market solutions, and government interventions alone might not be sufficient to address these challenges. A major part of such a transformation is the need to design innovative business models to act as the architecture with a social purpose (Raith and Seabold, 2018).

This chapter focuses on the concept of social business models to address some of the challenges of socio-economic development, including open innovation systems and the design of business models to address market failures. The chapter also discusses the often-unquestioned assumptions of the benefits of value creation and delivery for addressing socio-economic development, which might have unintended consequences in terms of winners and parts of society that might be left behind. The chapter makes the case for a more holistic approach to business model design in order to address some of these socio-economic issues.

8.1 Social Business Models

The Aravind Eye Hospital in India provides an example of a social business model, having adopted a mission to cure blindness through a combination of a market-oriented approach and a social purpose (Aravind Eye Care System, 2011; Rangan, 2009). There are 24 million blind people in the world and one-third of these cases are curable. Asia has two-thirds of the blind population in the world, with approximately three-quarters living in India. Dr Venkataswamy (also affectionately known as "Dr V") and David Green, an entrepreneur in

---

[1] Income inequality is often measured using the Gini coefficient, which ranges between 0 and 100, where 0 indicates that income is shared equally among all people and 100 indicates that income is concentrated on one individual.

the United States, came together to revolutionise the eye-care delivery system. Dr V had a vision of delivering eye care with the efficiency and scale of McDonald's fast-food chains. In 1976, the Aravind Eye Care System was formed as a hybrid business with hospitals, education and training programmes and a research foundation. David Green partnered with Aravind through Aurolab, which manufactures intraocular lenses at around $4 each in India, compared to $100 in the USA, meaning it was able to supply affordable lenses and related services. This partnership meant that Aravind was able to perform a high volume of eye surgery at a low cost.

This high volume provides surgeons with the training and experience to perform eye surgery with effectiveness rates that match many of the best eye hospitals in the world. Surgeons at Aravind perform over 2,000 surgeries a year, compared to a normal average of around 250–400, by adopting standardised processes and systems. Increasingly, telemedicine technologies are being used to reach remote areas. About 70 per cent of the surgeries are performed for free or below cost, while the remaining 30 per cent of patients are charged above cost. This allows the hospital to maintain a 50 per cent profit margin, which results in profits being ploughed back into the business to build capability and capacity. Aravind trains nurses for two years by recruiting students with the requisite education from local villages; all of the doctors work full-time. Moreover, the doctors and nurses are encouraged to adopt a culture of service called the "Arvind Way of Life."

The Aravind Eye Hospital adopts a social business model design. As shown in Figure 8.1, a social business model can be distinguished from other forms of business. On the one hand, as shown in the top-right quadrant of Figure 8.1, organisations can be seen as profit maximising, whereby their objective is to maximise financial return with a view to providing a return on the capital to shareholders. The second type of organisation, as shown in the bottom left of Figure 8.1, is a not-for-profit organisation, where the objective is to provide some social purpose (social profit maximisation), but not with a view to recovering the invested capital. Social businesses, as shown in the bottom-right quadrant, maximise social objectives while making a return on the capital investment, with a view to reinvesting in the business (Yunus et al., 2010). Hence, social business can be self-sustaining while the benefits are passed on to the target group of social undertaking in the form of lower prices, better service or greater accessibility (Yunus et al., 2010).

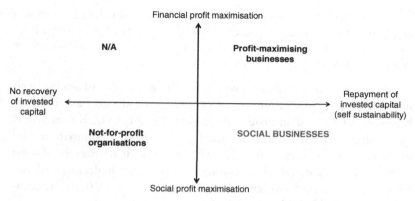

Figure 8.1 Social business versus other types of business
Source: Yunus et al. (2010)

Another example of a social business model is Danone, a multinational food-product corporation based in Paris (*Danone*, 2012). In 2006 Danone partnered with Grameen (microcredit) Bank in Bangladesh to form Grameen Danone Foods Ltd (GDFL) in Dhaka. Franck Riboud (then chairman and CEO of Danone) formed the social business model of GDFL following a discussion with Muhammad Yunus, the founder of Grameen Bank and subsequently a Nobel Peace Prize winner (Yunus et al., 2010). The mission of GDFL was to fight poverty and malnutrition in Bangladesh and to create a positive social impact. This vision is reflected in the statement by Muhammad Yunus (Danone Communities, 2020):

Grameen Danone Foods is a unique opportunity to create a company with a strong social dimension, a business whose goal is not to maximise profits but to serve the interests of the population, yet without sustaining losses. This small-scale project may be the start of a whole new type of market that will change the economic foundations of the world.

Franck Riboud went on to articulate the strategic imperative for Danone to create a new type of business model (*Emerging Markets Daily News*, 2006).

I strongly believe that our future depends on our ability to explore and invent new business models and new types of enterprise. For Danone, this partnership with a company as iconic and visionary as Grameen Bank is a great opportunity to make progress in that direction and take another huge step towards fulfilling our mission: to bring health through food to as many people as possible.

Grameen Danone Foods Ltd works on the principles of social business for profit-making, where the profits are ploughed back into the business. GDFL's main product is Shokti Doi, a type of yogurt aimed at children. Children in Bangladesh suffer from malnutrition and are underweight; it is estimated that 54 per cent of preschool-aged children, approximately 9.5 million youngsters, are malnourished and 56 per cent are underweight (Danone Communities, 2020). In addition, Bangladeshi children also suffer from high rates of micronutrient deficiencies, particularly vitamin A, iron, iodine and zinc; these deficiencies have an impact on the child's physical and cognitive development. The aim of Shokti Doi is to deliver 30 per cent of the daily requirement for iron, zinc, vitamin A and iodine at an affordable price through a distribution system based on – primarily women – entrepreneurs, called "Grameen ladies," who sell the yogurts in cooler bags door to door in both urban and rural populations. Grameen Bank provides microcredit to women entrepreneurs to enable them to conduct the business of distributing Shokti Doi. GDFL initially built a factory in Bogra, Bangladesh, to produce the yogurt. The Bogra factory is built to local specification and uses locally sourced milk products, thereby supporting local farmers by educating and training them to produce milk to the required specification. GDFL has provided a broad positive social impact to 300,000 children in Bangladesh while creating sustainable revenue for over 500 farmers and 200 Grameen ladies (Danone Communities, 2020).

Social business models often operate by serving less affluent communities (Seelos and Mair, 2007). There are many challenges inherent in serving such communities, as the market might not exist or consumers might not be in a position to consume. The market might be constrained by availability, whereby the supply chain, governance and institution might not be in existence – also called institutional voids (Khanna et al., 2010). Moreover, there could be an awareness issue, where customers might not have the knowledge to recognise the benefits of the product or service offering. In addition, from the point of view of the consumer, there is a challenge of affordability (consumers

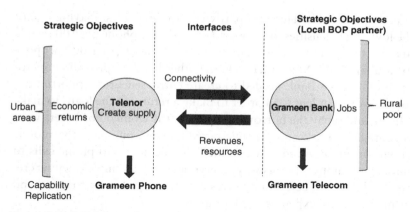

Figure 8.2 Grameen and Telenor – creating the supply chain
Source: Adapted from Seelos and Mair (2007)

not being able to pay), production and acceptability (whether consumers are willing to buy given the other demands on their resources). A social business model design has to address these market and consumer challenges, as illustrated in the case vignettes on Grameen and Telenor – in terms of creating the supply chain and Map Agro and Waste Concern – in terms of creating demand.

During the 1990s Telenor, the incumbent telecoms operator in Norway, was facing a growth challenge as a result of the saturation of its home market (Seelos and Mair, 2007). The CEO of Telenor at the time, Tormod Hermansen, received a call from the ambassador of Bangladesh in Norway to help develop the mobile phone market in Bangladesh. After some due diligence and learning more about Bangladesh, Telenor decided to partner with Grameen Bank. In 1997 the firms formalised their partnership via a joint venture by forming two separate organisations, Grameen Phone and Grameen Telecom, as shown in Figure 8.2 (Seelos and Mair, 2007). Grameen Phone was run by experienced telecoms managers from Telenor as a profit-making organisation focusing on the urban market. Grameen Telecom partnered with a Grameen microfinance initiative to create jobs for millions of poor people in over 60,000 villages across Bangladesh. Many people in rural Bangladesh did not have easy access to telephone services at that time and would often have to travel for more than eight hours, incurring the equivalent cost of over US$10 to make a phone call. This was partly due to Bangladesh having one of the lowest teledensities in the world – less than 1 phone per 100 people in the country; and even less accessibility – 1 phone per 1,000 people – in rural areas (GSMA, 2021). On the other hand, in providing micro-credit, Grameen Bank needed to create entrepreneurial opportunities for the women it lent to in order to make a return on the loans to make a living and repay the borrowings. Hence, the women borrowers were encouraged to take up the microcredit loans, purchase the mobile phones from Grameen Telecom and provide access to phone calls to rural communities. In this way, everyone gains, as employment is created and the rural community saves money by not having to travel and incur inordinate expenses to make a call.

Grameen Phone has been able to build up the middle-class community across villages in Bangladesh, becoming profitable and self-sustaining financially and having over 79 million subscribers in 2020 (Grameenphone Annual Report, 2020). Grameen Telecom focused on providing a profit-driven telecoms service to the urban community but also built up the telecoms infrastructure throughout Bangladesh, which in turn helped to reinforce the business of Grameen Phone. The positive feedback loop between Grameen Phone and Grameen Telecom helped to build the supply chain for telecoms services in Bangladesh and eventually enabled the joint ventures to become one of the largest taxpayers in the country. They did so by emphasising income-generation activities by gaining preferential access to the high-income segment in urban areas by serving the rural areas.

In the mid-1990s, the 10 million citizens of Dhaka produced over 4,500 tonnes of waste per year (IESE Insights, 2006). The city municipality could only collect and dispose of less than 40 per cent of the total solid debris generated, and much of the waste was not disposed of in a sanitary way. This left a considerable amount of uncollected rubbish, and during monsoon periods the waste contaminated the groundwater, leading to public health hazards. The city authorities had neither the budget nor the resources to address this challenge. In 1995, two entrepreneurs, Iftekhar Enayetullah and Maqsood Sinha, studied Dhaka's unacceptable conditions and set up Waste Concern (Seelos and Mair, 2007). The budding social entrepreneurs discovered that 76 per cent of the waste produced by the residential sector in Dhaka had organic content, which was suitable for transformation into compost for farmers (IESE Insights, 2006). It turns out that the soil in Bangladesh suffered

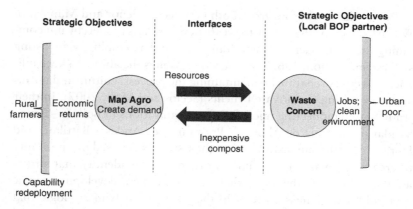

Figure 8.3 MAP Agro and Waste Concern – creating demand
Source: Adapted from Seelos and Mair (2007)

from intense chemical fertiliser use, which could reduce the crop yield in the long run despite the increased demand for agricultural produce to feed the growing population.

Waste Concern collects waste from households at a nominal charge using rickshaw vans. Despite Waste Concern initially having issues in terms of land use, it managed to obtain preferential access to land through donations made by the local government. The waste is composted in small, decentralised composting plants near residential areas. The firm uses an aerobic composting technique known as the Indonesian Windrow technique, which produces excellent compost material with little odour. Waste Concern also formed a partnership with local chemical fertiliser producer MAP Agro, which invested in a nutrient-enrichment plant in order to enrich the compost acquired from Waste Concern and used the vast distribution network of its parent group, ALPHA Agro, to sell to farmers. Waste Concern calls the business model "urban–rural symbiosis," with food transported from farmlands to urban areas and its remains constituting waste that is converted into compost for use in rural agricultural businesses – as shown in Figure 8.3. MAP Agro, in turn, is able to mark up and sell the enriched compost to farmers, which contributes to increased productivity of the farmlands. In addition, Waste Concern has also increased public awareness of the hazards of dumping waste, while valuing its organic waste, and public agencies are able to reduce landfill use.

One of the key lessons from both Grameen/Telenor and Map Agro/ Waste Concern is the ability to create new business models by not combining too many elements simultaneously and assembling via existing subsystems (Simon, 1962). The second lesson is the ability to keep alliance objectives separate by maintaining the process, culture and norms and maximising the private benefits (Seelos and Mair, 2007). In their study of two pioneering microfinance organisations in Bolivia – Banco Solidario and Caja de Ahorro y Prestamo Los Andes – Battilana and Dorado (2010) demonstrated that their success is based on the ability to create and maintain a common organisational identity that strikes a balance between the logics that they combine: a development logic that guides their mission to help the poor and a banking logic that maintains profitability and their fiduciary duty to make a financial return. In doing so, it is important for the social business to actively develop spaces for negotiation, where the tensions that naturally arise between managers with a profit objective can be discussed and the differences negotiated (Battilana et al., 2019). The hiring and socialisation policies are important in maintaining this balance between the logics. In terms of hiring, the focus on socialisation over-ability is an important driver. Socialisation allows the organisation to recruit people with no experience in either banking or development, enabling the firm to develop a culture of serving both objectives more effectively. Moreover, the compensation and promotion system was developed based on the joint objectives of approving loans targeted at the poor, as well as managing delinquent rates of these loans to ensure appropriate financial returns.

In contrast, Aspire – a British firm that employed homeless people in a door-to-door catalogue business selling fair-trade products – failed as a result of its inability to manage these competing logics effectively (Tracey and Jarvis, 2006). First, Aspire adopted the franchising model early, which created conflict among franchisees with a need to balance making a sufficient financial return and the overall social objectives. Second, the firm employed many homeless people with little work experience and often troubles of their own, which could make it more difficult for them to focus their efforts on achieving the mission. Aligning business models and organisational design for social businesses requires an understanding of two principal dimensions (Santos et al., 2015). The first dimension is the extent to which the value created automatically spills over to the relevant parties and communities compared to being contingent upon interventions. For example, the provision of microcredit to women might create employment, which is direct, but the indirect benefits in terms of the surplus spillovers could be beneficial for society in terms of better healthcare and education for families.

The second dimension is whether the clients are the same as the beneficiaries. There may be segments of the population that are unable to pay or gain access or who do not sufficiently value the benefits, which creates a dichotomy between clients and beneficiaries. On the one hand, mission drift is lowest in the case where the clients are the beneficiaries and the benefits spill over automatically. On the other hand, mission drift is highest when clients are not the beneficiaries and the benefits are contingent upon specific interventions, which might require close management of operational and impact KPIs.

In order to address some of these organisational challenges, a number of countries have developed legal structures for social businesses. For example, in the UK there are community interest companies, sociétés à mission in France, social enterprises in South Korea and benefit corporations in certain states in the United States. The legal structures are the first step, but social businesses need a change in mindset among corporate leaders, as well as creating a new norm that will evaluate the performance of firms based on financial results, and social and environmental impacts (Battilana, 2021). This will require appropriate metrics to be developed to measure the social and environmental impact, as well as the right funding opportunities for these social businesses. This also requires a change in mindset among not only corporate leaders but also investors and public authorities. And, to facilitate this change, we need to create a new norm, one that will dictate that we assess the performance of a firm based on not only its financial results but also its social and environmental impacts.

Moreover, managing social business models requires the careful management of tensions, including: performing tensions – managing the differing valuations of goals and achievements; organising tensions – managing the organisational cultures, priority-setting and resource allocation; belonging tensions – managing identity-related issues; and, finally, learning tensions – managing the tension between short-term financial and longer-term social outcomes (Smith et al., 2013). Balancing these tensions results in multiple ways in which social business models could be configured as activity systems with different configuration logics that could experience various ways of evolving over time (Tykkylainen and Ritala, 2021).

8.2 Open Innovation and Social Business Models

Open innovation is an approach to designing products and services to leverage knowledge from a variety of sources to develop and exploit innovation (Ahn et al., 2018; Chesbrough, 2003). Openness has been shown to increase the rate of innovation (Murray et al., 2016). For example, in 1988, Harvard University granted a patent for the "OncoMouse," a genetically engineered mouse. Du Pont funded research by Professor Phil Leder at Harvard Medical School and was given an exclusive licence to patent and hence control openness. Du Pont paid a fee to Harvard for the latter to disclose experimental progress, with the rights to follow-on commercial applications. In 1999, the restriction was lifted by Du Pont following pressure from the academic community. There were two effects of this openness. First, there was an increase in follow-on research (new researchers and new institutions), and, second, there was an increase in entirely new research lines (diversity of both horizontal explorations and vertical exploitation). Firms have adopted the concept of open innovation to increase the speed of product and service innovation. This is driven by increased globalisation, resulting in higher mobility of capital and labour coupled with higher technology intensity with a shorter product life cycle and complexity of R&D initiatives. These forces have led firms to innovate their business models using open innovation as a result of shifting industry borders from technology fusion across traditionally defined industry sectors. Studies have shown that there is a trade-off between the increased benefits of discovery and the costs of divergence in managing a large pool of stakeholders and the associated coordination costs (Boudreau, 2010; Laursen and Slater, 2006).

For example, in 2000 P&G set a target to source more ideas from outside the organisation as a result of the stagnation of its R&D productivity (Huston and Sakkab, 2006). A. G. Lafley, the CEO of P&G, made it a goal to source 50 per cent of innovations from outside the firm as part of its Connect and Develop (C&D) Strategy. When P&G wanted to develop Pringles potato crisps with trivia jokes printed on them, it discovered from its European network that a small bakery in

Bologna (Italy), run by a university professor, had already developed the edible ink. Ordinarily, it would have taken P&G over two years to develop such an ink, but, through the process of C&D, it was able to leverage the edible ink technology – with the Bologna bakery compensated appropriately – and develop a successful product quickly. There are two forms of open innovation: inbound open innovation; and outbound open innovation (Chesbrough, 2003). Inbound open innovation involves leveraging the discovery of others, while in outbound open innovation, an external organisation's business model might be better suited to commercialising the innovation compared to the focal firm.

The concept of open innovation has been studied extensively in relation to firms' economic performance and resilience (Ahn et al., 2018). These include, among others, GE's First Build – an open innovation platform for designers and engineers to share ideas with other members to create new home appliances; and LEGO Idea – where customers can create their own LEGO sets, which are voted upon by other users before being selected for production (Chesbrough et al., 2017). More recently, scholars and practitioners have become increasingly interested in how open innovation could be used to develop innovative business models to address society's grand challenges by leveraging the diverse set of collaborative partners (Ahn et al., 2019). For example, governments have increasingly been using open social innovation initiatives to address public needs (Mair and Gegenhuber, 2021). Governments worldwide typically have data sets that could be turned into applications to serve citizens' needs. Governments in Malaysia, India and Poland have created portals that allow data sets to be used free of charge. The city of Toronto organised a hackathon in 2015 by encouraging the public to delve into open data to fix Toronto's traffic troubles. The city governments in Denmark and Austria have created open government labs to stimulate social innovation by creating spaces for experimenting and developing propositions to address social problems via crowdsourcing ideas.

Crowdsourcing for social innovation has also led to innovative business model design (Kohler and Chesbrough, 2019), for example, Travel to Change (T2C). T2C was initially developed as an integrator platform to organise week-long volunteer trips. Creators would submit ideas, which would be voted upon; a jury would then select the travel idea to develop and a travel partner would develop the trip. The first iteration did not succeed, as it was based on volunteer trips to contribute to social change. The pivot is where participants pay for hours-long (within the day) and impactful activities. Participants can create a list of activities that they want to undertake, which is then vetted by T2C and provided by local communities via a matching process on a multi-sided platform. The participants pay for the service, which covers the cost of the T2C platform. Activities include cleaning up beaches that have marine debris or supporting the craft of growing chocolate among cocoa farmers in Hawaii.

Another example of an open innovation business model for social purposes is the OpenMRS initiative, which was used for different forms of inbound and outbound open innovation as it grew from a local to a global provider of healthcare software. The OpenMRS mission was to "Write Code, Save Lives" and it was founded by doctors. It is a free open-source software initially created to address the burdensome administrative procedures needed to handle data for treating AIDS patients in Kenya following the increased financial commitment provided by the US president's Emergency Plan for AIDS Relief and a non-profit organisation for distribution of the ART drug. OpenMRS can be adopted and modified based on open-source principles, is suitable for use in resource-poor environments and can be modified easily without programming through the addition of new data items, forms and reports.

There are four major challenges in open-innovation-based social business model development: (a) causality identification – it is often not clear what impact can be attributed to which cause; (b) attribution – it is difficult to attribute impact, as it can be diffuse, complex and contingent; and (c) evaluation timescale – premature impact measurement may result in policies that overemphasise the short-term results (Ahn et al., 2019). There are tools being developed such as Corporate Social Performance, which provides a qualitative measurement of the environment, governance and social performance of firms. Although still focused on the organisation, these frameworks will need to be developed further in light of the various case experiences in order to more comprehensively develop and measure the performance of the social business models.

8.3 Market Failures and Corrective Business Model Design

There are instances where the market is unable to serve recognised or unrecognised needs that could significantly improve the welfare of society. An example of this is the case of agricultural output. In India, two-thirds of the population is dependent on agriculture for a livelihood; however, agriculture is a risky business that is subject to price, climate, geological and biological risks (Banerjee and Bhattacharya, 2011). Moreover, many farmers have small landholdings of less than one hectare, with a growing share of small landholdings over time (Banerjee and Bhattacharya, 2011). One of the consequences of this is that farmers do not plough the full acreage of their farms in order to hedge against various risks, depending on the type of crops, resulting in severe economic hardship. The incomplete utilisation of the land implies a loss of agricultural output, and hence productivity, and the market forces do not necessarily have a mechanism to correct such challenges in resource utilisation.

Indian agriculture production and income suffer from large year-to-year fluctuations because of the variability in distribution and timeliness and variations in rainfall, prices and availability of input that are necessary for each crop (Banerjee and Bhattacharya, 2011; Rathore et al., 2011). To address these risks, the Indian government introduced various crop insurance schemes, such as the one by the General Insurance Corporation of India in 1972, which was modified and remodified as the Comprehensive Crop Insurance Scheme (CCIS) in 1985 and the Experimental Crop Insurance Scheme (ECIS) in 1997. These programmes required farmers to pay a premium, with a certain insured sum for the loans they were taking, with pay-out contingent upon risks such as adverse weather conditions, cyclones and floods. The programmes were not scalable, as they were run for specific crops in certain geographical regions. The National Agricultural Insurance Scheme (NAIS), or "Rashtriya Krishi Bima Yojna," was introduced in 1999–2000 in order to scale up the previous CCIS and ECIS programmes (The World Bank, 2012). It was taken over by the Agricultural Insurance Company of India in 2003. All of these types of crop insurance protected farmers against crop-yield fluctuations. In the case of NAIS, the farmers' premium was subsidised and aggregate claims over the farmers' premium were jointly funded by the national and state governments, respectively. Although various schemes have been tried, their success has been mixed – with low take-up due to a lack of awareness, a lack of full coverage across states, and the selection of coverage for larger farmers, among others.

New business models might be required to overcome such challenges in providing agriculture insurance schemes (Shah et. al., 2008).

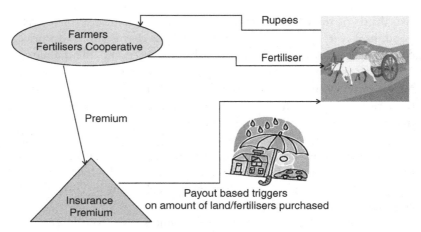

Figure 8.4 Weather risks for farmers
Source: Adapted from Shah et al. (2008)

One example of such a scheme considered ways to enhance the take-up of weather-related insurance products without increasing the cost for farmers, as illustrated in Figure 8.4. A large proportion of fertilisers is purchased via the Farmers' Fertiliser Cooperative. Farmers are automatically insured for their crops based on the amount of fertiliser purchased each season – assuming that a farmer with a larger landholding will buy greater amounts of fertiliser. The pay-out for farmers is based on certain rainfall thresholds and dependent on the fertiliser purchased. The protection of downside risk for farmers without incurring additional costs would most likely incentivise them to increase the acreage planted on their land. Part of the increased revenue received from the increased volume of fertiliser purchases by the Farmers' Fertiliser Cooperative is channelled into an insurance company as the insurance premium that is used for the pay-outs, depending on the weather outcomes. This is an innovative business model design that is, in principle, able to increase insurance coverage for all farmers purchasing fertilisers without increasing their costs, which could contribute to increased agricultural output while protecting farmers against adverse economic conditions. The success of such a venture will principally be dependent on the elasticities of increased fertiliser purchase, in addition to the actuarial risks related to the weather.

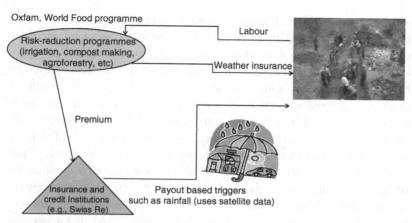

Figure 8.5 Horn of Africa Risk Transfer for Adaptation (HARITA) programme
Source: Adapted and recreated from Oxfam (2009)

A variation of such a business model innovation that aligns incentives to solve agricultural risk is through leveraging under-utilised resources. Farmers often face risks but are unable to pay the premiums for weather-related insurance policies, and climate change is driving an increase in the frequency and intensity of such weather-related risks. Oxfam, a global charitable organisation, and Swiss Re, a global reinsurance company and its partners, addressed this through a novel solution in the drought-prone northern state of Tigray in Ethiopia through improved risk reduction, risk transfer and managed risk-taking via resource management, insurance and microcredit, respectively (Oxfam, 2009). The programme was called the Horn of Africa Risk Transfer for Adaptation (HARITA), as illustrated in Figure 8.5. The farmers came up with the suggestion of using their labour time to contribute to building irrigation systems, compost-making and soil management, which contributes to a reduction of risk from the unpredictable weather. In turn, funds donated via charitable agencies such as the Rockefeller Foundation are donated to a risk-transfer company such as Swiss Re, which pays out to farmers if there is a drought and the rainfall drops below a certain predetermined threshold. Such a scheme, which has a unique business model combining a charitable and a profit-making organisation, protects farmers from having to sell productive assets and enables them to buy the seeds needed to plant the following year's crops.

Market price fluctuations constitute another risk that farmers face. For example, in India farmers often have poor access to information that could help them with cultivation, as well as selling their produce. Often, farmers have to take their produce to nearby markets that might be several miles away; sometimes markets have an oversupply, resulting in a significant reduction in market prices, and sometimes there is insufficient supply, with prices tending to increase significantly. Moreover, there are often middlemen who take advantage of the lack of market price information to take an extraordinarily high proportion of the final customer price, leaving farmers with subsistence-level incomes. In order to overcome such a challenge, in October 2007 Thomson Reuters set up Reuters Market Light (RML), a mobile-based information service for farmers (Velu and Prakash, 2010). RML provided a personalised professional information service to the farming community ($5 per quarter), including spot crop prices, localised weather forecasts, crop advisory and commodity news and information. The service was initially delivered by mobile phone subscriptions in local languages to more than 1 million farmers in over 35,000 villages, and to a selected number of states, before rolling out nationally. The advantages of RML have been significant, with benefits within five years of $2–3 billion in income for farmers, while over 50 per cent of them reduced their spending on agricultural input. This is exemplified by the following quote by a farmer on the benefits of having market prices: "Knowledge of market prices has made it easier to sell produce at good rates." And on the benefits of weather forecasts: "RML's weather forecasts have made it much easier to protect my crops. [And] RML's crop advisories are excellent. I have learnt a lot. My tomato plants are lasting longer now because I know the right fertilisers and medicines for them" (Velu and Prakash, 2010, pp. 80–81).

A related concept that fosters business model innovation is frugal innovation, which is characterised by a low-cost, flexible and inclusive approach. There are various related innovation concepts that encapsulate "do-it-yourself" improvisation, including *jugaad* innovation in the Indian context, *gambiarra* or *jeitinho* in Brazil, *kanju* in parts of Africa, *juakali* in Kenya and *jiejian chuangxin* in China (Prabhu and Jain, 2015; Radjou et al., 2012). An example of frugal innovation is the business model developed by SELCO, a rural energy service company in India (Prabhu and Jain, 2015). SELCO's mission was to provide solar lighting solutions to Indians living in rural areas who do not have access to electricity and who use kerosene lamps to light their homes. SELCO needed to make solar lamps as cheap as kerosene lamps in order to make them affordable for the rural community, so it devised an innovative business model. The company trains local people in rural villages to manage and maintain solar panels and batteries; and an arrangement is made with a bank for local people to take out a loan guaranteed by SELCO. The local person becomes an entrepreneur by setting up a shop with solar panels, which are used to charge lamps supplied by SELCO at an affordable price. The lamps are rented to local villagers at a cost per lamp that is equivalent to kerosene lamps; the villagers are therefore incentivised to rent the lamps and the local entrepreneur makes enough returns to be able to pay back the loan. In this innovative approach, SELCO, a profit-making entity, is able to deliver solar lighting to the rural community, which has the benefit of being more economical, healthy, not a fire hazard and brighter than kerosene lamps.

The concept of frugal innovation has also been adopted by large multinational firms, such as Tatas, with Tata Nano and GE's Mac 400 ECG machine. Tata Nano was a compact city car priced affordably for Indian consumers.[2] GE's Mac 400 electrocardiograph (ECG) low-cost handheld machine was developed in the Indian market to enable examinations to be carried out at the homes of patients who would otherwise have had to travel long distances to medical centres to receive treatment. The portable ECG machine first developed in India enabled GE to adopt a reverse innovation process to take the product to developed countries (Immelt et al., 2009). Frugal innovation propositions in the healthcare sector have also been shown to create value for the entire healthcare system by generating overall efficiency gains (Winterhalter et al., 2017). This is achieved by allowing basic examinations to be done outside hospitals, which frees up specialists in hospitals to focus on severe health cases, enabling the efficient distribution of scare resources in the local healthcare system.

---

[2] Tata Nano was loss-making for Tatas and was closed for production in 2018. There are various analyses for why Tata Nano did not take off, among them technical faults and being less than comfortable. In addition, prospective Indian consumers did not want to be seen to acquire the "cheapest" car, which denotes a lowly status. Instead, Tata Nano was seen to have niche appeal among the wealthy, being seen as cute and funky (*The Wire*, 2018).

8.4 Discussion

Organisations that work with the world's poor need to measure their success to ensure that they provide the feel-good factor that is needed to continue to drive the success of their initiatives (London, 2009). VisionSpring provides a case vignette for how to measure the success of these social development initiatives. VisionSpring sells reading glasses through a microfranchising programme, hiring poor people, training them to become vision entrepreneurs and providing them with a business in a backpack, which contains reading glasses. The vision entrepreneur goes to a village and sets up "camp" for three days in order to test the eyesight of the villagers. Many of the villagers are tailors, mechanics and artisans, meaning clear sight is needed to continue their livelihoods and support their families. The mission of VisionSpring is to provide vision to these villagers in order to reduce poverty through the sale of affordable glasses. Its success can be measured broadly in three main areas: changes in economics; changes in capabilities; and changes in relationships across the key stakeholders such as sellers, buyers and communities.

For example, for sellers, measures of success include increased income to be able to support their families, which in turn might improve communication skills and an improved role in the family, as there will be less financial stress. For buyers, it could contribute to increased productivity from their jobs, improved contentment due to better vision and, finally, a better professional reputation. Finally, from a community perspective, there could be increased interest from other businesses due to the improved productivity of the artisans, in addition to the high aspirations of the women in the community, which could lead to greater gender equality. Therefore, tracking such performance indicators must cover both quantitative and qualitative indicators to be able to share the positive results and hence motivate the immediate stakeholders and the wider community.

Studies have also highlighted the stance taken by both managers and scholars to address the challenging aspects of designing business models for social and economic development. The book *Fortune at the Bottom of the Pyramid* (BOP)[3] by C. K. Prahalad highlighted that large multinational companies should not view people who live on

---

[3] Also known as the base of the pyramid.

less than $2 a day as marginal to the process of globalisation, rather embracing them as resilient entrepreneurs and value-conscious customers (Prahalad, 2006). Gupta (2020) provides a reasoned critique of such a view of the reification of consumers at the bottom of the pyramid as having "entrepreneurial" traits that need to be harnessed for the betterment of society given the right incentives. Such a view might overly attribute the locus of social problems such as poverty and joblessness to individuals themselves, as opposed to institutional, social, political and economic dysfunctions; hence, unwittingly it might desensitise poverty and normalise economic upheavals and life at the BOP. This, in turn, might limit the field of possible actions that can be initiated by the vulnerable people at the bottom of the pyramid. Therefore, it is important for managers to think reflexively when designing social business models about the implications of the power balance between partners in order to ensure that there is a fair outcome for society as a whole.

Studies have highlighted the need to examine business models that might cause oppression (human stakeholders) or depletion (non-human stakeholders) exclusion in certain communities (Marti, 2018). For example, new business models able to respond appropriately to a scarcity of minerals and metals with complex business models might not fully appreciate how they translate into practices of child labour, low salaries or hazardous working conditions at the end of the complex supply chain. Moreover, some microfinance initiatives might exclude certain strata of society based on gender and other communal strictures and practices, which reinforces some of the deprivation that the programme set out to address. To address these concerns, business models designed to address the grand challenges[4] of society need to have four elements: participatory forms of architecture – whereby there are structures and rules to enable diverse and heterogeneous actors to interact constructively; multivocal inscription – capturing the need to combine all opposing perspectives to get a better idea of the main problems; scaffolding – unlocking entrenched social norms and building alternative social orders; and proximity – building the ethics of care and concern for others as neighbours in a moral sense (Marti, 2018).

---

[4] Grand challenges are complex problems with significant implications and no clearly defined solutions (Ferraro et al., 2015).

Scholars have also highlighted that BOP initiatives need to focus on capability development and social capital-building as part of poverty alleviation and the role of business in empowering communities (Ansari et al., 2012). The focus of the traditional welfare approaches of choice and desire fulfilment might be inadequate (Putnam, 1995; Sen, 1985). For example, Hindustan Unilever's "Fair and Lovely" skin-whitening face cream, a profitable brand, may have reinforced beauty stereotyping in India based on the premium placed on fair skin compared to dark skin. In this context, business models targeting the BOP need to be evaluated on the basis of how well they advance capability transfer, diffusion and retention by preserving and enhancing social capital within the community, as well as other resource-rich networks.[5]

Conclusion

Market solutions and government interventions alone are inadequate to solve major global issues such as healthcare, poverty, education and general well-being (George et al., 2012); and such problems are more complex in countries with limited resources. A major part of addressing these challenges is the need to design innovative business models to build markets where there could be institutional voids, whereby certain institutions that typically provide the legal structure and set the rules of exchange might not exist (Khanna et al., 2010). In addition, these markets could display a lack of knowledge from both the supply and demand perspectives (Seelos and Mair, 2007). Business models need to be interactive by functioning with, and within, the ecosystem in order to help develop the resources and institutions by working with partners and even competitors (Howell et al., 2018).

The Trans-African Hydro-Meteorological Observatory (TAHMO) illustrates the importance of designing business models by developing markets to overcome institutional voids and working with an ecosystem of partners (Howell et al., 2018; Van de Giesen et al., 2014). TAHMO stepped in to provide a public good, as the governments in Africa were cutting down on their provision of reliable weather

---

[5] These include structural social capital – the ties and network configuration of the society, relational social capital – pertaining to trust and the type of relationship; and cognitive social capital – covering shared language, identities, beliefs and norms (Ansari et al., 2012).

data, which is crucial for the productivity of farmers in Africa, having over 65 per cent of the world's arable land (African Development Bank, 2016). TAHMO was started by Delft University of Technology and Oregon State University in order to improve the poor weather-monitoring practices on the African continent through the deployment of low-cost, simple and robust ground-weather stations. TAHMO uses high-technology sensors through frugal engineering to monitor weather using ground stations. Ground stations use solar panels and mobile networks and have integrated sensors that measure rainfall, shortwave radiation, wind speed, wind direction, barometric pressure, air temperature and relative humidity; they have no moving parts and are low maintenance.

Formally, TAHMO is a registered international NGO but it adopts a commercial approach to the diffusion of weather stations by combining education for schools with the sale of data to different service providers across various African countries. The weather data from the local stations needed to be enhanced with specific niche requirements and hence needed different ecosystems of partners. TAHMO started with a "buy-one, pay-two" programme, whereby schools in a developed country pay for the cost of two schools, with the second school located in Africa, which hosts the ground station. The programme allows schools to enrich their curriculum with lessons about the environment, weather, electronics and computer science. For example, the data collected by the ground stations is then sold to an IT start-up in Rwanda that provides simple SMS-based weather-prediction information to small farmers. In East Africa the data is sold to Acre, a micro crop insurance company that uses more accurate weather data to reduce the premiums on weather insurance for farmers. The weather data typically allows the insurance of crops with a value that is multiple times the cost of the station. TAHMO aims to resolve the major issue of a lack of weather forecasting for farmers in Africa to manage climate mitigation and adaptation. However, the distribution of data requires access to the Internet, which not all farmers have. This could promote less inclusion, which is a major problem that needs to be addressed.

There are a number of areas for further investigation of business model innovation for socio-economic development, with the first being how frugal innovation business models for socio-economic development could affect the mental models of the population. For example, there have been claims that the low-cost and low-resource nature of *jugaad* innovation, which focuses on improvisation, might instil a mental model of "making do" (Nelson, 2018). However, the case of TAHMO shows that frugal innovation can be based on the most advanced technology coupled with innovative business models. The second area is how business models developed for socio-economic development might create inequality as a result of exclusion. The additional complication for socio-economic business models needs to factor in the lack of knowledge and resources, which could have unintended negative consequences or even reinforce certain cultural norms and practices, thereby worsening the existing socio-economic development issues. Hence, entrepreneurs and established firms need to recognise these issues when designing and managing business models for socio-economic development purposes. The third issue is how better to manage the tension between the business and social objectives in start-ups compared to established firms. What are the leadership and organisational issues to enable such paradoxes to be managed efficiently? Are the mechanisms different or similar among start-ups and established firms? Is there a basis for theorising the management of the paradoxes as a duality in such a way as to enhance the value creation and value capture from such socio-economic business models?

This chapter has provided an overview of the opportunities and challenges of addressing socio-economic development issues such as healthcare, education and poverty through business model innovation. These issues need to be addressed to ensure an inclusive growth agenda for the world to maintain economic growth and well-being within a peaceful environment. We propose a number of key research issues on this topic.

References

African Development Bank. (2016). Retrieved from: www.afdb.org/en/news-and-events/world-food-day-adapting-africas-agriculture-to-the-exigencies-of-climate-change-16218 (accessed 6 March 2022).

Ahn, J. M., Mortara, L., and Minshall, T. (2018). Dynamic Capabilities and Economic Crises: Has Openness Enhanced a Firm's Performance in an Economic Downturn? *Industrial and Corporate Change* 27: 49–63.

Ahn, J. M., Roijakkers, N., Fini, R., and Mortara, L. (2019). Leveraging Open Innovation to Improve Society: Past Achievements and Future Trajectories. *R&D Management* 49(3): 267–278.

Ansari, S., Munir, K., and Gregg, T. (2012). Impact at the "Bottom of the Pyramid": The Role of Social Capital in Capability Development and Community Empowerment. *Journal of Management Studies* 49(4): 813–842.

Aravind Eye Care System. (2011). Northeastern University, Boston, USA. www.northeastern.edu/sei/2011/10/aravind-eye-care-system-case/ (accessed 20 January 2022).

Banerjee, D. and Bhattacharya, U. (2011). Innovations in Agricultural Insurance in India: Retrospect and Prospect. *Indian Journal of Agricultural Economics* 66(3): 457–471.

Battilana, J. (2021). For Social Business to Become the Norm, We Need to Build a Social Business Infrastructure. *Stanford Social Innovation Review*, May 19. https://doi.org/10.48558/DDR9-1169

Battilana, J. and Dorado, S. (2010). Building Sustainable Hybrid Organizations: The Case of Commercial Microfinance Organizations. *Academy of Management Journal* 53(6): 1419–1440.

Battilana, J., Pache, A-C., Sengul, M., and Kimsey, M. (2019). The Dual-Purpose Playbook. *Harvard Business Review* 97(4): 124–133.

Boudreau, K. (2010). Open Platform Strategies and Innovation: Granting Access vs Devolving Control. *Management Science* 56(10): 1849–1872.

Chesbrough, H. W. (2003). *Open Innovation: The New Imperative for Creating and Profiting from Technology*. Boston, MA: Harvard Business Press.

Chesbrough, H. Vanhaverbeke, W., and West, J. (2017). *New Frontiers in Open Innovation*. Oxford: Oxford University Press.

Danone. (2012). Sustainability Report: Strategy and Performance, pp. 1–175.

Danone Communities. (2020). Grameen Danone, Fighting against Malnutrition in Bangladesh. Danone. www.danone.com/integrated-annual-reports/integrated-annual-report-2019/sustainable-projects/danone-communities-grameen.html (accessed 28 January 2022).

Emerging Market Daily News. (2006). Danone Launches Innovative JV in Bangladesh, pp. 1–2.

Ferraro, F., Etzion, D., and Gehman, J. (2015). Tackling Grand Challenges Pragmatically: Robust Action Revisited. *Organization Studies* 36(3): 363–390.

George, G., McGahan, A. M., and Prabhu, J. (2012). Innovation for Inclusive Growth: Towards a Theoretical Framework and a Research Agenda. *Journal of Management Studies* 49(4): 661–683.

Grameenphone Annual Report. (2020). Connecting Possibilities.

GSMA. (2021). Country Overview: Bangladesh: Mobile Industry Driving Growth and Enabling Digital Inclusion, London.

Gupta, S. (2020). Understanding the Feasibility and Value of Grassroots Innovation. *Journal of the Academy of Marketing Science* 48: 941–965.

Howell, R., van Beers, C., and Doorn, N. (2018). Value Capture and Value Creation: The Role of Information Technology in Business Models for Frugal Innovations in Africa. *Technological Forecasting & Social Change* 131: 227–239.

Huston, L. and Sakkab, N. (2006). P&G's New Innovation Model. An Excerpt from Connect and Develop: Inside Procter & Gamble's New Model for Innovation. *Harvard Business Review* 84(3): 58–66.

IESE Insights. (2006). The Value of Organic Waste. https://ieseinsight.com/doc.aspx?id=565&ar=17 (accessed 4 February 2022).

Immelt, J. R., Govindarajan, V., and Trimble, C. (2009). How GE Is Disrupting Itself. *Harvard Business Review* 87(October): 3–10.

Khanna, T., Palepu, K. G., and Bullock, R. (2010). *Winning in Emerging Markets: A Road Map for Strategy and Execution.* Boston: Harvard Business Press.

Kohler, T. and Chesbrough, H. (2019). From Collaborative Community to Competitive Market: The Quest to Build a Crowdsourcing Platform for Social Innovation. *R&D Management* 49(3): 356–368.

Laursen, K. and Salter, A. (2006). Open for Innovation: The Role of Openness in Explaining Innovation Performance among U.K. Manufacturing Firms. *Strategic Management Journal* 27: 131–150.

London, T. (2009). Making Better Investments at the Base of the Pyramid. *Harvard Business Review*, May: 106–113.

Mair, J. and Gegenhuber, T. (2021). Open Social Innovation. *Stanford Social Innovation Review* Fall: 26–33.

Marti, I. (2018). Transformational Business Models, Grand Challenges, and Social Impact. *Journal of Business Ethics* 152: 965–976.

Murray, F., Aghion, P., Dewatripont, M., Kolev, J., and Stern, S. (2016). Of Mice and Academics: Examining the Effect of Openness on Innovation. *American Economic Journal: Economic Policy* 8(1): 212–252.

Nelson, D. (2018). *Jugaad Yatra: Exploring the Indian Art of Problem Solving.* New Delhi: Aleph.

Oxfam. (2009). Horn of Africa Risk Transfer for Adaptation (HARITA) Project Brief, August 2009. Project Brief, *Oxfam America.*

Prabhu, J. and Jain, S. (2015). Innovation and Entrepreneurship in India: Understanding jugaad. *Asia Pacific Journal of Management* 32: 843–868.

Prahalad, C. K. (2006). *The Fortune at the Bottom of the Pyramid, Eradicating Poverty Through Profits.* Upper Saddle River, NJ: Wharton School Publishing.

Putnam, R. (1995). Bowling alone: America's declining social capital. *Journal of Democracy* 6: 65–78.

Radjou, N., Prabhu, J., and Ahuja, S. (2012). *Jugaad Innovation: Think Frugal, be Flexible, Generate Breakthrough Growth*. San Francisco: Jossey Bass.

Raith, M. G. and Siebold, N. (2018). Building Business Models Around Sustainable Development Goals. *Journal of Business Models* 6(2): 71–77.

Rangan, V. K. (2009). *Write Code, Save Lives: How a Community Uses Open Innovation to Address a Societal Challenge*. Harvard Business School 593–098: 1–20.

Rathore, V. S., Burark, S. S., and Jain, H. K. (2011). Performance of Crop Insurance Scheme in Udaipur District of Rajasthan. *Agricultural Economics Research Review* 24: 25–35.

Santos, F., Pache, A-C., and Birkholz, C. (2015). Making Hybrids Work: Aligning Business Models and Organizational Design for Social Enterprises. *California Management Review* 57(3): 36–58.

Seelos, C. and Mair, J. (2007). Profitable Business Models and Market Creation in the Context of Deep Poverty: A Strategic View. *Academy of Management Perspectives* 21(4): 49–63.

Sen, A. (1985). Wellbeing, Agency and Freedom: The Dewey Lectures 1984. *Journal of Philosophy* 82: 169–221.

Shah, H., Pan, T.C., Li, B. and Wagh, S.S. (2008). Micro Insurance for Natural Disasters: Concepts, Present and Future Outlook, The 14th World Conference on Earthquake Engineering October 12–17, Beijing, China

Simon. H. (1962). The Architecture of Complexity. *Proceedings of the American Philosophical Society* 106(6): 467–82.

Smith, W. K., Gonin, M., and Besharov, M. L. (2013). Managing Social-Business Tensions: A Review and Research Agenda for Social Enterprise. *Business Ethics Quarterly* 23(3): 407–442.

The Wire. (2018). Tata Nano – Why Did the People Not Want the People's Car? https://thewire.in/business/tata-nano-why-did-the-people-not-want-the-peoples-car (accessed 3 March 2022).

The World Bank. (2012). National Agricultural Insurance Scheme in India (2012).

Tracey, P. and Jarvis, O. (2006). An Enterprising Failure Why a Promising Social Franchise Collapsed. *Stanford Social Innovation Review* 2006 (Spring): 66–70.

Tykkylainen, S. and Ritala, P. (2021). Business Model Innovation in Social Enterprises: An Activity System Perspective. *Journal of Business Research* 125: 684–697.

United Nations. (2020). The Sustainable Development Goals Report, pp. 1–64.

Van de Giesen, N., Hut, R., and Selker, J. (2014). The Trans-African Hydro-Meteorological Observatory (TAHMO). *WIREs Water* 1: 341–348.

Velu, C. and Prakash, S. (2010). Reuters Market Light: Business Model Innovation for Growth. *Effective Executive* 13(2): 78–83.

Winterhalter, S., Zeschky, M. B., Neumann, L., and Gassmann, O. (2017). Business Models for Frugal Innovation in Emerging Markets: The Case of the Medical Device and Laboratory Equipment Industry. *Technovation* 66–67: 3–13.

Yunus, M., Moingeon, B., and Lehmann-Ortega, L. (2010). Building Social Business Models: Lessons from the Grameen Experience. *Long Range Planning* 43: 308–325.

9 | Conduct Risk and Business Models

It is better to be roughly right than precisely wrong.

John Maynard Keynes

Introduction

The global financial crisis (GFC) of 2008 had a significant impact on the operation of both financial and other markets around the world (Bernanke et al., 2019). The collapse of Lehman Brothers on 15 September 2008 sent shock waves around the world, resulting in a significant decline in the stock markets globally. The GFC was extremely detrimental to borrowers, investors and other stakeholders, including the freezing of financial markets through misinformation and conflicts of interest (Meeks and Velu, 2018).[1] One of the major developments following the crisis has been the focus on the notion of conduct risk, which is broadly defined as any action of a regulated firm or individual that leads to customer detriment or which has an adverse effect on market stability or effective competition (FCA Handbook, 2021). Customer detriment occurs when customers are damaged or harmed, financially or non-financially. It is important to emphasise that non-financial detriment includes psychological effects, including distress and inconvenience, and that customers need not necessarily be aware that they have suffered detriment. The UK regulatory authority, the Financial Conduct Authority (FCA), were the pioneers in developing the framework for regulating conduct risk (*Financial Times*, 2012).

Conduct risk can be seen as different to the conventional risk that financial services firm usually manage, such as market risk, credit risk

---

[1] This chapter is based on research and executive education courses on conduct risk delivered together with Professor Geoff Meeks to some of the major global financial institutions. I would like to express my grateful thanks to Professor Meeks for sharing his wealth of knowledge and insights on this topic.

and operational risk, which are internally focused and have an immediate effect on the profits of the bank from a failure to manage them
well. Conduct risk, unlike the other types, relates to the external risk
to protect consumers, financial markets and competition. Conduct risk
arises as a result of information asymmetry and conflicts of interest;
hence, it has significant implications for the design of business models
(Meeks and Velu, 2018). This chapter provides an overview of how
information asymmetry and conflicts of interest arose in the subprime
mortgage supply chain. We then look at the business model design of
the major investment banks and other firms within the supply chain
in order to examine the business model design underpinning some of
the conduct-related issues. We draw lessons from other industries in
order to overcome such conflicts of interest with a view to designing
appropriate business models. The next section reviews the subprime
mortgage market and goes on to discuss how conflicts of interest arose
from the design of business models. The subsequent section discusses
the implications for business model design to manage conduct risk
before the chapter concludes.

9.1 Subprime Mortgage Supply Chain

Financial institutions play an important part in the intermediation
between borrowers and savers of funds by managing the appropriate
transformation of the various risks, such as liquidity, market prices
and credit, among others. In doing so, they provide an important service to the economy in order to ensure the appropriate returns to savings and to fund economic growth and development. However, the
very act of financial intermediation could contribute to information
asymmetry and conflicts of interest. Information asymmetry arises
when information is distorted or withheld by the bank from the client
and/or the market; and conflicts of interest arise as a result of the interests of the bank and employees – or the bank and clients – being in
conflict (Meeks and Velu, 2018). Let us examine the subprime mortgage supply chain to see how such information asymmetry and conflicts of interest might arise.

Let us assume that Betty wants to buy a house and does not have
enough savings to do so. Lucy, on the other hand, has funds to save
and wants a good return on her savings. Lucy could lend directly to
Betty but would not want to do so, as this would expose Lucy to the

risk of default by Betty. Hence, the banks and other related financial institutions act as intermediaries in order to transform such direct
lending risks. In 2001 the George Bush administration pushed hard
to expand home ownership, especially among minority groups in the
United States. This quote from President George Bush in 2002 encapsulates this policy (*New York Times*, 2008):

We can put light where there's darkness, and hope where there's despon-
dency in this country. And part of it is working together as a nation to
encourage folks to own their own home.

Almost every case of detriment actually begins with good intentions –
a product or service designed to benefit the customer. However, in
the process of intermediation, various information asymmetries and
conflicts of interest cause detriment to customers and markets.

Returning to our case, Betty embraces the Bush administration's
policy of home ownership and borrows money from New Century, a
major mortgage provider in the United States. New Century originates
Betty's mortgage and bundles it with some 5,000 others. Citigroup
buys the bundle of mortgages and issues securities backed by the
mortgages, called mortgage-backed securities (MBS). Citigroup asks
Moody's, the credit rating agency, to rate the mortgages. Strategos, an
investment advisory firm in the real-estate securities market, then buys
a portion of a lower-rated tranche of Citigroup securities, bundles
them with similar tranches of low-rated MBS and funds the collateralised debt obligations (CDOs) with bonds. Strategos similarly asks
Moody's to rate these CDO securities. Lucy then buys some of the
CDOs as an investment vehicle for her savings in order to get a healthy
return. In doing so, Lucy has, through the intermediation enabled by
the mortgage supply chain, indirectly lent her savings to Betty to buy a
house. The mortgage value chain is summarised in Figure 9.1.

The mortgage originators had developed a product called option
adjustable-rate mortgages (option ARMs), where borrowers had
a reduced interest rate to pay in the initial years, which made them
affordable, and were then charged above the average rate thereaf-
ter. In fact, borrowers could choose how much to pay each month
as part of the "Pick a Pay" scheme. Any shortfall was added to the
principal through a negative amortisation scheme. The option ARM
was a widely used product among mortgage originators such as New
Century, Washington Mutual and other firms in the United States

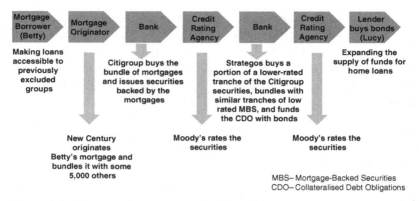

Figure 9.1 Subprime mortgage supply chain
Source: Adapted and recreated from FCIC Report (2011)

ahead of the crisis in subprime mortgages. When the low initial interest rates increased, borrowers could: (1) refinance with another initial
rate mortgage; (2) sell their homes and repay their mortgage; or (3)
default – and the lender would sell the house to recoup the lending.
The mortgage originators earned substantial origination fees, which
were often added to the principal being borrowed. In addition, there
were substantial interest rate margins once the teaser period had
elapsed. Finally, there were capital gains if the home was repossessed
and sold at a profit in a rising market. Hence, the mortgage originators
provided substantial incentives for sales staff to sell option ARMs, as
they were very profitable. For example, Countrywide option ARMs
retained on the balance sheet grew from $5 billion in 2004 to $26
billion in 2005 and $33 billion in 2006. The CEO of Countrywide,
Angelo Mozilo, said (Financial Crisis Inquiry Commission (FCIC)
Report, 2011, p. 105):

Countrywide was one of the greatest companies in the history of this country and probably made more difference to society, to the integrity of our
society, than any company in the history of America.

The mortgage originators, in turn, had an incentive to sell these mortgages to banks such as Citibank to free up their balance sheets to
obtain new funds in order to originate even more mortgages.

Credit-rating agencies, such as Moody's, played a role in enabling
this securitisation of mortgages to take place across the mortgage

supply chain. The central role of the rating agencies was to mitigate information asymmetry. Banks, in turn, needed their ratings to determine what amount of capital to hold, as BBB-rated securities required five times as much capital as AAA- and AA-rated securities. Many investors relied on these credit ratings because they had neither access to the same data nor the capacity and analytical ability to assess the securities they were purchasing (Financial Crisis Inquiry Commission (FCIC) Report, 2011, pp. 118–122). The lower-rated mortgage-backed securities were more difficult to sell given the restrictions placed on some institutional investors, such as pension funds, to hold only A-rated securities and above.

Collateralised debt obligations (CDOs) are structured financial instruments that pool these lower-rated mortgage-backed securities. The CDO manager buys lower-rated mortgage-backed securities and bundles them together to get diversification benefits. CDO securities were sold in tranches, with risk-tolerant investors securing a higher yield but taking the first hit should the underlying investments perform badly, with the risk-averse investors getting a lower yield but taking the last hit. These CDOs were then rated again by Moody's. For example, 88 per cent of one of the CDOs, Kleros III bonds, were being AAA-rated when they were composed of mortgage-related securities, of which 45 per cent were rated as BBB or lower and 16 per cent as A. Moody's reasoned that pooling many BBB-rated mortgage-backed securities would lead to additional diversification benefits: if one security went bad, the second had only a very small chance of going bad at the same time. Only those investors at the bottom would lose money (and were compensated by a higher yield). It was reasoned that there would be few defaults at any one time. Moody's model "had put little weight on the possibility that prices would fall nationwide." "Even as housing prices rose to unprecedented levels, Moody's never adjusted the scenarios to put greater weight on the possibility of a decline." "Moody's position was that there was not a … national housing bubble" (FCIC Report, 2011, pp. 120–121). This was because, in the preceding 50 years, there had never been an instance where all parts of the United States had exhibited a fall in house prices simultaneously. Moody's model and data were based on this assumption and did not factor in the possibility of falling house prices simultaneously across the United States, which is what happened during the global financial crisis. Of all mortgage-backed securities that it had rated triple A in

2006, Moody's (subsequently in the crash) downgraded 73 per cent to junk (FCIC Report, 2011, p. 122).

Moody's income was driven by rating MBS. The fee for rating MBS was as much as three times the fee for rating corporate bonds; half of Moody's ratings income in 2007 came from rating MBS. Hence, it was conflicted in its business model by relying heavily on the income being paid by the issuers of the securities. The investment banks threatened to withdraw their business if they did not get their desired rating. This was encapsulated in a comment from Gary Witt, Moody's former team managing director covering US derivatives (FCIC Report, 2011, p. 210):

Oh God, are you kidding? All the time. I mean that's routine. I mean they would threaten you all of the time.... It's like, "Well, next time, we're just going to go with Fitch and S&P."

Richard Malek, former Moody's vice president and senior credit officer, said (FCIC Report, 2011, p. 210):

The threat of losing business to a competitor, even if not realised, absolutely tilted the balance away from an independent arbiter of risk towards a captive facilitator of risk transfer.

Moreover, there was evidence that the investment banks were selling securities to investors as agents and trading in them as principals, as noted in the quote below from Senator Carl Lewin questioning the CEO of Goldman Sachs, Lloyd Blankfein (Louis and Zinkin, 2019, p. 30):

Goldman was selling securities to people and not telling them that they were taking and intending to maintain a short position against those same securities.

There was evidence that the conflict of interest was showing up among some of the more sophisticated clients in Bear Sterns' Structured Credit Fund, which made good returns when the credit market was booming between 2004 and 2006. However, in early 2007 the sub-prime mortgage market started to turn down and the price of mortgage securities began to decline. Investors were demanding their money back as the value of the funds started to decline rapidly. Employees of Bear Sterns tried to soothe them by saying that the funds offered an "...awesome opportunity..." and that "...we're very comfortable with where we are...." However, in private emails to colleagues, they expressed their concerns: "...I'm fearful of these markets..." and "...It's either a meltdown or the greatest buying opportunity ever. I'm leaning more towards the former..." (Mintz, 2008). The next section seeks to better understand how information asymmetry and the design of the business model resulted in such conflicts of interest and hence contributed to the increase in conduct risk, with the consequence of being detrimental to clients and markets, respectively.

9.2 Business Models and Conflicts of Interest

In a written testimony dated 7 December 2011 by Professor Arthur E. Wilmarth Jr (Professor of Law, George Washington University Law School, Washington, DC) to the Subcommittee on Financial Institutions and Consumer Protection on Banking, Housing and Urban Affairs, United States Senate, the professor said:

The financial crisis has also proven, beyond any reasonable doubt, that large financial conglomerates operate based on a hazardous business model that is riddled with conflicts of interest and prone to speculative risk-taking.

Financial conglomerates have never demonstrated that they can provide beneficial services to their customers and attractive returns to their investors without relying on safety net subsidies during good times and massive taxpayer-funded bailouts during crises. It is long past time for LCFIs (Large, Complex Financial Institutions) to prove – based on a true market test – that their claimed synergies and their supposedly superior business models are real and not mythical.

Arguably, there is some merit in Professor Wilmarth's statement about the business models among the LCFIs, as there could be a tendency to take excessive risks during good times if firms believe that they will be bailed out using taxpayers' money during less sanguine times. This is what economists term the moral hazard problem, whereby firms might lack the incentive to guard against risk when they are effectively protected from its consequences by a form of government insurance (Pauly, 1968). In order to examine this phenomenon, it is worth exploring in more depth the failure of Lehman Brothers and the other associated firms during the global financial crisis.

The excerpts from Management's Discussion and Analysis of Financial Condition and Results of Operations from the *2007 Annual*

Table 9.1 *Income statement of Lehman Brothers*

Lehman Brothers Income statement			
in US$ million	2005	2006	2007
Net revenues	14,630	17,583	19,527
Net income	3,260	4,007	4,192

Source: Annual Reports of Lehman Brothers

Report of Lehman Brothers, which was the last report before the Chapter 11 bankruptcy protection, mentions:

On the basis of a record first half and a reasonably successful navigation of difficult market conditions in the second half, we achieved our fourth consecutive year of record net revenues, net income and diluted earnings per common share in 2007.

The statement in the Management Discussion appears to be consistent with the results reported by Lehman Brothers, as shown in Table 9.1.

In addition, the *Auditor's Report* by Ernst & Young LLP from the *2007 Annual Report* stated:

We also have audited, in accordance with the standards of the Public Company Accounting Oversight Board (United States), the consolidated statement of financial condition of the Company as of November 30, 2007 and 2006, and the related consolidated statements of income, changes in stockholders' equity, and cash flows for each of the three years in the period ended November 30, 2007 of the Company and our report dated January 28, 2008 expressed an unqualified opinion thereon.

The auditors, Ernst & Young, had provided an unqualified opinion on the last financial statement of Lehman Brothers, implying that the figures showed a true and fair view of the business performance of Lehman Brothers and that there were no material misstatements. It is therefore puzzling that Lehman Brothers collapsed a few months after such a positive financial performance. To explore this, let us get a better understanding of its business model. There was a significant shift in the business model of Lehman Brothers before the GFC from acting as an agent to becoming a principal. This is encapsulated in the statement below (FCIC Report, 2011, p. 177):

Then, in its March 2006 "Global Strategy Offsite," CEO Richard Fuld and other executives explained to their colleagues a new move toward an

Table 9.2 *Balance sheet of Lehman Brothers*

Lehman Brothers Balance sheet			
in US$ billion	2005	2006	2007
Assets	410	503	691
(*of which Financial instrument other inventory position owned*)	177	227	313
Liabilities and Equity			
ST Debt	339	403	546
LT Debt	54	81	123
Total Debit	393	403	669
Shareholders' equity	17	19	22
Total Liab & SE	410	503	691
Debt/equity	23.1	25.5	30.4

Source: Annual Reports of Lehman Brothers

aggressive growth strategy, including greater risk and more leverage. They described the change as a shift from a "moving" or securitization business to a "storage" business, in which Lehman would make and hold longer-term investments.

In order to see the implications of this shift in strategy, and hence business model, we need to examine closely the balance sheet of the firm, which is shown in Table 9.2.

The balance sheet shows that Lehman Brothers was increasingly holding assets for its own position – as the principal – as opposed to being a broker, namely, as an agent. This was a deliberate strategy, as noted above in the shift from a "moving" to a "storage" business. In order to better understand the difference, it might be worth examining an analogy in the real-estate market. Imagine Ann wants to buy a house similar to the one that Tom lives in. Incidentally, Tom wants to sell his house in the process of moving to a larger one to accommodate his growing family. Typically, Ann might not know that Tom wants to sell his house and approaches a real-estate agent to indicate her preference for the type of house she is looking for. Equally, Tom does not know that Ann is looking to buy a house similar to the one he lives in and approaches the real-estate agent to put his house up for sale on the market. The real-estate agent advertises that Tom's house is up for sale. Ann approaches the real-estate agent to view the property, happens to like the property and agrees to buy the house. The agent then matches the buyer, Ann, with the seller, Tom, and makes a commission from the sale of the house, charging the buyer, the seller, or both, depending on the practice in each country.

Let us assume that the real-estate agent observes that the price of houses is generally going up. Moreover, it is often the case as the business grows that the real-estate agent might not be able to find a buyer immediately when a seller wants to sell their house. Hence, the estate agent reasons that it might not be a bad idea to buy the house from the seller and hold it on its own books, selling it when a buyer comes along sometime in the future. In this way, the estate agent makes a return twice, first on the commission and second on the difference between the buying and selling price of the house as the prices rise. However, the estate agent does not have the funds to buy the house and borrows from the bank to do so, in the process leveraging themselves up. The real-estate agent has effectively transformed its business model from agent to principal, investing in houses and hoping to make a handsome return. The new business model works as long as house prices continue to increase. However, when house prices start to tumble, the estate agent makes a loss from its inventory of houses, which might not be easy to dispose of; hence, the agent might get into a liquidity crisis with the bank by breaking the terms of the loan covenant. This could result in the bankruptcy of the estate agent.

This is essentially what happened to Lehman Brothers. Table 9.2 shows us that Lehman Brothers increased the assets held on its own account as inventory from US$177 billion in 2005 to US$313 billion in 2007, an increase of US$136 billion. There was a large holding of MBS and CDOs. Much of this increase was funded with short-term loans, which increased by US$207 billion in the same period, from US$339 billion in 2005 to US$546 billion in 2007. These short-term funds were often borrowed from the inter-bank market for periods of up to one day. As a result, Lehman Brothers' leverage ratio, indicated by the debt-to-equity ratio, increased from 23.1 to 30.4 between 2005 and 2007, respectively. The highly leveraged position was partly responsible for the stellar performance of Lehman Brothers for the few years preceding its bankruptcy. However, when the housing market started to decline, with the corresponding value of securities, including declines in the value of MBS and CDOs, Lehman Brothers were caught holding these declining assets, which could not be sold easily.

Banks such as JP Morgan, which had lent the short-term funds to Lehman Brothers, called in their loans one Friday afternoon, on 12 September 2008, which left Lehman in a liquidity crisis and having to file for Chapter 11 bankruptcy on Monday 15 September 2008.

The change in the business model of Lehman Brothers, which was riddled with conduct risk and caused significant detriment to customers and markets, was exacerbated by a number of practices. First, there was an opportunity to arbitrage the capital requirements, as noted in the *FCIC Report* (2011, p. 100):

Banks could reduce the capital they were required to hold for a pool of mortgages simply by securitizing them, rather than holding them on their books as whole loans. If a bank kept $100 in mortgages on its books, it might have to set aside about $5, including $4 in capital against unexpected losses and $1 in reserves against expected losses. But if the bank created a $100 mortgage-backed security, sold that security in tranches, and then bought all the tranches, the capital requirement would be about $4.10.

Second, Lehman Brothers understated its leverage at the end of each reporting season by merely selling and repurchasing the securities held in order to temporarily remove assets from its balance sheet under an accounting gimmick called "Repo 105" (FCIC Report, 2011, p. 177). Third, Lehman Brothers relied on credit default swaps, which were a type of insurance contract meant to pay out in the case of default. These credit default swaps were sold by an insurance company, AIG, which had to be bailed out by the US government. It turns out that AIG's business model was also based on unsound foundations, as noted below (FCIC Report, 2011, p. 140), namely, leveraging the parent's strong credit rating of AAA in order to provide credit insurance relatively cheaply:

Relying on the guarantee of its parent, AIG [which had a AAA rating], AIG Financial Products became a major over-the counter derivatives dealer, eventually having a portfolio of $2.7 trillion in notional amount.

AIG Financial Products issued credit default swaps guaranteeing debt obligations held by financial institutions and other investors. Because credit default swaps were not regulated insurance contracts, no reserve requirement was applicable.

AIG FP predicted with 99.85 per cent confidence that there would be no realized economic loss on the supposedly safest portions of the CDOs on

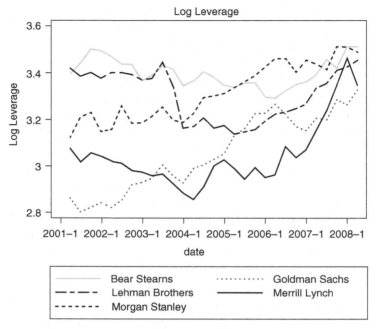

Figure 9.2 Leverage of US investments banks
Source: Adrian and Shin (2010)

which they wrote CDS protection, and failed to make any provisions what-soever for declines in value – or unrealized losses – a decision that would prove fatal to AIG in 2008.

The practice of increased financial leverage through short-term bor-rowing and changing the business model from principal to agent cre-ated a conflict of interest. Moreover, asymmetric information played a part too – the superior information of the bank acting as dealers in the market gave them an advantage in taking security positions that were contrary to customers' interests.[2] However, this practice was prevalent among all of the major US investment banks, as shown in Figure 9.2 by their increase in leverage from 2004. This is because these invest-ment banks effectively persuaded the US Securities and Exchange

---

[2] The banks could see the "colour of the market" better than any individual customers, as they act as the intermediary of the transactions in the marketplace.

Commission (SEC) in 2004 that they were not deposit-taking institutions, and hence had low risk in terms of deposit runs, whereby investors lose confidence and remove deposits all at once (Adrian and Shin, 2010). The SEC was suitably convinced and allowed the investment banks to determine their capital requirements based on their own risk models. This favourable change to the reserve requirements partially incentivised the banks to increase their leverage and shift their business models from agent to principal. It seems that such a practice was also prevalent among retail banks such as Barclays, which were able to use their retail deposits to fund taking positions as principal in the investment banking business rather than funding such operations through the inter-bank wholesale markets.

9.3 Implications for Business Model Design

The global financial crisis (GFC) and some of the related financial misconduct resulted in significant costs to various stakeholders (Meeks and Velu, 2018). First, customers lost access to finance, as banks significantly curtailed their lending. Second, employees lost their jobs, as was the case with Lehman Brothers and other banks. The banks had to pay fines of up to £260 billion globally between 2012 and 2016. Third, the operations of the market and competition were significantly affected. The Nobel Laureate, George Akerlof, highlighted the costs of such information asymmetry using the analogy of the sale of "lemons" in the used-car market (Akerlof, 1970). A second-hand car dealer – who will inevitably have more information about a used car – who sells a decrepit old car, a "lemon," portraying it as a good car, will contribute to two types of cost of such misinformation. First, there is the cost to the customer who buys the lemon and incurs costs later when the car develops issues. The second cost is the loss that arises from driving legitimate business out of existence, as customers lose faith in the second-hand-car market and hence withdraw from buying used cars. The cost of driving such legitimate business out of the market often exceeds the costs of any individual customer who has been cheated. A similar phenomenon happened during the GFC; for example, some financial markets such as the REPO market froze and stopped functioning (FCIC Report, 2011, p. 136). Studies have shown that uninformed investors could rationally withdraw from the market as a result of information asymmetry, which could then deprive the market of the risk transformation function of financial markets (Lev, 1988). Moreover, the US government had to bail out some of the major financial institutions with funds of over US$2,700 billion (FCIC Report, 2011).

The FCA considers business model analysis and business model challenge to be key to identifying the drivers of a firm's conduct risks. Moreover, the FCA and the Prudential Regulation Authority in the UK have a number of prescribed responsibilities as part of the Senior Managers' Certification Regime (SMCR), which includes: "Responsibility for the development and maintenance of the firm's business model by the governing body" (FCA Handbook, 2021, SYSC 24.2.6).

The SMCR places personal accountability on senior directors/ managers in terms of managing conduct-related risks, among other responsibilities. One of the aims of the SMCR, as noted by Jonathan Davidson, Director of Supervision – Retail and Authorisations at the FCA, is to deter business models that create commercial behaviour leading to poor outcomes for customers and the associated pay structure that rewards such misconduct (Davidson, 2017). In doing so, the SMCR explicitly makes senior managers accountable not only for taking responsibility for their own actions but also in leading the institution in terms of the formulation of strategy and business model design. A failure to do so can result in personal fines.

There has been an increase in information asymmetry over time as a result of structural changes in the financial sectors causing incentive misalignments and hence contributing to conduct risk. For example, the crisis in the Lloyds insurance market has been linked to the growth of the market weakening the personal links and ties of trust between client and firm, and formal information channels did not keep pace (Duguid, 2014). In the retail market for mortgages, potential customers used to have to build a savings record with – and become known to – a building society before they could get a loan – a far cry from the multi-layered supply chain in the US case, where the originators and the ratings agencies failed to bridge the information gap (Wigand et al., 2005). It is incumbent upon the senior managers of firms to develop their strategy and design business models in such a way as to reduce conduct risk by minimising information asymmetry and aligning incentives between customers and the firm. In the spirit of doing just that, it is instructive that Vikram Pandit, the CEO of Citigroup at the time, made the following remark: "It's all about clients,"… In place of a business model that was largely dependent on making quick gains, he is trying to revive a banking culture based on cultivating long-term relationships with Citi's customers. Vikram Pandit goes on to say, "Once you make your business all about relationships, conflicts of interest are not an issue" (Cassidy, 2010). Three principles stand out in the statement by Vikram Pandit, which are worth emphasising in terms of how banking business models should be designed. These are how to align customers' interests with the firm's interest, reducing conflicts of interest and cultivating long-term relationships.

In order to address these principles, it is worth looking at other industries where such conflict-of-interest-driven business models, combined with information asymmetry, have resulted in customer detriment – and how the issue was addressed by redesigning the business model. The two examples involve servitisation-based business models in capital equipment such as aero engines or earth-movers. In the earth-moving equipment market, Caterpillar used to earn four times more from providing spare parts over the life of the product compared to the initial sales. Hence, the business model was dependent on the failure of the equipment and customer detriment and therefore ridden with conflicts of interest and information asymmetry. Customers with important contractual deadlines, such as major building projects, often incurred significant penalties as a result of the breakdown of this earth-moving equipment. These customers were increasingly unhappy with the product provided by firms such as Caterpillar, which prompted the firm to embed sensors into the earth-moving equipment to monitor its performance and effectively predict when the machines were likely to break down (Baines and Lightfoot, 2013). In this way, Caterpillar has been able to provide an integrated-solution optimal use of machine, as well as repairs, optimised the coordination of machines in the worksite (e.g., quarry) and even moved to a model of charging customers based on the price per tonne of material mined. Moreover, Caterpillar's dealers assume responsibility for a portfolio of equipment, including multi-vendor products (e.g., John Deree, Volvo equipment), which allows them to be replaced with the manufacturer's own products later.

In the same way, Rolls-Royce, one of the major providers of aero engines, was dependent on engine breakdowns to generate income, which was resisted by some of the major airlines (Smith, 2013). Rolls-Royce subsequently adopted a servitised business model, whereby its

TotalCare programme provides support and service by embedding sensors into the aero engine, and it is paid for by the hour that the engine is flown: the power-by-the-hour model. Rolls-Royce is able to monitor the engines remotely and hence provide advice on how best to use the aircrafts and which routes optimise engine performance. These servitised business models of Caterpillar and Rolls-Royce provide better alignment of customers' interests with those of the firm and therefore reduce conduct-related risks.

Similarly, business models based on better alignment of customer and bank interests are beginning to emerge, such as the loan provided by the French bank BNP Paribas to JetBlue, a major domestic airline in the United States. JetBlue announced that it would be "carbon-neutral" on its flights in the United States by 2040 by purchasing more efficient engines and using biofuel blends. There was a financial incentive to follow through on its public commitment to reduce its carbon footprint. JetBlue signed a new credit facility – the first of its kind in the airline industry. The credit facility is a $550 million sustainability-linked loan arranged by BNP Paribas: the interest rate will go up or down in conjunction with JetBlue achieving its environmental, social and governance score, as determined by Vigeo Eiris, a Paris-based sustainability research group owned by Moody's (*Financial Times*, 2020).

The shift to solutions-based business models requires a transformation from products to solutions, transactions to relationships, and from suppliers to a network of partners (Martinez et al., 2017). In addition, appropriate business model designs could align customers' and firms' interests in complex products; services also need to have concertive controls, which are a negotiated consensus on values that workers use to infer proper behavioural premises for self-control and team management. Concertive controls are often practised by firms in the hospitality industry, such as Ritz Carlton (Barker, 1993; HBS Case, 2005). They call upon employees to be counted on to respond to, and anticipate, individual customer wants and needs. Employees need to do the right thing in the right way, even when the right thing has not been specified. Such values play to the spirt of Mark Twain's quote "Laws control the lesser man.... Right conduct controls the greater one." The critical question becomes not whether one can legally make a transaction but rather whether one should ethically make a transaction (HBR Case, 2014).

Conclusion

Conduct risk encompasses the need to prevent detriment to customers and markets. It can be seen as the preservation of the customer and markets and maintaining adequate competition so that there will be fair customer outcomes. Hence, conduct risk can be seen as the external-facing risk for firms and could manifest itself in terms of the impact on the performance of firms in the medium to long term. Although conduct risk has always been prevalent, the global financial crisis brought it into sharp contrast, as the global impact on financial markets and the real economy was significant. The *Salz Review* pointed out that regulation alone is insufficient to address conduct-related issues (Salz and Collins, 2013, p. 6):

It is understandable, and in many respects necessary, that since the start of the financial crisis, there has been an explosion in new regulation and in the intrusiveness of regulators. However, regulation alone cannot address the fundamental underlying causes that led to the business practices which are in the spotlight – the cultural shortcomings we found.

Conduct risk is particularly problematic when there is asymmetric information and conflicts of interest. Although financial regulators such as the Financial Conduct Authority (FCA) in the UK were pioneers in developing the set of guidelines for managing conduct risk among financial institutions, the issue of conduct risk is just as important in other industries where there are conflicts of interest. For example, KPMG was fined a record £13 million in 2021 following a case of misconduct dating back to 2011. This is because KPMG had acted as advisors for Silentnight, a bedding company, and HIG, a private equity firm, with significant conflicts of interest. KPMG helped to push Silentnight into insolvency so that HIG could buy the assets out of administration and sell off the costly pension scheme of Silentnight (*The Guardian*, 2021).

The issue of conduct risk needs to be managed effectively as firms respond to digital technologies such as artificial intelligence (AI) and machine learning (ML). Although AI and ML enhance customer solutions, they are also prone to creating new types of asymmetric information, as well as conflicts of interest. For example, the Open Banking initiative in Europe requires banks to open up customer data (if the customer consents) to third-party – typically banks/finance companies/

tech groups using application programme interfaces (APIs) – protocols that transfer data automatically from one piece of software to another. This would allow third parties to "aggregate" data from all customer accounts and advise on which products are most suitable. The idea is that the customer benefits, as there would be greater transparency and better value for money. Some banks have, in response, launched platforms that enable third-party organisations to develop applications – including Open Banking.

There are several challenging business model design issues to consider. For example, should the firm launch the new business as a separate business unit or within its existing business; and what are the associated implications for conduct risk? As discussed in Chapter 3, the organisational design to accommodate new business models could have an impact on customer outcomes. For example, the fulfilment of orders using Tesco's physical stores by its online business, Tesco.com, could have a detrimental impact on customers coming into stores to shop, as they would need to manoeuvre around the trolleys being used to fulfil the online orders. Similarly, banks need to pay close attention to the organisational design of new business models as a result of the adoption of digital technologies such as blockchains, artificial intelligence and quantum computing, among others, in order to manage conduct-related risks. Such risks are not exclusive to financial institutions, with other industries just as prone to them as they adopt new business models.

There are a number of areas that warrant further investigation of business model design and conduct risk. The first is to better understand how new digital technologies such as blockchains, artificial intelligence and quantum computing might contribute to conduct risk and the implications for business model design. In particular, how could firms systematically learn from industries that are ahead in the adoption curve of these digital technologies? Hence, how does one manage such conduct-related risks and the associated implications for business model design? The second area is the design issues related to new business model development and the associated conduct risk. How does one manage the conflicts that arise between the new business model and the existing business model? The introduction of new business models could result in conflicts with the existing business model and also increase information asymmetry between the customer and the firm – and hence contribute to customer detriment. Moreover, the introduction of new business models could increase the conflicts between various departments within an organisation, such as marketing and new product development, which might also lead to increases in conduct risks. How does organisational design launch new business models in order to manage conduct risk? Third, digital technologies increasingly call for collaborative business models, whereby conduct-related risks are dependent on a series of firms within the ecosystem. Are there lessons to be learnt from managing other types of systemic risk? This calls for managing conduct risk at ecosystem rather than firm level. Further research needs to be conducted to better understand the business model design implications for managing systemic conduct-related risks.

This chapter has provided an overview of the opportunities and challenges of conduct risk and business model design and proposed some outstanding research issues on this topic.

References

Adrian, T. and Shin, H. S. (2010). Liquidity and Leverage. *Journal of Financial Intermediation* 19: 418–437.

Akerlof, G. A. (1970). The Market for "Lemons": Quality Uncertainty and the Market Mechanism. *The Quarterly Journal of Economics* 84(3): 488–500.

Baines, T. and Lightfoot, H. (2013). *Made to Serve: How Manufacturers can Compete through Servitization and Product Service Systems*. Chichester, UK: John Wiley & Sons.

Barker, J. (1993). Tightening the Iron Cage: Concertive Controls in Self-Managing Teams. *Administrative Science Quarterly* 38(3): 408–437.

Bernanke, B. S., Geithner T. F., and Paulson. H. M. (2019). *Firefighting: The Financial Crisis and Its Lessons*. New York: Penguin Random House.

Cassidy, J. (2010). What Good Is Wall Street? Much of What Investment Bankers Do Is Socially Worthless. *The New Yorker*.

Davidson, J. (2017). Culture and Conduct – Extending the Accountability Regime. Speech delivered at City and Financial Summit, London, 20 September 2017.

Duguid, Andrew. (2014). *On the Brink: How a Crisis Transformed Lloyd's of London*. Basingstoke, UK: Palgrave Macmillan.

FCA Handbook. (2021). SYSC 24 Senior managers and certification regime: Allocation of prescribed responsibilities.

Financial Crisis Inquiry Commission (FCIC) Report. (2011). *Final Report of the National Commission on the Causes of the Financial and Economic Crisis in the United States*, Official Government Edition.

Financial Times. (2012). FSA Slams "Aggressive" Selling of Retail Investments, 13 March.

Financial Times. (2020). JetBlue Signs Loan Linked to ESG Goals, 23 February.

HBR Case. (2014). Goldman Sachs: Anchoring Standards After the Financial Crisis, Case Number: N9-514-020.

HBR Case. (2005). The Ritz-Carlton Hotel Company, Case number: 9-601-163.

Lev, B. (1988). Toward a Theory of Equitable and Efficient Accounting Policy. *The Accounting Review* 63(1): 1–22.

Louis, J. and Zinkin, R. (2019). *Better Governance across the Board: Creating Value through Reputation, People, and Processes.* Walter De Gruyter, Boston, USA.

Martinez, V., Neely, A. Velu, C., Leinster-Evans, S., and Bisessar, D. (2017) Exploring the Journey to Services. *International Journal of Production Economics* 192: 66–80.

Meeks, G. and Velu, C. (2018). Ten Years from the Crash: Time to Row Back on Financial Regulation and Compliance? *LSE Business Review.*

Mintz, Robert. A. (2008). Business Failure Are Not a Crime. *Wall Street Journal*, 26 June 2008.

New York Times. (2008). White House Philosophy Stoked Mortgage Bonfire, 21 December.

Pauly, M. V. (1968). The Economics of Moral Hazard: Comment. *The American Economic Review* 58(3): 531–537.

Salz, A. and Collins, R. (2013). An Independent Review of Barclay's Business Practices. *Salz Review*, Barclays PLC, London, UK.

Smith, D. J. (2013). Power-by-the-Hour: The Role of Technology in Reshaping Business Strategy at Rolls-Royce. *Technology Analysis & Strategic Management* 25(8): 987–1007.

The Financial Crisis Inquiry Report – FCIC Report. (2011). *Final Report of the National Commission on the Causes of the Financial and Economic Crisis in the United States* Washington, DC: Financial Crisis Inquiry Commission.

The Guardian. (2021). KPMG Fined £13m over Sale of Silentnight to Private Equity Firm, 6 August.

Wigand, R. T., Steinfield, C. W., and Markus, M. (2005). Information Technology Standards Choices and Industry Structure Outcomes: The Case of the United States Home Mortgage Industry. *Journal of Management Information Systems* 22(2): 165–191.

10 | *Conclusion*

Simplicity is the ultimate sophistication.

Leonardo da Vinci

Introduction

New business models are created in response to a combination of society's explicit or implicit needs and technological developments. Hence, to better understand the overall evolution of business models, it is worth reviewing the broader technological progress that has enabled value to be created and captured by businesses – and the role of the state and the market in facilitating such an exchange. In this concluding chapter we first provide a historical overview of the technological developments that created the techno-economic foundations for business model innovation. We briefly discuss the impact of the COVID-19 pandemic on business models before reviewing the role of the state and the economic system in nurturing and accommodating business models. In doing so, we highlight the importance of business model design in distributing value among stakeholders in order to ensure fairness in society as the world we live in embraces further prosperity and well-being.

This chapter provides a broad overview of business model developments going from the industrial revolutions that started in Britain in the eighteenth century to the more recent digital technology era. The following section reviews the impact of the pandemic on business model innovation and some of the initial lessons for firms. The chapter then discusses how the role of the state and the economic system are key to influencing the design and evolution of business models. The concluding section discusses the imperative of the distribution consequences of business models and the implications for economic growth in an equitable society.

10.1 Industrial Revolution and Business Models

The reasons why the Industrial Revolution – a more mechanised production system with features related to technological, socio-economic and cultural change – took place in Britain in the eighteenth century, and not elsewhere, continue to be a major bone of contention[1] (Allen, 2009, 2011). The reasons are varied and have been attributed to the British constitution, culture and science, among other things (Crafts, 2018; Hartwell, 1967; Mokyr, 1993). The crux of the argument relies on whether it is the factors that are conducive to a greater supply of inventions or the drivers that encourage a favourable cost and commercial environment that create a demand for inventions. On the one hand, the supply-side proponents say that there was a period of "industrial enlightenment," driven by British society's willingness to apply scientific discoveries to social and economic problems, which provided the incentive for the supply of inventions (Mokyr, 2010).

On the other hand, the demand-side thesis says that Britain had a more pressing economic need for labour-saving technology – the spinning jenny, the steam engine and coke smelting, among others – compared to other countries because of its higher wages and lower energy costs (Allen, 2009). The higher wages were due to Britain's unique position in international trade in the late eighteenth century and early nineteenth century, while the lower energy costs were a result of the abundant supply of coal in Britain. These factors gave Britain the economic incentive to develop energy using technology that would substitute capital for labour. Hence, despite the more advanced state of science in some European countries, such as France, there was a greater need to mechanise production and displace labour in Britain. Some scholars have said that it is probably the combination of supply and demand conditions that formed the basis for Britain leading the Industrial Revolution (Crafts, 2018). In time, the Industrial Revolution was diffused to other European nations, such as France and Germany.

Before the mid-nineteenth century, there were no multi-functional, multinational and multi-product enterprises administered by professional managers (Chandler, 1986). The enormous increase in volume

---

[1] Arnold Toynbee used the term Industrial Revolution to describe Britain's economic development from 1760 to around 1840 (Britannica, The Editors of Encyclopaedia, 2023).

and output that led to these types of firm arising was not due to the First Industrial Revolution, which took place between the mid-eighteenth and mid-nineteenth centuries in Europe, led by Britain. The concept of mass-production techniques that led to the development of modern large-scale business enterprises did not take place until after the 1840s, led by the United States. The increase was a result of the Second Industrial Revolution, from the mid-nineteenth to the early twentieth centuries, when the emergence of transportation, communication technologies (such as the telegraph) and stable energy (first in the form of coal and then electricity) enabled such firms to emerge (Chandler, 1977). The European economies had a more fragmented market than America and were also dominated by family-owned and -managed firms. Hence, European economies, together with Japan, were slower to adopt mass-production techniques, coupled with large marketing and purchasing organisations.

In contrast, American firms often developed machinery based on European inventions, as the latter were more technologically advanced. Alfred Chandler, in his influential book *The Visible Hand*, argued that American firms were the first to adopt large-scale managerial capitalism, whereby firms were run by professional managers administering them as a result of their growth in terms of both vertical and horizontal integration (Chandler, 1977). This was partly due to the significant growth in the American markets, which became large, homogenous and open to international trade, between the American Civil War[2] and World War I (WWI). Hence, there is merit in studying the development and growth of American corporations to better understand the mechanisms driving business model innovation.

Alfred Chandler showed that production and distribution in the United States were primarily carried out by family-owned general merchants in the late eighteenth century until the 1840s (Chandler, 1977). From the period of ratification of the US Constitution, from the 1790s onwards, the legal and political development of the national economy provided the impetus for the growth of goods that were produced and distributed. However, the businesses that were conducting these production and distribution activities continued to be traditional single-unit enterprises, which remained the dominant business organisation

[2] The American Civil War took place between 1861 and 1865 and World War I between 1914 and 1918.

until the 1840s, when new sources of energy such as coal, transportation provided by railroad and telecommunication through the telegraph provided the catalyst for change in business enterprises in the US.

Between the 1790s and 1840s in the US, there were exceptions such as armouries and textile mills, where there was evidence of the subdivision of labour and the integration of several production processes within a single establishment. The armouries were able to grow as a result of the guaranteed market enabling them to cover production and distribution costs. The textile market manufacturers relied on the large flowing rivers to generate power. For example, because of the growing demand for clothing, Lowell's Boston Manufacturing integrated weaving and spinning in a single factory and had a higher productivity rate than any other textile factory in the United States[3] (Chandler, 1977, p. 58). However, for most industries during this period, the growth of the economy was driven by business enterprises that displayed increasing specialisation of particular activities and relied on the market to conduct transactions between enterprises. For example, specialised business enterprises focused on manufacturing, distribution and financing activities. The growth of these enterprises made the transactions less personalised, with the merchants often not knowing the producers and consumers across the long chain of activities in moving the goods through the economy. However, the basic business enterprise remained small and was managed personally because the volume of business did not require a large hierarchical management.

10.1.1 Mass Production and Distribution

Mass-production techniques were first used in industries processing liquids or semi-liquids such as crude oil (Chandler, 1977) because such industries had a steady flow of raw materials that needed to be worked on through the use of continuous process machinery. The flow of activities was less continuous and related to less controllable factors such as biological constraints and weather in industries such as agriculture and construction. The application of continuous process machinery enabled the integration of tasks and the reorganisation of the factory system to increase throughput and hence productivity. This resulted

---

[3] The owner, Francis Cabot Lowell, had smuggled the plans for the power loom out of Britain (Chandler, 1977, p. 58).

in improvements in technology in terms of efficient machinery, the quality of raw materials and intensified application of energy. Such technological innovation, in turn, called for organisational innovation to arrange the artefacts and coordination of materials and workers. From the 1840s to the 1870s, the combination of coal to reliably produce heat, and the development of the rail system for transportation and the telegraph for communication, enabled better coordination of input and output, which further stimulated the development of mass-production factories. The speed of production through the use of continuous production methods was responsible for the increased productivity. However, the textile industry, beyond the integration of spinning and weaving, experienced a slower rate of adoption of continuous production methods.

The steel industry followed the adoption of mass-production techniques in the 1870s in the United States. In the 1830s and 1840s the steel industry started to disintegrate from the "iron plantation" facilities as a result of the availability of coal. Coal permitted greater and steadier output, enabling specialisation in blast furnaces, forges, rolling and finishing mills. However, the reintegration of the steel mills started with the adoption of the Bessemer steel process, where the co-location of the different processes for steel-making resulted in continuous production processes and increased productivity. One of the first examples of such a factory was the Edgar Thomson Works (E.T. Works) of Andrew Carnegie, which opened in 1875 in Pennsylvania. Andrew Carnegie had adopted administrative procedures to manage the business from his previous experience in the railroad industry. These integrated iron works, together with more systematic management procedures, brought about business model innovation in the steel-making industry, with significantly improved productivity and profitability for the business. In the metal-working industries that produced many of the tools and mass-produced metal works (e.g., for armoury), there was a type of business model innovation involving "inside contracting"; the owners sub-contracted to skilled mechanics a specified number of parts over a specified period of time (e.g., one year), were credited for the value and charged for the cost of providing the floor space, machinery, power and other related materials. At the end of the period any surplus was paid to the contractor as profits. This way, the owner needed to provide only light supervision of the overall process of manufacturing.

However, the period from the 1870s resulted in a slowdown in economic growth, and hence demand, which put additional pressure on firms to manage and contain costs. To improve productivity, factories started to share the benefits of productivity improvements with employees and managers, which resulted in the development of the Taylorist management approach, which is often seen as the beginning of the scientific management system.[4] However, the increased mechanisation and capital intensity of mass-production industries resulted in increased fixed costs. Hence, to keep the machinery, workers and managers fully employed, there was increased pressure on the owners of these firms to control the supply of raw materials and semi-finished components, as well as the marketing and distribution of their products. This economic pressure resulted in business model innovation in the form of vertical integration of production and distribution.

Vertical integration enabled increased profitability through decreasing costs and increasing productivity. The completion of the railroad and telegraphic network went into full operation in the 1870s and 1880s in the United States. The growth of railroads lowered the barriers to transportation and enabled small enterprises to compete on a nationwide scale. Moreover, the development of the telegraph and then the telephone enabled the centralised supervision of geographically dispersed operations of these businesses. The prices of products started to decline as a result of the combination of increased competition – due to the development of transportation and communication technologies – and the economic depression that began in 1873. This economic pressure prompted firms to integrate horizontally in order to maintain profits by controlling the prices and output of the operating units. American manufacturers operationalised such horizontal integration predominantly through mergers. Many of the firms that grew via horizontal integration through mergers remained profitable only if they followed their consolidation with a strategy of vertical integration forward into marketing and backward into purchasing raw or semi-finished goods. These integrated enterprises replaced the

---

[4] The Taylorist management system was introduced by Frederick W. Taylor at the Midvale Steel Company; a paper was written in 1895 and was termed "scientific management." Several papers discuss the merits and shortcomings of the Taylorist approach (Wagner-Tsukamoto, 2007).

invisible hand of market forces with the visible hand of management in coordinating the flow from the suppliers of raw materials to the consumer (Chandler, 1977, p. 315).

The emergence of business models of integrated firms took place at different speeds across various industries. The industries that adopted the continuous flow technologies, such as petroleum, food and complex but standardised machinery, were the first to successfully adopt the integrated-firm business model structure. Industries that needed labour input or complex products, which could not use continuous process machinery for production, were slower to adopt such a model. The increased production rate from large-batch continuous process machinery meant that firms needed to coordinate the production and sales of their output, and therefore they tended to internalise the marketing and sales channels. Moreover, these firms needed to develop management skills that enabled the coordination, monitoring and planning of these operating units in order to achieve improved performance compared to the constituent operations or firms, with such operations working independently. The key factor that determines profits in these large-batch, continuous-flow industries is not capacity but throughput, which requires management expertise to coordinate the production processes with distribution and marketing (Chandler, 1986).[5] Therefore, the locus of competition shifts from the price of the product to all stages of production and distribution, including the availability of credit and aftersales service. For example, Singer developed an extensive sales distribution channel for its sewing machines and aftersales service in repair and maintenance.

The increased adoption of salaried managers required two basic functions of management to be sharpened and improved in these large integrated organisations. First, it was necessary to coordinate and monitor the current production and distribution of goods and services. Second, there was a need to allocate resources for future production and distribution. However, managers tended to focus on current

---

[5] Management expertise is needed to ensure such coordination to achieve and maintain production and distribution at the minimum efficient scale – the volume of the operations that archives the lowest unit costs. Therefore, it is posited that economies of scale are technological, while throughput is organisational (Chandler, 1986).

operations rather than long-term planning. Moreover, firms started to diversify from their own specific technological base: Du Pont from its nitrocellulose chemistry into paint, dyes, films and fibres; and General Motors from using knowledge in diesel automotives to diesel locomotives.

There was a severe recession in 1920–1921 after WWI, which caused firms to rethink their management approaches. Firms adopted techniques to improve the coordination of forecasting and planning for demand changes. Du Pont adopted the integrated autonomous divisions for different product lines from the functional departmental structure, which helped to improve its profitability. General Motors adopted the committee structure to coordinate across functions and the flow of current and future demand. Hence, the administration systems in the large integrated American firms were improved after WWI, permitting middle managers to focus on coordinating the current flows and top management to focus on evaluating, planning and allocating resources. Hence, the first modern enterprises created to administer the new railroad and telegraph firms in the nineteenth century came to be adopted by integrated multi-product managerial enterprises in the twentieth century. These firms dominated American industry post-World War II (WWII) – the 200 largest industrial firms in the United States accounted for 47.2 per cent of the total corporate manufacturing assets in 1947, 56.3 per cent in 1963 and 60.9 per cent in 1968 (Chandler, 1977, p. 482).

The economist view, based on Adam Smith's invisible hand of the market, whereby improved technology and markets result in increased specialisation and hence vertical disintegration, was increasingly questioned (Chandler, 1977, p. 490). Such a dictum overlooks the important aspect of administrative coordination, where the speed and regularity with which goods flow through the process of production and distribution, and the ways in which these flows are organised, affect the volume and unit costs[6] – the choice of business model design affects productivity (Wannakrairoj and Velu, 2021). There are alternative perspectives on the role of administration and coordination on business model design.

[6] Economists traditionally classify this organisational and managerial aspect of the firm as a residual effect of the production function, which is the proportion of output not explained by input (Wannakrairoj and Velu, 2021).

10.1.2 *An Alternative Theory for Vertical Integration*

Langlois (1988, 2003) had a different conceptualisation of the vertically integrated firm that Chandler (1977) had described in response to achieving high-throughput production as a result of the emergence of the railroad for transportation, the telegraph for communication and coal as a source of heat energy. Langlois argued that, as the population and income grow, and technology and legal barriers decline, the process of the division of labour will result in finer specialisation of function and increased coordination through markets. However, the components of the process, such as technology, organisations and institutions, tend to change at different rates. Hence, Langlois (2002, 2003) argued that the vertically integrated firms that Chandler described were an organisational response to overcoming the imbalance at the time between the needs of high-throughput technologies and the ability of existing markets and institutions to meet this demand. Thompson (1967) had argued that organisations tend to buffer uncertainty in the environment by surrounding the technical core of their production process with input and output components. The role of management in such a process is to act as an information-processing function, managing uncertainties by translating complex information into routine information that the production system can use. Integration and management are ways of controlling or buffering product flow uncertainties due to the higher fixed costs of a vertically integrated system compared to a decentralised system. This management function enables the firm to create and capture value in such a way as to deliver the most utility to customers at the lowest cost.

Levinthal and March (1993) go further, invoking Herbert Simon's (1962) notion of a nearly decomposable system, with modularisation enabling components to become independent of one another and interactions happening within modules, while interactions among modules are kept to a minimum and managed through formal interfaces. Modularisation enables loose coupling, whereby each function can concentrate on the local rather than global consequences of the information that it receives. This nearly decomposable system is akin to Adam Smith's view of specialisation – and hence the advantages of the invisible hand of the market. The Chandlerian vertical integrated firm can then be explained in terms of dynamic transaction costs, with the need to coordinate and systematically reorganise production and distribution requiring centralised organisation, which surpasses the benefits of decentralised organisation, with a focus on specialisation. When many components of the system need to be changed simultaneously as a result of new technologies or market needs, the centralised vertical integrated structure reduces the dynamic transaction costs of systemic change. These vertically integrated firms were initially geared towards the management of economies of scale. However, the lumpiness of resources, and the resultant excess capacity, encourage firms to diversify into adjacent markets, which increases the economies of scope, resulting in diversified enterprises (Penrose, 1959).[7]

However, the charmed life of US corporations in the 1950s/1960s was disrupted by new technologies, particularly digital technologies, in the 1970s/1980s. The impact of these new technologies, which was the premise of the new digital economy, was effectively to simplify and reduce scale in some aspects while increasing the benefits of scale in other respects. Moreover, digital technologies enabled better mass customisation, which required firms to increase the variety of their product offering. In particular, the benefits of vertical integration reduce with the increasing need to be more responsive to changes in the growing markets for customised products. The variation induced by such mass customisation implies the need for the system to be responsive to changes in demand and supply, which results in the unbundling of the vertical structure of the managerial corporation. Increasingly, firms across industries, from pharmaceuticals and semiconductor manufacturing to automobiles, were outsourcing parts of their production and marketing functions to specialist firms, and these firms were becoming general specialists by diversifying their portfolios to serve multiple industries (Langlois, 1999, 2003). In doing so, they were able to smooth demand and facilitate high-throughput production through a more decentralised modular system, the aim of which is to standardise the more abstract visible design rules of the system rather than the products and processes (Baldwin and Clarke, 2000).

In conforming to the visible design rules, it is not necessary for each participant to disclose its activities, which become hidden design

---

[7] Economies of scale and economies of scope are ultimately related to the need for the same structure of knowledge and the need to increase efficiency: economies of scale are due to increasing production of the same product, while economies of scope increase the production of something different that requires similar knowledge (Langlois, 1999).

parameters, and yet they can achieve mass customisation by reducing product standardisation. This was evident in the way that Dell was able to sell customised personal computers from standardised components. However, firms are able to exert considerable administrative control over the stages of production that they do not control, effectively creating the benefits of vertical integration. The benefits of information-improving innovation on the market structure, such as the degree of vertical integration, are ambiguous. The trade-off depends on whether the information-improving innovation renders the cost of organising internally within the firm greater than reducing organisation in markets. The major technology that enabled information-improving innovation in the late twentieth century was the digital computer and the Internet. Next, we review the historical development and impact of the digital computer and the Internet on information, communication and coordination mechanisms, and their influence on firm structure – and hence business models.

10.2 The Advent of the Digital Computer

There was an explicit plan led by the US government and other allied forces to ensure that the technological inventions from WWII should have benefits for society (Bush, 1945).[8] One of the major technological breakthroughs was the development of digital computers for business applications based on principles developed during WWII. The first digital computer developed in the United States was the ENIAC machine, at the University of Pennsylvania, to calculate artillery firing tables for the US Army Ballistic Research Laboratory in 1945. In the UK, a secret programme was developed to crack the German Enigma code during the war, which led to the development of the Colossus.[9]

---

[8] Hence, the commercial development of technologically complex products, such as synthetic rubber, high-octane gasoline, radar, electronic antisubmarine devices and other related war-time technologies, led to the systematic application of science to industry. This resulted in the development of various chemical and synthetic materials, as well as a wide range of electronic products.

[9] There was a computing machine – a precursor to Colossus – called Bombe, developed by Alan Turing that was used to decode the German Enigma machine. Bombe was initially based on electromagnetic relays (relays with small switches of metal rods that opened and closed based on electrical circuits), although later versions of the Colossus were based on valves or vacuum tubes that operate many times faster, as the only moving part is a beam of electrons.

Colossus was the first large-scale electronic digital computer, which was operational in December 1943.[10]

In the years following WWII, the American mathematician John von Neumann was influential in building the first stored-program digital computer, the EDVAC, at the Institute for Advanced Studies at Princeton.[11] The EDVAC was influential in terms of early US computers and the precursor to the IBM 701, the company's first mass-produced stored programme computer. In the UK, following WWII, expertise for the development of the digital computer was taken up by the National Physical Laboratory and called the Automatic Computing Engine machine (Copeland, 2005). Subsequently, there were developments at Manchester and Cambridge universities, with the Manchester Mark 1 and Electronic Delay Storage Automatic Calculator, respectively. The work at the University of Cambridge led to the development of the Lyons Electronic Office, the first digital business computer. These basic developments, combined with application use cases demanded by government and businesses, led to the proliferation of digital computers around the world. At the end of 1968 IBM announced that it would unbundle its software with its hardware, which until then had been coupled together (Ceruzzi, 1998).[12] This enabled the firm to charge separately for the software packages. This decision effectively opened up software development to a myriad of third-party developers, which led to a plethora of applications, particularly to solve business problems. Moreover, there was a move to connect these disparate computers in order for them to work more effectively. There were several private- and public-sector

---

[10] Before the 1970s, few knew about the use of electronic computation during WWII, as the Colossus was kept secret by the British government. It was not until 2000 that the US and Britain declassified the information about Colossus, which was developed by Thomas Flowers, from the Post Office Research Station, and Cambridge mathematician Max Newman (who subsequently led the computing effort at Manchester University). The lack of knowledge about Colossus led some to, understandably but erroneously, think that the ENIAC was the first electronic computing machine (Copeland, 2005).

[11] The stored-programme digital computers were envisioned by Cambridge mathematician Alan Turing in his 1936 paper on computable numbers and subsequently developed further by John Van Neumann as part of the EDVAC (Copeland, 2005).

[12] This was a result of the pressure from the US government to untie the monopoly that IBM had on the computer industry.

initiatives to link these computers and enhance communications between them. Chief among these was an initiative to link the computers under the ARPA programme funded by the US Department of Defense, ARPANET (Campbell-Kelly and Garcia-Swartz, 2013). The combination of these initiatives with the Transmission Control Protocol/Internet Protocol and the World Wide Web led to the emergence of the Internet.

The early uses of digital computers were for engineering and scientific applications, later moving to commercial business applications (Cortada, 2003, 2005); the digital computer collects, stores, analyses and produces information. Simon (1973) highlighted that organisational design should be based on dividing the work in such a way as to make them as independent as possible, while reducing the need to manage the coordination between parts. In a world that is becoming more information-driven, the focus of organisational design needs to shift from dividing the work to produce output in the most efficient way to dividing while factoring in decision-making, because post-industrial society is shifting from producing goods to services – or from producing houses to housing.[13] The anatomy of an organisation that is viewed as a collection of people that need to be subdivided will look very different to an organisation viewed as a decision-making and information-processing system. A goods-producing organisation will be divided into tasks in departments that can be as independent of one another as possible, with coordinating mechanisms. An information-processing organisation's division of labour means the decision needs to be made in relatively independent subsystems in order to minimise concerns about interactions with others. The reason for this is the limited processing capacity of the man or machine in comparison with the magnitude of the decision problem that the organisation needs to undertake. Therefore, the number and interdependencies of the decision need to be minimised in order to have a coordination mechanism within manageable bounds. The computer then acts as a memory and processing unit. As a memory unit, the computer acts as a means of storing potential information, which, if indexed appropriately, can be available at a reasonable cost. The computer as a processing unit models complex situations and

---

[13] This has also been termed the service dominant logic (Vargo and Lusch, 2016).

infers the consequences of alternative decisions through models that calculate optimal decisions, simulate the consequences of alternative decisions and even help to make decisions.

Firms initially used digital computers to reduce operational costs. The applications of digital computers were threefold: first, they helped to reduce the labour content of some activities (e.g., data entry); second, they lowered the operating overheads (e.g., the cost of inventory); and, third, they led to more effective work performance (e.g., modelling production schedules in manufacturing). The adoption of digital computers, combined with complementary digital technologies and the emergence of the Internet, enabled more customisation of products and services. Furthermore, the increased data from the combination of Internet usage, sensors, mobile devices and other related sources has increased the demand for artificial intelligence and machine learning capabilities; and the combination of these technology trends has increased the demand for new business models. Moreover, the sheer volume and complexity of data requirements are creating the demand for quantum computers and related quantum-enabled technologies for communications, sensing and imaging, and also for position, navigation and timing. These technology developments provide the foundations for more personalisation of value to customers, which could take the form of personalised medicine, design and delivery of goods and services based on a segment of one. Such personalisation will incentivise the design of revolutionary business models to help improve society and well-being. We saw a glimpse of such a trend in the recent COVID-19 pandemic, which caused major disruptions to supply chains and increased reliance on digital transformation, which we discuss below.

10.3 The Pandemic and Business Model Innovation

The COVID-19 pandemic created a period of unprecedented uncertainty that affected both the demand and supply of goods and services simultaneously (Said et al., 2022). Firms had to respond very quickly to this economic downturn, while leveraging the opportunity to contribute to the healthcare challenges (Chesbrough, 2020; *Financial Times*, 2020; von Behr et al., 2022). For example, some firms in the aerospace sector managed to adapt their products to provide healthcare equipment such as ventilators to the healthcare industry. Other firms took the opportunity to rethink their core capabilities and diversified their product offering to other sectors, as the civil aerospace industry experienced a dramatic reduction in air travel. Research shows that small and medium-sized enterprises (SMEs) that invested in intangible capital, such as human, organisational and information capital, demonstrated effective leadership by engaging and empowering their employees prior to the pandemic, and they were the ones that were most able to make these types of business model change during the pandemic (Said et al., 2022). Hence, firms and governments should continue to invest in programmes to help strengthen the intangible capital of SMEs.

Firms had to respond to major restrictions such as social distancing requirements and working from home directives. They responded to the impact of the pandemic in two principal ways (Popper and Velu, 2021), the first being to make supply chains more agile. For example, many supply chains were configured for a "just-in-time" delivery model based on optimisation methods enabled by digital technologies. Firms are reconsidering building supply chains based on "just-in-case" principles, whereby inventory is held on the assumption that it might be needed urgently in the case of supply chain disruptions. However, "just-in-time" has benefits, such as being less tolerant of defective parts, thereby improving both quality and the relationship between partners from the close collaboration (Yoffie, 2022). Hence, firms might want to adopt the best of "just-in-time" while incorporating some of the principles of "just-in-case." Moreover, firms have also begun to build supply chains that are more focused on domestic supply rather than relying on international supply. However, the IMF has recently warned that such domestically reliant supply chains might not be as robust as diversified supply chains, which could be more resilient to global disruptions (*Wall Street Journal*, 2022).

The second way that firms responded to the impact of the pandemic was to cut out the middleman to get closer to the customer. For example, a large European personal-care company developed a direct customer model without the need to sell through retailers by developing its investment in "virtual tryouts" (such as mixing hair colouring), which allow customers to apply beauty products digitally while receiving real-time advice. Moreover, a US-based multinational conglomerate decided to remove long-standing intermediaries from its distribution channels and go direct to customers, similar to Amazon's business model. The firm felt that intermediaries provided fewer insights, such as whether the products were bought for stock or immediate use, especially during the crisis period. These two principal approaches require firms to adopt a more agile strategic planning process, which is just as much about stopping doing an initiative as it is about starting to develop new business models as firms prepare for a more volatile crisis-management environment. Moreover, the possibilities that biology and biotechnology might bring to solve various problems of humankind were highlighted by scientists even before the pandemic, for example, the benefits arising from the convergence of biology with engineering (Hockfield, 2019). Such a promise became a reality with the sheer speed of development of the COVID-19 vaccines, especially the promise that mRNA vaccines as a foundational technology might bring to society.[14]

In addition, one of the key lessons arising from the crisis is for firms to think in a more allocentric[15] manner, to work more collaboratively across firms and other stakeholders to address future crises in the most efficient and effective manner (Pedersen et al., 2020). Hence, it is important, as firms develop the new normal and build back better after the crisis by adopting digital technologies, for such an allocentric model to become one of the basic principles for new business model design. We next review the role of the state and economic systems in designing and accommodating business models for the benefit of society.

10.4 State Capitalism and Business Model Design Choices

The East India Company (EIC) provides the principles to examine such issues, as it was one of the major corporations that started as a private company before being run as a state-owned institution, accounting for half of the world's trade during the mid-1700s and early 1800s (Farrington, 2002). Adam Smith, in his famous treatise

---

[14] The standard conventional vaccine works by injecting a dead or weakened form of a pathogen into the body, which then trains the immune system to recognise and respond to the infection. In contrast, RNA vaccines introduce a messenger RNA (mRNA) sequence that contains the genetic instructions for the body to produce the vaccine antigens and generate an immune response to the infectious agent (Pardi et al., 2018).

[15] Allocentric implies a community minded approach, whereby a firm's interest is centred on other firms' objectives as well.

on *The Wealth of Nations*, was critical of the EIC (Smith, 1776).[16] The EIC was granted a licence to trade in 1600 with the objective of procuring goods (such as silk) and food items (such as spices) from the then wealthy states in the East Indies – the Indian subcontinent and South East Asia. The British government had to renew the charter of the EIC every 20 years, as it viewed the firm as a low-cost source of finance and a way of outsourcing the objective of pursuing its interests in Asia. Although the EIC was seen as economically successful in its first decade, the company got into financial difficulties in the mid-1700s because of its monopoly power and poor governance structure[17] (Robins, 2006).

The EIC had obtained *Diwani* rights in Bengal in 1765. Diwani was a grant to collect taxes by the Mughal emperor, who remained the nominal sovereign of Bengal and received geographical protection from the EIC. One of the main bones of contention was whether a private company such as the EIC should have sovereign rights to the lucrative patronage of collecting taxes. If the UK Crown or Parliament gained control of this patronage, it would be likely to have enormous influence as an arbiter of British politics. Hence, freedom was given to the EIC in order to retain the balance of power in Britain, with the consequence of not being able to resolve the mismanagement of affairs in India. However, the Seven Years' War (1756–1763) left Britain victorious but nearly bankrupt.[18] The British Prime Minister at the time, William Pitt, saw the Diwani as a divine intervention to fill the coffers of the Treasury.

As part of this initiative, in 1766 the company agreed to pay the Treasury an annual tax, which then permitted the firm to pay an annual dividend of 12.5 per cent. However, the EIC collapsed in

---

[16] The East India Company was originally chartered as "Governor and Company of Merchants of London Trading into the East-Indies" and is also known as "The John Company."

[17] For example, the EIC had directors who leased their vessels to the company, which resulted in the firm renting more vessels than needed at a higher price. These directors were often shareholders, and hence the rental of the vessels can be seen as a redistribution of corporate rents, as they could maximise personal gains by trading off losses from the EIC against the higher rental income (Hejeebu, 2015).

[18] The Seven Years' war was a global conflict between Great Britain and predominantly France but also with other European countries for global pre-eminence.

Figure 10.1 Belvedere House in Calcutta

1772 and needed a bailout of government loans. This was granted after much debate in Parliament, which gave the British government effective control over the EIC.[19] Warren Hastings was the first governor general of India; his official residence was Belvedere House in Calcutta, as shown in Figure 10.1. Although the EIC was effectively transferred to the British government, the company continued to have a level of independence in administrative affairs in India. It even had its own armed forces to protect its interests and govern the territories under its control in India and elsewhere. However, the level of unequal trading in the relationship contributed to a continual drain of resources, resulting in harm to the traders and producers in India. Moreover, the continued engagement in a series of wars by the EIC resulted in significant expenditures that could not be recovered from revenue. Therefore, the EIC changed its business model in the late

---

[19] Parliament would appoint a governor general of India (the first was Warren Hastings) who had authority over all three presidencies in India: Calcutta, Bombay and Madras. Also, there would be a five-person council, with three of the members being appointed by Parliament.

1700s by emphasising the private or privileged trade model, which allowed its executives to buy goods in India on their own account and to use the shipping facilities of the company to transport them for sale.[20] This inverted the EIC from being a trading business on its own account, employing servants as factors, to a situation whereby the servants traded on their own account and used the company as agent and factors by paying a commission[21] (Marshall, 1981). However, this new business model was barely profitable and was unable to save the firm from its difficult financial situation.

Following the Indian Rebellion or Indian Mutiny of 1857, under the provision of the Government of India Act, the British government nationalised the East India Company, which was dissolved in 1858; the British government, through the India Office, then took over its assets, administrative powers and its armed forces. The EIC is an example of a firm that started as a private company and increasingly became government-owned until its full nationalisation. The degree of arms-length governance arrangement, partial ownership and then full nationalisation by the British government influenced the design and objectives of the firm, and hence its business model, including how value was created and distributed among its stakeholders. The case of the EIC shows that state capitalism can determine the economic and well-being outcomes of countries.

---

[20] Such private trade was allowed among the captains, officers and crew of the EIC based on a sliding scale of cargo value and space, respectively, depending on their rank. Although the EIC allowed private trade between its officers and the local merchants in India, which sometimes contributed to corruption and abuse of power, scholars have argued that such a practice was the basis of the success of the English East India Company in the eighteenth century compared to the Dutch East India Company (Verenigde Oostindische Compagnie – VOC) and the French East India Company (Compagnie Royale des Indes Orientales), which initially did not permit such trading but subsequently allowed the practice. Private trade was seen as a strategic complement to company trading, as it allowed the EIC to attract and retain servants as an inducement to enhance their own earnings, as well as providing information on the network of trading patterns, which was beneficial for the performance of the company (Berg et al., 2015; Hejeebu, 2005).

[21] Edmund Burke, a Member of Parliament in the House of Commons in Great Britain (Marshall, 1981), was a major critic of this business model of the EIC and its unequal power over India. Moreover, there was general disagreement between members of the Court of Directors of the EIC about permitting such private trade (India Office Records, 1800–2).

The structure of state capitalism could influence how firms are owned by the government for certain strategic purposes, to pursue economic or political goals (Musacchio et al., 2015). Hence, the business model design of state-owned enterprises will have implications for how value is created and distributed to stakeholders. Although there are generally accepted definitions of state capitalism, a country can be considered state capitalist if the government has an ownership stake in, or significant influence over, more than one-third of the 500 largest companies – by revenue – in that country (Kulantzick, 2016). Under this definition, some of the major global economies, such as China, Brazil, India and Russia, practise state capitalism, to different degrees. State-capitalism-based firms could have both positive and negative consequences. For example, over three decades ago the Brazilian government provided aircraft manufacturer Embraer with lucrative contracts and related subsidies in order to compete with Boeing and Airbus in producing regional jets. This government ownership, combined with preferential treatment, enabled Embraer to become the world's largest producer of regional jets and the third-largest producer of civil aircraft after Boeing and Airbus. In the 2000s and 2010s, Russia developed a reputation for using its state-controlled natural gas giant, Gazprom, which has the largest gas reserves in the world, as a means to curtail the power of other states, such as Ukraine. For example, during 2013–2015 Russia used Gazprom to threaten the supply of gas to the Kremlin-opposed regime in Ukraine and its allies in Western Europe.[22]

There are four major perspectives when it comes to accounting for state capitalism's strategic behaviour: the managerial view, the social view, the political view and the institutional-based view (Mussacchio et al., 2015). The first three imply a negative relationship because of the liability of state-ness, while the fourth implies a positive relationship between state ownership and profitability. According to the managerial view, state-owned enterprises (SOEs) will face conflicts between managers and government objectives; in the social view the government will use SOEs to pursue social objectives; and in the political view politicians will use these SOEs to direct political gain. According to

---

[22] Russia invaded Ukraine in February 2022, resulting in major economies such as the United States and United Kingdom promising to stop buying hydrocarbon-based products such as natural gas from Russia (*Financial Times*, 2022).

the institution-based view, SOEs could fill institutional voids in certain countries that lack appropriately developed product, labour and financial markets, hence reducing transaction costs and improving productive efficiency, which contributes to increased profitability. Hence, the degree of state ownership between the wholly owned, state as a majority investor,[23] state as minority investor[24] and state strategic involvement,[25] to direct industrial policies, could influence the degree to which the four major perspectives on state capitalism's strategic behaviour plays out in terms of business model design, with consequences for value creation and distribution. Some scholars have argued that there is an increasing resurgence of state capitalism seeking to learn from past failures of the liabilities of state-ness, while leveraging the benefits (Kulantzick, 2016). In addition, some scholars have studied the impact of privatisation – the transfer of ownership of state-owned organisations to private stakeholders – on the efficiency and effectiveness of the business model, whereby a balanced view is called for so that society is not in a situation where profits are privatised and losses are socialised (Radic et al., 2021).

Some scholars have argued that the liberal market structure of the United States has contributed to the increased financialisation of US corporations as they have transitioned from the old economy to the new digital economy (Lazonick, 2010). The new economy, based on digital technologies, requires a more open architecture, with less proprietary technology, compared to the old economy and the focus on organisational learning as the core competencies. The new economy has led to vertical specialisation compared to the more vertical integration of the old economy model. The inter-firm mobility of labour and liquid capital markets were needed to grow the new economy firms. Professional, technical and administrative staff needed to eschew the security of the established old economy of job security for the

---

[23] For example, firms with majority state ownership include oil majors such as Rosneft in Russia, Petrobas in Brazil and Sinopec in China. Banking firms include Sberbank in Russia, the Bank of China and the State Bank of India.

[24] For example, firms with minority state ownership include Deutsche Telecom and France Telecom in Europe and the Life Insurance Corporation of India.

[25] For example, the South Korean model of development involves the state acting as a country-level catalyst of private entrepreneurship in order to encourage the development of certain strategic industries by taking a minority stake in certain firms.

inducement offered by stock options based on potential initial public offerings (IPOs). As a result, there has been increased financialisation of the business models of US corporations, whereby the performance of the firms is measured by financial measures such as earnings per share. The inducement of executive compensation via stock options fuelled firms to adopt a programme of stock buy-backs to boost their respective share prices. This separates the interests of those who exercise strategic control from the rest of the corporation, sacrifices the interests of employees for the sake of booking profits, and reduces the financial commitment to invest in innovation. Such trends have exacerbated inequity because certain groups are able to extract more value and instability, with this value extraction undermining the ability to invest in productive capabilities. It has been argued that the financialisation of the business models of US firms might restrict the potential for economic growth (Lazonick, 2010).

10.5 Discussion

The basic premise of the business model is to ensure that the benefits of science, technology and knowledge for human progress in other dimensions of the humanities and the social sciences are translated into value for society to foster economic, social and general well-being. In doing so, we must remember that business models are the mechanisms that enable value to be created, delivered and captured through a collaborative network of stakeholders. On the one hand, the financial crisis of 2008 showed how the design of the mortgage value chain, whereby individual firms had business models designed to maximise their own returns, collectively resulted in amplifying risks, which contributed to the failure of firms, to the detriment of the market. On the other hand, the architecture of the market could also contribute to the sustained operations of firms that are inherently unprofitable. For example, in the 1990s General Electric (GE) built a financial services firm to provide financing for its aero-engine business to airlines (Dissanaike et al., 2022). The leasing and services business of General Electric Commercial and Aviation Services developed a significant market share between 2000 and 2008, to the extent that GE could benefit from aftersales services, including spare parts and repairs. The GE leasing services business could provide good terms, partly driven by the ability to convert capital expenditure for the airlines into operating expenses through sale and lease-back-style leases, thereby benefiting from tax savings.[26] This enabled GE to have exclusivity and priority with the aircraft manufacturer to choose the GE engine, resulting in the firm having more than a 65 per cent market share in large aircraft engines during the early 2000s.[27]

Airlines were not making profits because of severe competition and reduced prices, which benefited consumers. However, GE was able to use its power in the marketplace to provide funding to these airlines and redeploy aircrafts between airlines more seamlessly. This meant that the less profitable airlines could continue in business. However, the financial crisis brought this practice of enabling unsuccessful firms to survive to a screeching halt, with General Electric needing to be bailed out as a result of its heavily leveraged financial services business.[28] The case vignette shows that the design of the business model within a wider supply chain could result in allocative inefficiencies but provide efficiency through creditor concentration in preventing the premature bankruptcy of the firms, with the consequent loss of consumer welfare.

The design of economic systems themselves could foster different business models and hence outcomes for society. It is worth noting that two prominent scholars, Adam Smith and Karl Marx, studied the trading rights afforded to the East India Company and came up with different formulations of an ideal economic system (Robins, 2006). The shares of the EIC plummeted significantly after 1769 following a period of speculative trading that created a bubble in the share price following the news of the Diwani reaching London in 1766. This fall in the share price of the EIC nearly ruined several elites who were shareholders in London. Adam Smith, observing the financial crash of the EIC, viewed its monopoly powers as the bane of preventing the full forces of the market power to operate and called for more free-market-based economic systems in his classic treatise, *The Wealth of Nations* (Smith, 1776).

---

[26] GE also leveraged its AAA credit standing to borrow money from the capital markets on favourable terms.

[27] The bundling of financing with the sales of the aircraft engine also enables GE to provide other aftersales services such as spare parts and repairs.

[28] GE resorted to an emergency stock sale, including a portion to Berkshire Hathaway, because of cashflow insolvency at GE's financial services business, GE Capital.

The EIC's monopoly privilege on Indian trade was lifted in 1813 and opened up to private competition under certain conditions, except its monopoly of Chinese trade, predominantly in tea.[29] Leveraging its privilege to trade in China, the EIC developed the opium trade by growing opium in Bengal and exporting it to China, which became increasingly lucrative,[30] albeit illegal (Gao, 2019). Karl Marx went on to write a series of articles in the early to mid-1850s in *The New York Daily Tribune* – the world's bestselling newspaper at the time – about how the EIC, while openly preaching free trade, was defending the monopoly of the manufacture of opium (Marx, 1853). Moreover, Marx went on to argue that the control of the EIC by the British government enabled it to plunder the Indian subcontinent and benefit a small portion of the wealthy society in Britain (Marx,1858). Based on these insights and other observations of the factory-based industrial system, Marx argued in his general writings against the benefits of the free-market capitalist economy based on private profit, particularly in his famous book *Das Kapital* (Marx, 1867).[31]

One aspect that the above analysis brings to the fore is the meaning of profit. There are two theoretical positions provided by economics: the neoclassical economics of marginalism; and the classical political economy perspectives (Tinker, 1980). In the neoclassical view, firms trade in factor and product markets, and profit is therefore an indication of the firm's market viability and social efficiency in utilising these resources. According to the political economy view, profit is conceptualised as the social power of capitalism. Therefore, in the political economy view, the rate of profit provides an indication of the social, institutional and monopolistic power of the stakeholders, with capital rather than social efficiency and productive efficiency. The traditional emphasis of neoclassical economics is predominantly on production and exchange, with less focus on the distributional conditions. The

---

[29] This monopoly privilege was removed from the EIC in 1833.

[30] Although the trade in opium was illegal, the term "unauthorised trade" was commonly used. The EIC was finding it difficult to sell British goods in China in order to buy tea for sale in Britain, which became Britain's favourite drink by the end of the eighteenth century. In order to address this commercial problem, the EIC developed opium production in its colony in Bengal and sold it to private merchants on credit, who in turn sold it to the Chinese. The Chinese then paid the EIC representatives in Canton, who used the money to purchase tea.

[31] The first volume of *Das Kapital* was published in 1867.

political economy view brings to the forefront the distribution aspects (Cooper, 1980). In fact, arguments have been put forward by more left-leaning economists that all creation of wealth from history is based on a collective process of the division of labour, the use of natural resources and the accumulation of knowledge, and hence it should be more equally divided (Piketty, 2022). However, more recently there has been a resurgence in the emphasis on the distributional implications among mainstream economics (Galor, 2022; Rajan, 2019). Rajan (2019) highlights the importance of understanding the economic impact on communities, and hence the distribution of value, as the third pillar, in conjunction with the traditional view of analysing markets and the state. Increasingly, these two views, based on market efficiency and social power perspectives, are seen as complementary, which could have enormous consequences for the design of business models.

The different views from the perspective of business model design choices can be explored in the "Cambridge capital controversy"[32] (Harcourt, 1969). At the heart of the matter is how to determine the rate of return to capital – profit accruing to providers of capital. The rate of return on capital will determine the proportion of labour and capital used for production and hence contribute to economic growth and employment. On one side, there are the neoclassical economists from Cambridge, Massachusetts, in the United States. The neoclassical school assumes that the rate of return to capital is based on the marginal revenue from the use of capital, which is assumed to be exogenously given, and the firm then chooses the technique of production that maximises returns subject to paying for the other factor input, such as labour with the wage rate.

On the other side, there is the post-Keynesian economist from Cambridge, England, who argued that the rate of return on capital could only be determined by calculating the value of the capital

---

[32] The Cambridge capital controversy was a dispute between the proponents of two differing theoretical positions in economics in the 1950s–1960s, between economists such as Joan Robinson and Piero Sraffa at the University of Cambridge in England, on the one hand, and economists such as Paul Samuelson and Robert Solow at the Massachusetts Institute of Technology, in Cambridge, the United States, on the other. The English Cambridge economists were often labelled "post-Keynesian" and the US Cambridge side "neoclassical."

(Tinker, 1980). However, the value of the capital would be based on the present value of the income stream that is due to the capital-holders (Robinson, 1953), but determining such an income stream requires an assumption about how the income is distributed between labour and capital, and no rationale can be provided for choosing one distribution over another. Therefore, the neoclassical view of being able to determine the rate of return to capital based on the marginal revenue product is indeterminate unless a distribution of income is assumed beforehand. However, the distribution of income for capital is what the analysis seeks to identify in arriving at the rate of profit – and hence the return to capital (Harcourt, 1969). Therefore, there are in-built assumptions – which might be difficult to defend – inherent in some of the production function models related to determining productivity and the corresponding rate of growth of the economy.

The Cambridge capital controversy highlights that the chosen blueprint of the technique of production would determine the distribution of income between labour and capital – and hence the rate of return on capital.[33] Chandler – through detailed case studies of the changes to business models through both vertical and horizontal integration to get the benefits of economies of scale and scope – shows how the tension between labour and capital in manufacturing drove the design of incentives and business models, which led to the growth of American business (Chandler, 1977). Studies have shown that the choice of business model design and the boundary of the firm could have an impact on productivity, and hence economic growth (Coyle, 2019; Wannakrairoj and Velu, 2021). Moreover, there has been much debate in the literature about whether mission-oriented state investment is needed to take discoveries from science to innovation that are useful to society or whether state intervention alone is sufficient to address market failure (Mazzucato, 2013; Mowery, 2010). There

---

[33] Robert Allen coined the term Engel's pause (based on Friedrich Engels, *The Condition of the Working Class in England* in 1844, where he argued that labour was losing out to capitalism as part of the Industrial Revolution) to describe the two-stage growth in labour's share of income in nineteenth-century England (Allen, 2009). In the early part of the nineteenth century, the growth of capital as part of the Industrial Revolution caused output to increase and the share of income to capital to increase, at the expense of labour income – hence, "Engel's pause." However, once the capital accumulation took place as part of the Industrial Revolution, the share of wages in income grew in line with labour productivity.

are ample examples from history that strategic state interventions to address grand themes on societal challenges – such as national development, national security, poverty alleviation, health challenges, and others – can be powerful at a system-wide level and can overwhelm any calculations based on welfare economics and market failure (Janeway, 2018; Lerner, 2009). This comparison between mission-oriented state policies and market failure interventions could have significant implications for business model design choices.

Concluding Remarks

This book has proposed that it is necessary to have a holistic-systems-based perspective to enable business model innovation – a perspective that highlights the hierarchical nature of business models, whereby the combination of activities comprises subsystems, which, in turn, can be connected to other subsystems. A change in one component of the system could have complex effects on other components, which contributes to new business model innovation. Hence, the design and adoption of new business models require leadership that combines an understanding of techno-economic and political challenges. The adoption of new business models is key to tackling the opportunities provided by digital technologies and to addressing issues related to sustaining the leadership of incumbent firms, scaling up start-up firms and promoting the competitiveness of SMEs. These business models are required to tackle some of the most challenging issues faced by society today, including climate change and various socio-economic development issues; they need to be managed bearing in mind the conduct-related issues of maintaining fair customer and market outcomes.

It is imperative that the business model, which acts as the blueprint for strategic change, be designed by not only paying attention to the architectural configuration at the firm level but also by looking within the industrial system and the economic system that they operate. This multi-level systems perspective of the design of business models is needed to address some of the most pressing challenges that humans face today in terms of climate change, healthcare, education, economic inequality and achieving emotional and mental well-being, among others. We are fortunate to have the benefit of digital technologies and other emerging technologies from both the physical and biological sciences to address these challenges by designing suitable business models. We hope that this book provides some of the basic conceptual frameworks for designing business models to inspire those in academia, industry and government to work collectively to foster economic and social development that is fair and just for all.

References

Allen, R. C. (2009). Engels' Pause: Technical Change, Capital Accumulation, and Inequality in the British Industrial Revolution. *Explorations in Economic History* 46: 418–435.

Allen, R. C. (2009). *The British Industrial Revolution in Global Perspective.* Cambridge, UK: Cambridge University Press.

Allen, R. C. (2011). Why the Industrial Revolution Was British: Commerce, Induced Invention, and the Scientific Revolution. *The Economic History Review* 64(2): 357–384.

Baldwin, C. Y. and K. B. Clark. (2000). *Design Rules: The Power of Modularity,* Vol. 1. Cambridge, MA: MIT Press.

Berg, M., Davies, T., Fellinger, M., Gottmann, F., Hodacs, H., and Nierstrasz, C. (2015). Private Trade and Monopoly Structures: The East India Companies and the Commodity Trade to Europe in the Eighteenth Century. *Chartering Capitalism: Organizing Markets, States, and Publics Political Power and Social Theory* 29: 123–145.

Bush, V. (1945). *Science, the Endless Frontier: A Report to the President.* Washington, DC: US Government Printing Office.

Britannica, The Editors of Encyclopaedia. (2023). "Industrial Revolution." *Encyclopedia Britannica,* 26 Sept 2023, www.britannica.com/money/topic/Industrial-Revolution (accessed 18 October 2023).

Campbell-Kelly, M. and Garcia-Swartz, D. (2013). History of the Internet: The Missing Narrative. *Journal of Information Technology* 28: 18–33.

Ceruzzi, P. (1998). *A History of Modern Computing.* Cambridge, MA: The MIT Press.

Chandler, A. D. (1977). *The Visible Hand: The Managerial Revolution in American Business.* Cambridge, MA: Harvard University Press.

Chandler, A. D. (1986). The Beginnings of the Modern Industrial Corporation. *Proceedings of the American Philosophical Society* 130(4): 382–389.

Chesbrough, H. (2020). To Recover Faster from Covid-19, Open Up: Managerial Implications from an Open Innovation Perspective. *Industrial Marketing Management* 88(20): 410–413.

Cooper, D. (1980). Discussion of towards a Political Economy of Accounting. *Accounting, Organizations and Society* 5(1): 161–166.

Copeland, J. (2005). *Alan Turing's Automatic Computing Engine: The Master Codebreaker's Struggle to Build the Modern Computer.* Oxford: Oxford University Press.

Cortada, J. W. (2003). *The Digital Hand: Volume I: How Computers Changed the Work of American Manufacturing, Transportation, and Retail Industries.* Oxford: Oxford University Press.

Cortada, J. W. (2005). *The Digital Hand: Volume II: How Computers Changed the Work of American Financial, Telecommunications, Media, and Entertainment Industries.* Oxford: Oxford University Press.

Coyle, D (2019). Do-It-Yourself Digital: The Production Boundary, the Productivity Puzzle and Economic Welfare. *Economica* 86(344): 750–774.

Crafts, N. (2018). *Forging Ahead, Falling Behind and Fighting Back: British Economic Growth from the Industrial Revolution to the Financial Crisis.* Cambridge, UK: Cambridge University Press.

Dissanaike, G., Jayasekera, R., and Meeks, G. (2022). Why Do Unsuccessful Companies Survive? US Airlines, Aircraft Leasing and GE, 2000–2008. *Business History Review* 96(3): 615–642.

Encyclopedia Britannica. (2022, March 13). "Industrial Revolution." www.britannica.com/event/Industrial-Revolution.

Farrington, A. (2002). *Trading Places: The East India Company and Asia 1600–1834.* London, UK: The British Library Publishing Division.

Financial Times. (2020). IMF Warns Global Economy to Suffer Deepest Plunge since the 1930s, 14 April.

Financial Times. (2022). US and UK Ban Russian Oil and Gas Imports in Drive to Punish Putin, 9 March.

Galor, O. (2022). *The Journey of Humanity: The Origins of Growth and Equality.* London, UK: Penguin Random House.

Gao, H. (2019). The EIC versus Free Traders. In: *Creating the Opium War British Imperial Attitudes towards China, 1792–1840.* Manchester, UK: Manchester University Press.

Harcourt, G. C. (1969). Some Cambridge Controversies in the Theory of Capital. *Journal of Economic Literature* 7(2): 369–405.

Hartwell, R. M. (1967). *The Causes of the Industrial Revolution.* London, UK: University Paperbacks.

Hejeebu, S. (2005). Contract Enforcement in the English East India Company. *The Journal of Economic History* 65(2): 496–523.

Hejeebu, S. (2015). Own, Rent, or Rent-Seek? Vertical Integration in Historical Chartered Monopolies. *Chartering Capitalism: Organizing Markets, States, and Publics Political Power and Social Theory* 29: 177–206.

Hockfield, S. (2019). *The Age of Living Machines: How Biology Will Build the Next Technology Revolution.* New York and London: W W Norton & Company.

India Office Records. (1800–2). Letters of the Directors of the East India Company held at the British Library, Mss Eur D107: 1800–1802.

Janeway, W. (2018). *Doing Capitalism in the Innovation Economy*. Cambridge, UK: Cambridge University Press.

Kulantzick, J. (2016). *State Capitalism: How the Return of Statism Is Transforming the World*. Oxford: Oxford University Press.

Langlois, R. N. (1988). Economic Change and the Boundaries of the Firm. *Journal of Institutional and Theoretical Economics* 144(4): 635–657.

Langlois, R. N. (1999). Scale, Scope and the Reuse of Knowledge. In: S. C. Dows and P. E. Earl (eds), *Economic Organization and Economic Knowledge: Essays in Honour of Brian Loasby*. Aldershop: Edward Elgar, pp. 239–254.

Langlois, R. N. (2002). Modularity in Technology and Organization. *Journal of Economic Behavior & Organization* 49: 19–37.

Langlois, R. N. (2003). The Vanishing Hand: The Changing Dynamics of Industrial Capitalism. *Industrial and Corporate Change* 12(2): 351–385.

Lazonick, W. (2010). Innovative Business Models and Varieties of Capitalism: Financialization of the US Corporation. *Business History Review* 84(4): 675–702.

Lerner, J. (2009). *Boulevard of Broken Dreams: Why Public Efforts to Boost Entrepreneurship and Venture Capital Have Failed – And What to Do about It*. New Jersey: Princeton University Press.

Levinthal, D. A. and March, J. G. (1993). The Myopia of Learning. *Strategic Management Journal* 14: 95–112.

Marshall P. J. (ed.) (1981). *Writings and Speeches of Edmund Burke*, vol. 5. Oxford: Clarendon Press.

Marx, K. (1853). The East India Company – Its History and Results. *New York Herald Tribune*.

Marx, K. (1858). Free Trade and Monopoly. *New York Daily Tribune*.

Marx, K. (1867). *Das Kapital: Kritik der politischen Oekonomie. Vol. 1: Der Produktionsprozess des Kapitals* (1st ed.). Hamburg: Verlag von Otto Meissner.

Mazzucato, M. (2013). *The Entrepreneurial State*. London: Anthem.

Mokyr, J. (1999). The New Economic History and the Industrial Revolution. In: J. Mokyr (ed), *The British Industrial Revolution*. New York: Routledge, pp. 1–127.

Mokyr, J. (2010). *The Enlightened Economy: An Economic History of Britain 1700–1850*. New Haven and London: Yale University Press.

Mowery, D. C. (2010). Military R&D and Innovation. In: B. H. Hall and N. Rosenberg (eds), *Handbook of the Economics of Innovation*, 2 vols. Amsterdam: Elsevier, pp. 1219–1256.

Musacchio, A., Lazzarini, S. G., and Aguilera, R. V. (2015). New Varieties of State Capitalism: Strategic and Governance Implications. *Academy of Management Perspectives* 29(1): 115–131.

Pardi, N., Hogan, M. J., Porter, F. W., and Weissman, D. (2018). mRNA Vaccines – A New Era in Vaccinology. *Nature Reviews Drug Discovery* 17(4): 261–279.

Pedersen, C. L., Ritter, T., and Di Benedetto, C. A. (2020). Managing through a Crisis: Managerial Implications for Business-to-Business Firms. *Industrial Marketing Management* 88: 314–322.

Penrose. E. T. (1959). *The Theory of the Growth of the Firm*. Oxford: Basil Blackwell.

Piketty, T. (2022). *A Brief History of Equality*. Boston, MA: Belknap Press.

Popper, C. and Velu, C. (2021). The Impact of the Pandemic on Digital Transformation. *Conference Board Report*.

Radic, M., Ravasi, D., and Munir, K. (2021). Privatization: Implications of a Shift from State to Private Ownership. *Journal of Management* 47(6): 1596–1629.

Rajan, R. (2019). *The Third Pillar: The Revival of Community in a Polarised World*. London: Harper Collins.

Robins, N. (2006). *The Corporation that Changed the World: How the East India Company Shaped the Modern Multinational*. London: Pluto Press.

Robinson, J. (1953). The Production Function and the Theory of Capital. *The Review of Economic Studies* 21(2): 81–106.

Said, F., Page, A., Salter, L., and Velu, C. (2022). Intangible Capital and Reorienting of Manufacturing during a Pandemic. In: E. Gallitto, M. Massi, and P. Harrison et al. (eds), *Consumption, Production and Entrepreneurship in the Time of Coronavirus*. Palgrave Macmillan, Cham, Switzerland, pp. 127–149.

Simon, H. A. (1962). The Architecture of Complexity. *Proceedings of the American Philosophical Society* 106: 467–482.

Simon, H. A. (1973). Applying Information Technology to Organization Design. *Public Administration Review* 33(3): 268–278.

Smith, A. (1776). *An Inquiry into the Nature and Causes of the Wealth of Nations*. New York: The Modern Library, 1994.

Thompson, J. D. (1967). *Organizations in Action: Social Science Bases of Administrative Theory*. New York: McGraw-Hill.

Tinker, A. M. (1980). Towards a Political Economy of Accounting: An empirical Illustration of the Cambridge Controversies. *Accounting, Organizations and Society* 5(1): 147–160.

Vargo, S. L. and Lusch, R. F. (2016). Institutions and Axioms: An Extension and Update of Service-Dominant Logic. *Journal of the Academy of Marketing Science* 44: 5–23.

von Behr, C-M., Semple, G. A., and Minshall, T. (2022). Rapid Setup and Management of Medical Device Design and Manufacturing Consortia: Experiences from the COVID-19 Crisis in the UK. *R&D Management* 52(2): 220–234.

Wagner-Tsukamoto, S. (2007). An Institutional Economic Reconstruction of Scientific Management: On the Lost Theoretical Logic of Taylorism. *Academy of Management Review* 32(1): 105–117.

Wall Street Journal. (2022). Supply-Chain Woes Won't Be Solved by "Reshoring," Report Says, April 12.

Wannakrairoj, W. and Velu C. (2021). Productivity Growth and Business Model Innovation. *Economics Letters* 199, 109679: 1–5.

Yoffie, S. (2022) Commentary: Pandemic Shortages Haven't Shattered the Case for "Just-in-Time" Supply Chains. *Wall Street Journal*, 30 January.

Index

T2C. *See* Travel to Change (T2C)
tactical responses, 13–14, 18
TAHMO. *See* Trans-African Hydro-
   Meteorological Observatory
   (TAHMO)
Taobao, 123
Tata Nano, 219
Taylorist management approach, 254
Telenor and Grameen partnership
   (Grameen Phone & Grameen
   Telecom), 207–208
temporal agency, 42
Tesco, phased separation strategy,
   60–61
Tesla development, analogical
   reasoning and, 34–35
Thompson, J. D., 54, 74, 257
transaction costs theory, 85–86
transaction platforms, 115, 116, 120
transaction-free zones, 86
transactions, 86
Trans-African Hydro-Meteorological
   Observatory (TAHMO),
   222–223
Travel to Change (T2C), 213–214

Uber, 130, 133, 134
   AI and, 93–94
UNFCCC, 167
Unilever, 180
unitisation process, schemas, 33
unsupervised learning, 93
US investments banks, leverage of,
   240–241

value capturing, 2, 4, 5, 6, 27, 46, 64,
   80, 85, 90, 154, 257
   in digital platforms, 112, 115,
   118–119, 122, 127

value creation, 2, 4, 5, 6, 27, 46, 64,
   72, 80, 85, 90, 92, 124, 154,
   170, 210, 268
   for circular economy, 171
   in digital platforms, 112, 118–119,
   122, 127
value destruction, 170
value propositions, 2, 3, 4, 5, 6, 8, 13,
   14, 18, 54, 69, 72, 80, 81, 86,
   88, 101, 154, 184
   Blockbuster, 15
   changing meaning of, 31–32
   digital platform generativity and,
   116–118
   Hertz, 14
Van de Ven, A., 17
Velu, C., 8, 122
VisionSpring, 220
Vodafone, 87
Volvo Cars, digital platform in,
   124–126
von Neumann, J., 260

Waste Concern and Map Agro,
   208–210
watch market, 31–32
WR Hambrecht + Co, 39

Xerox, 10, 11, 12
   914 dry copier, 10–11
Xerox PARC, 10, 11

Yang, M., 176

Zara, 141
ZEBs. *See* zero-emission buses (ZEBs)
zero-emission buses (ZEBs), 193–194
Zipcar, 13–14, 131
Zott, C., 8, 154

Printed in the United States
by Baker & Taylor Publisher Services